THE WORLD BOOK OF PEOPLES

THE WORLD BOOK OF PEOPLES

by *Albert J. Nevins, M.M.*

Our Sunday Visitor, Inc.
Huntington, Ind. 46750

Nihil Obstat:
REV. LAWRENCE GOLLNER
Censor Librorum

Imprimatur:
✝LEO A. PURSLEY, D.D.
Bishop of Fort Wayne-South Bend

ISBN: 0-87973-876-6
Library of Congress Catalog Card Number: 73-86975

Portions of this book originally appeared as "The Maryknoll Book of Peoples." It has been completely revised, re-edited and updated by the original author from the earlier edition.

The author wishes to acknowledge his indebtedness to Florence Robbins of the Maryknoll Photo Library for invaluable pictorial research; and to the following members of Our Sunday Visitor: Larry Lewis for textual research; John Zierten for additional pictorial research; and to James McIlrath for additional art and the cover design.

Published and printed in the U.S.A. by
Our Sunday Visitor, Inc.
Noll Plaza
Huntington, Indiana 46750
876

CONTENTS

PART I

PART II

VIGNETTES

Part 1

What This Book Is About

WHEN I WAS a boy, I used to hate to visit one of my grandmothers because she lived on the top floor of an apartment house and the only way to reach her was up many dark flights of stairs. I used to grope my way up the stairs, clutching the bannister to avoid a misstep.

Looking back now, I realize why I was afraid of those stairs and the darkness. I was afraid because they represented something unknown. The children who lived in the house had no such fears. They knew every step and turn.

It is much the same with people. We become suspicious and on our guard against people who are strange to us. Once we get to know those same people, our doubts and fears vanish. We find them very much like ourselves.

This then is the purpose of this book. It is to introduce you to many of the peoples of the world—people much like ourselves, people who cry when they are sad, and laugh when they are happy. People who love their children as we do. People who will remind us that we all belong to one family—the human family; that we have one common Father—God.

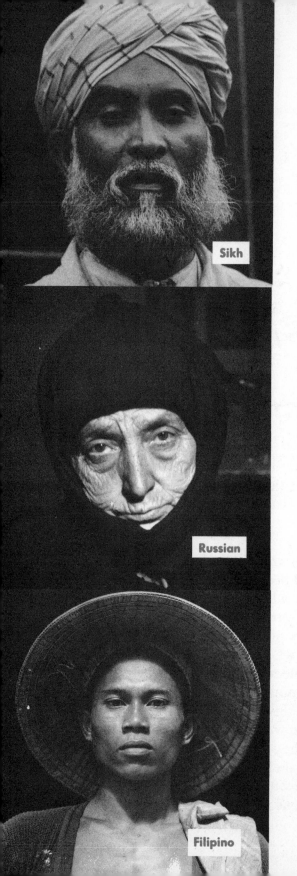

Sikh

Russian

Filipino

PEOPLE

There is a difference between a people and a race. If you live in an average large American city, it is possible to walk downtown and rub elbows with men and women from all parts of the world. These strangers may be foreign students, diplomats, businessmen, or just tourists. Few of us would guess that they are not Americans because our nation is made up of many races and peoples.

Race is a division of mankind on the basis of striking physical characteristics. Until recently, scientists divided the peoples of the world into color groups. Thus men were said to be Caucasian (white), Negro (black), Indian (red), Mongoloid (yellow) and Malay (brown).

In recent years, however, scientists have begun to base distinctions in race not on color but on the size and proportion of the human skull and on associated differences, such as the kind of hair and the composition of blood. Under this system, people of different colors can belong to the same race.

The term race is misused when we really mean a people. There is no such thing as the English race or the Jewish race. What we mean when we use such words is the English people or the Jewish people.

Races are different because of obvious physical differences. Peoples, on the other hand, are groups that are marked off from each other by less obvious physical differences but even more importantly by cultural differences such as languages and customs.

We may refer to a person as being an Indian. This is a racial reference. There are many kinds of Indians—Sioux, Cherokee, Pima, to mention only three. In Brazil, for example, there are almost three hundred and fifty different Indian peoples.

We must also be careful not to confuse nationality with race or people. Nationality is a political division, based on a country's boundaries. Actually, Britain contains many people—Anglo-Saxons, Celts, Irish, Scotch, Britons, English, Belgae, Manx, Welsh, and others.

It would be more correct to speak of the British family. The word family is a sort of middle ground between race and people. Thus the Aryan family is part of the Caucasian race. Members of the Aryan family include such diverse types as Germans, Persians, French and Hindustanis.

Over the years, peoples, families, and even races have tended to produce new groups because of intermarriage. By means of modern transportation, this process is being speeded up; as a result, any scientific account of races and peoples becomes complicated. This is particularly true in the United States.

The human race began from a single pair of ancestors, Adam and Eve. Over the centuries isolation caused peoples and races to develop. Today that process has been reversed. Someday in the distant future only the human race may remain.

Zulu

Briton

Aymara

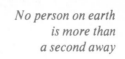

*No person on earth
is more than
a second away*

The WORLD is your neighbor

When future historians write the history of our own times, they will probably call the Twentieth Century the Age of Communications. The satellite and television have made the globe shrink. Once the interior of China was months away from your own backyard. Today it is only a fraction of a second away by TV, a matter of hours by airjet. What does this mean? It means that we of America are more closely joined with the people of the world. What happens in Timbuktu or Ranchipur is as important as what happens down our own block.

We Depend Upon People

"No man is an island."
The poet expresses well in these words how each of us is linked to other people. For no person is cut off from the rest of mankind.

In a material sense, we depend on men and women around the earth. Since the beginning of time, people have been borrowing new ideas from each other and better ways of fulfilling man's countless wants. Paper and printing, for instance, were known in China before the time of Christ. And the Chinese first knew how to make fine silk cloth, chinaware and explosives.

We often forget how much we owe to some people like the American Indians who first showed the white man how to grow Indian corn, beans and potatoes—crops which supply a large part of our diet today. Indians discovered the value of medicines, such as quinine, which relieve much human suffering. And they also taught us the use of such familiar things as rubber, tobacco and chocolate.

Just consider the origin of many of the dishes for which we thank God each day. A farmer in Dakota may have sown the wheat from which our bread is baked; someone in Italy perhaps grew the olives which grace the table; and the coffee we drink with gusto was ground from beans planted by a Negro in Brazil.

The ancient people of the Near East were great explorers and navigators. In small, sturdy, hand-carved boats they braved the Mediterranean Sea and the Indian Ocean.

This Latin American youth reflects the problems of unemployment and education which afflict much of the Third World. His idleness could become explosive.

What Other People Should Mean to Us

There is nothing more interesting than the study of mankind. No other science has as many people connected with it or as many divisions. Geographers study man in relation to his physical surroundings. Physical anthropologists regard man as a biological type. Sociologists pursue man's relationships with his fellow humans. Cultural anthropologists are concerned with such man-made characteristics as language and social institutions.

Today the world has become one neighborhood. People must learn to get along with other people. This is not too difficult for Americans because we are used to working shoulder to shoulder with men and women from many nationalities. But today events are bringing people together on a world scale.

As Christians, we've many reasons for being interested in other people, particularly those who are not of our nationality or race. Our religion teaches us to look not at the accidental differences between people, but at the essential sameness.

The soul of every man is made in the image and likeness of God, and we are therefore all alike. We are all children of a common Father. We believe that mankind has unity; that the human person is clothed in spiritual dignity; that the Gospel of Christ is based on love.

Our religion teaches us that the soul of every person is infinitely precious because Jesus Christ died for every human being who ever lived, is living, or will live. It was Christ Himself who commanded us to teach all mankind these truths.

Therefore, we are not interested in man as a biological specimen to be studied under a microscope. We are interested in mankind because God created all of us for an identical purpose and made all of us His children.

Guatemala's Mam Indians wear beads of gold and hand-embroidered costumes.

The Tragedy of Bernie Nunez

A YOUNG EX-GI arrived in New York City recently, having just been discharged from the United States Army after completing his two-year hitch of service. He was twenty-year-old Bernie Nunez, en route to his wife in California, where he had sent her to await the birth of their first child.

Bernie's only reason for stopping off in New York was to say "Hello" to an older brother who lived there and whom he had not seen in several years. During the course of his stay, Bernie and his brother visited some relatives. On the way back to the brother's house, they decided to stop at a tavern and play a few games of shuffleboard.

As they played, a group of men jeered at the brothers for speaking Spanish—the only language Bernie knew. The older brother left the game for a few moments; and when he returned, he found both Bernie and the men had gone. Thinking that Bernie had left for home, he started out after him. As he came out of the store, five men jumped on him, cursing and swearing at him because he was "a Spik who won't talk English." When the beating was ended, and he had regained his feet, he saw Bernie lying in the street, badly battered, his skull crushed in by repeated kicking. Thus death came to the young ex-GI, whose offense was that he knew only his own native language. For Bernie was a Puerto Rican. As an American citizen, he had been drafted like any other youth and he had served his country even though he couldn't speak the language of the majority.

It is difficult to say who were the real victims of this tragedy: Bernie, who was kicked to death for speaking Spanish; an innocent wife and orphaned, unborn child; or the seven men who were later arrested for homicide in connection with the attack. Regarding those seven, the tragedy is heightened when we read their names—names that indicate Irish and Italian ancestry—names that are Christian and probably Catholic. If we had to pick the real victims, we would choose those seven men, who will have to live out their lives knowing that they put a fellow human being to death solely from prejudice.

By their bigoted, senseless, and intolerant deed, those seven men allied themselves with the men who put Christ to death. By their act, they gave concrete denial to any belief in the essential Catholic doctrine of the Mystical Body. It is this doctrine that makes all of us one with Christ. It is this doctrine that teaches us that what happens to any man, anywhere, happens to each one of us.

As a result, each one of us had a share in the death of Bernie Nunez. Each one of us suffered a loss when the ex-soldier was cut off from the Mystical Body. In the death of Bernie Nunez, each one of us became a victim of ignorance and prejudice—the real reasons for the attack.

16

What happened to Bernie Nunez is the final demonstration of the ultimate effect of prejudice—a disease that comes on not of a sudden but one that is developed over years—a disease that is caught from elders, both parents and friends—a disease that twists and distorts—a disease that destroys Christ in the soul of a man, that makes him a traitor to the principles of his Church and his country.

Every decent person can but experience horror and repulsion when reading the story of Bernie Nunez. Yet how guiltless are we? If we have ever referred to other nationalities by opprobrious names, if we have ever discriminated against a person because of color or race, if we have ever suggested our own superiority, we have demonstrated a lack of comprehension of basic Catholic doctrine.

When the people of Ohio were petitioning Congress for statehood, one legislator objected to the request on the ground that the Ohio natives "are so uncouth, so rude, and so unlettered, that they will never make good citizens." Fortunately, the advice of that solon was not followed. Ohio was admitted to the Union, and later gave to our country seven Presidents.

Very often in discussions, when the subject of races or nationalities is mentioned, we hear people making remarks that have about as much sense as did the conclusion of the objecting Congressman. Few subjects are as misunderstood and surrounded by myths as is the subject of race.

To get a clear idea of what race is all about, we must examine the best scientific opinion found today. The following is what we find.

HUMAN LIFE probably began in western Asia; although recent discoveries have caused some scientists to consider central Africa as its source. The first human beings were neither white nor black, but somewhere in between. As men multiplied, they began to spread out, seeking new areas for food. Gradually over the long centuries, those groups took on special characteristics, due in part to intermarriage within each group. Climate, environment, and diet also were factors.

The people who were in northern Europe became lighter in color, because of loss of pigmentation. The people who were in tropical zones became darker. Among some groups, inbreeding produced a majority of people with curly hair; among others, the majority had straight hair. Inbreeding made some groups grow tall, and others grow smaller. Because children inherited the characteristics of parents, certain qualities, passed on through generation after generation, tended to become very strong.

In this manner were the various races of the world developed. Actually all mankind was (and is) still one, springing from the one common pair of ancestors. The differences that have come among men were accidental differences. In all basic essentials, they were (and are) still the same.

All members of the different groups, since they lived alone, were suspicious of any stranger from another group. The stranger represented something unknown, something that could not be predicted. Thus, racial and national prejudices began.

Most people have only the haziest knowledge of genetics and other scientific factors that must be considered in any study of race and heredity. Consequently, today we find much inaccurate and wrong talk. People use the word "race" to describe a nationality, such as the French race; or to describe a language group, such as the Latin race; or a geographical group, such as the Nordic race; or a religious group, such as the Jewish race. To speak in such a fashion, is to speak loosely and incorrectly. What are meant by such descriptions are ethnic and cultural groups, not races of mankind.

If this is so, then how many races are there? Once scientists made many divisions, but today anthropologists reduce the races of mankind to four groups. These divisions are not made on skin color alone, but on other physical characteristics such as eye and hair color, the amount of hair on the body, the formation of the bones in the face, the construction of the hair on the head, and the shape of the shin bone.

THESE FOUR GROUPS did not always exist, and at times there may have been more. The four groups that exist today are not static, but changing. There is every reason to believe that in the future the differences between these groups will become less and less, and that one day the differences may altogether disappear. We can see that at work in our own country, where more and more persons with some Negro blood, because of intermarriage and other factors, are passing over to what is called the "white race."

It is a sad travesty on the Christian doctrine of the brotherhood of man and the Fatherhood of God (to which science itself gives evidence), that far too many Christians look at only the accidental differences and do not consider the essential sameness. The soul of man is made in the image and likeness of God, and we are therefore basically all alike. To propound any other doctrine, is contrary to the best Christian teaching.

Yet there must be something wrong—if we are to judge from certain frequent remarks we hear made by people who call themselves Christian. Some grave fault lies in either their education or their personal prejudice. The error is not Christ's.

How many students in our schools, for instance, have even been told of the ancient African Negro civilizations? Many scholars hold that civilization descended down the Nile to Egypt from Central Africa. While our European ancestors were hiding in forests and worshiping spirits, Ahmed Baba, a Negro scholar, was building up a library of sixteen hundred volumes. The three great Negro kingdoms of Ghana, Mellestine, and Songhai were already highly developed. In Timbuktu, eight hundred years ago, there was a Negro university that exchanged its scholars with other schools. Historians tell us that Negroes developed the method of smelting iron, and contributed more than any other race to the advancement of the iron industry. While white peoples' ancestors were using stone hammers, Negroes were making delicate carvings with their metal tools.

The correct teachings on race must be spread everywhere: in the school, church, home, and factory. We must remind all men that we are children of a common Father; that mankind has unity; that the human person is clothed in spiritual dignity; that the Gospel of Christ teaches the law of love. Spreading these teachings is a project of education, not legislation.

There is a growing clamor in the United States for more and more legislation against racial and religious prejudices. While such legislation gives a greater public awareness of the evil and does prevent certain public prejudicial acts, legislation is no cure for bigotry and prejudice. The cure is much more gradual.

As the late Cardinal Cushing has stated, "The road to world peace is the street where we ourselves live." To find that road, we must understand a little more about ourselves and our neighbors.

Racial prejudice is not a disease in itself, any more than a running sore is the disease of leprosy. The running sore may be the effect of leprosy and an indication that the leprous bacilli are present in the blood stream. Putting ointments and bandages on the sore, cannot cure the leprosy. And legislating against racial prejudice cannot cure the basic weakness, of which prejudice is a symptom.

The disease of which race prejudice is but the symptom is a mental disease called "fear." Today people are afraid of losing their jobs to other people. They are afraid of losing social position. They are afraid of losing economic or political power. They are afraid of being punished for past injuries. All these fears build up conflicts and tensions. We seek a scapegoat on whom we can put the blame. To justify our fears, we pick on some minority group.

Fear is like a rat gnawing away in the dark. But when the light of knowledge and understanding is turned on, the rat flees. Fear is the child of ignorance. Dispel the ignorance, and you dispel the fear. Laws will not cure ignorance, nor will they cure fear. The remedy for racial prejudice is a long-term process of education. When we understand something, we may stand in awe of it, but we are no longer afraid.

We fear other people because they are strangers to us. We do not know them. We think that they are different from us. We are unable to predict their acts. But when we learn that human beings are the same the world over, that the most remote Africans and Asians are very much like ourselves, then we are on the road to understanding.

Catholics have addèd reason for understanding, because of the doctrine of the Mystical Body, which makes us all one with Christ. We can be bigoted and intolerant only by denying our Christian Faith.

VOICE NO PERSONAL opinion," the late Cardinal Cushing told a group in Boston, "but with the consecrated authority of my holy office, as a bishop of the Roman Catholic Church, and priest forever according to the order of Melchisedech, I declare to you that no Catholic can despise a fellow man and remain a true follower of his Lord and Saviour, Jesus Christ....

"Any Catholic who reviles or wrongs a brother because of his skin, because of race or religion, or who condemns any racial or religious group because of the mistakes or sins of a few individuals in that racial or religious group, ceases in that condemnation to be a Catholic and an American. He becomes a disobedient son of Mother Church and a disloyal citizen of the United States. The Catholic who fails to take a stand against racial or religious persecutions, is at once a slacker in the army of the Church Militant and a deserter from the battle of Christian democracy; turning his back to a brother of different color, race, or religion, wittingly or not, he turns his back to the flag and to the cross of Mount Calvary."

These are strong words from the Cardinal. They should be pondered by every Catholic. If all believed them, Bernie Nunez would not have been murdered.

The Bible Tells the Story

IN THE BEGINNING God created heaven and earth. And the earth was void and empty, and darkness was upon the deep; and the spirit of God moved over the waters. And God said, "Be light made." And light was made. God also said, "Let the waters that are under the heaven be gathered together in one place; and let the dry land appear." And it was so done. And God called the dry land, Earth; and the gathering together of waters, He called Seas. And God saw that all was good.

And He said, "Let the earth bring forth the green herb, and such as may seed. Let the waters bring forth the creeping creatures having life, and the fowl that may fly over the earth." And God saw that it was good. And He blessed them, saying, "Increase and multiply."

And God said, "Let the earth bring forth the living creatures in their kind, cattle and creeping things, and beasts of the earth, according to their kinds." And it was done. And God made the beasts of the earth according to their kinds. And God saw that it was good.

And He said, "Let us make man to our image and likeness: and let him have dominion over the fishes of the sea, and the fowls of the air, and the beasts, and the whole earth, and every creeping creature that moveth upon the earth." And the Lord God created man to His own image: to the image of God He created him: male and female He created them.

And God blessed them saying, "Increase and multiply, and fill the earth, and subdue it, and rule over the fishes of the sea, and the fowls of the air, and all living creatures that move upon the earth...." And God saw all the things that He had made and they were very good. And the Lord God had planted a paradise of pleasure from the beginning: wherein He placed man whom He had formed.

In the story of creation, there is no conflict between Scripture and science. The top scholars hold that the Scriptural "day" could actually mean millions of years.

Youth is the time for dreams of the future. This African youth has little future to look forward towards while this American boy can expect to go to a good college.

This Is How the Earth Was Inhabited

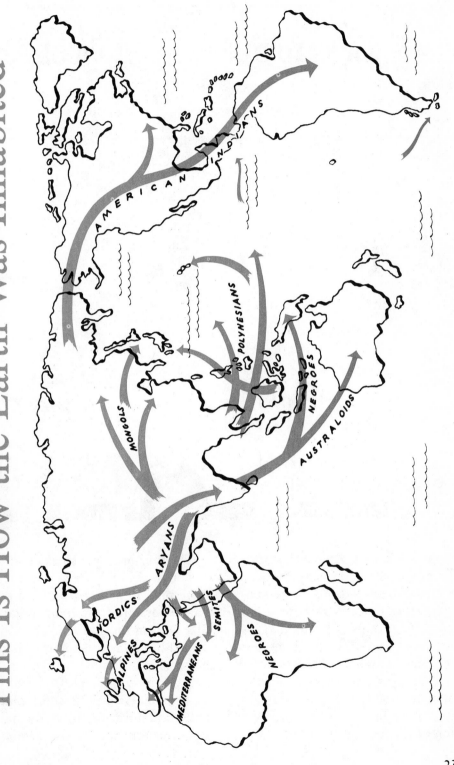

THE BASIC RACIAL

CAUCASOID

MONGOLOID

There are four basic racial stocks. Once scientists made many divisions of mankind but today the best opinion divides the world's population into four groups. This division is not made on skin color alone, but on other physical characteristics such as eyes and hair colors, the amount of body hair, the construction of the face, and the composition of the hair on the head.

The four principal stocks are:

1. *Caucasoid.* Here skin color is from pink to dark brown. Eye and hair colors are from light to dark. Size is from short to tall. The Caucasoid has a large amount of body hair; a high, thin nose; thin lips.

2. *Mongoloid.* Skin is from yellow to brown. He has straight black hair, and little or no body hair. Eyes are dark; and in some members

STOCKS OF MANKIND

NEGROID

COMPOSITE

of this group, the eyelids cover the corners so that eyes appear slanted. Height is from short to tall.

3. *Negroid.* Skin color is from light brown to blue-black. Hair is dark and curly. Lips are heavy, eyes dark. Size varies from very short to tall.

4. *Composite.* This type combines various characteristics of the three main stocks. For example, the Pol-

ynesians combined Mongoloid and Caucasoid traits, and some groups have Negroid features. Some anthropologists suggest that the Polynesians are the closest to earliest men.

The four groups that exist today are changing. There is every evidence to believe that the differences between these groups will become less and less, and that one day the differences may altogether disappear.

How the Earth Was Populated

Man is a great traveler. Since his first appearance on earth many thousands of years ago, man has been on the move. Scientists frequently disagree about our early history, but the best theory seems to be that the human race began somewhere in Asia Minor.

As people increased, they spread out, seeking regions where there were animals to provide them with food and clothing. They also had to settle near water.

From Asia Minor, the various tribes moved into Europe and Africa. They also advanced eastward across Asia and into the islands of the South Seas. About twenty thousand years ago, the first Asiatics crossed from Siberia to Alaska and began to march down North Amer-

ica. In 1932, a Professor Hrdlicka discovered on Kodiak Island the skeletons of an ancient, oblong headed people. By means of these skeletons, he was able to show that the California aborigines descended from one of the earliest migration waves from Siberia.

A strange example of how people get around was recorded by a French missioner, Father Grellon, who had worked among the Huron Indians in Canada. After the destruction of the Huron Mission in 1648, he was reassigned to work in Asia. One day in Central Asia, he met a Christian Huron woman. She told him that she had been taken prisoner in Canada and had been sold from tribe to tribe and thus eventually arrived deep in the interior of China.

The reasons for migrations are manifold. Some people move for religious, political and social reasons. The two main reasons, however, are the search for food and the need to escape a stronger enemy. It is probably the first main reason that is responsible for the spread of man over the earth. Down through the Stone Age, man had been merely a hunter or collector of food. Where game and wild food abounded he could live in moderate-sized communities. When the population grew too large, migration of some of the people became necessary.

Not all migrations have taken place outside of history. In the thirteenth century, Genghis Kahn and his Mongol tribesmen swept across Asia into Europe and set in movement vast masses of people. One of the greatest human migrations has been the populating of the Americas. People from many lands and races have poured into North and South America. In a little over a century and a half, the population of the United States increased by almost 150 million. Even in our own time, migrations are going on. Millions of people fled war in North and South Vietnam. Millions of people in India and Pakistan have been uprooted. Other millions of Chinese have fled to Hong Kong and Taiwan (Formosa).

Today migration is accomplished swiftly by means of ships and planes. In the days before recorded history, migration was a slow process, taking place in short, successive movements along the course of least resistance until mankind covered the earth.

BASIC MISTAKES ABOUT PEOPLE

1. There are pure races.

   FACT: *All people are of mixed ancestry.*

   •

2. Some races are superior.

   FACT: *Only individuals are superior, and they come from all races.*

   •

3. Race mixture produces inferior offspring.

   FACT: *Mixture only produces hybrid vigor.*

   •

4. Races do not change.

   FACT: *The evidence shows that races are constantly changing.*

   •

5. Some races lack the ability to succeed.

   FACT: *All races have the ability. Some lack the opportunity.*

   •

6. Physical racial differences are important.

   FACT: *Physical racial differences are only accidental and therefore unimportant.*

   •

7. The white race is superior because it has developed the highest known civilization.

   FACT: *The civilization known as the white man's is built on the contributions borrowed from many other peoples.*

   •

8. Each race has different blood.

   FACT: *There are only four blood types, called O, A, B, and AB. All races have these same blood types and within the types all human blood is the same.*

Why People Talk Differently

In the beginning, there was one language. Science is able to tell us little of the history of languages but if we accept the unity of the human race through Adam and Eve, it is reasonable to conclude that originally there was but one tongue. Then as migrations started and groups began to to live in isolation, that language changed, until new languages developed. We have examples of such changes in our own time. Italian is a development from ancient Latin. French spoken in Canada is different from Parisian French.

Today the peoples of our globe speak some 1,500 languages. Many of these languages are related to one another. English, for example, is Teutonic in origin and is closely related to Dutch and German. Yet many English words come from Latin.

Some languages are difficult to trace. Basque is a language used by some mountain people on the Spanish-French border. It has little in common with any other speech although some linguistic scholars claim that there is a relationship to the speech of the Ainu (Japan).

Every language possesses a large body of words. The average American knows about 30,000. A missioner among the Yaagans, a primitive tribe of Tierra del Fuego, compiled a dictionary of 30,000 Yaagan words.

There is also variety in a single language from district to district. Each variety is called a dialect. In China, for example, there are many dialects because the people of each region found it difficult to associate with the people of others. Class distinctions also created dialects. The English spoken by the Cockney of the London slums is far different from the English of the educated Londoner.

The Polynesians were the world's greatest navigators who spread out over the vast Pacific, inhabiting many islands. Today they continue to dwell close to the sea.

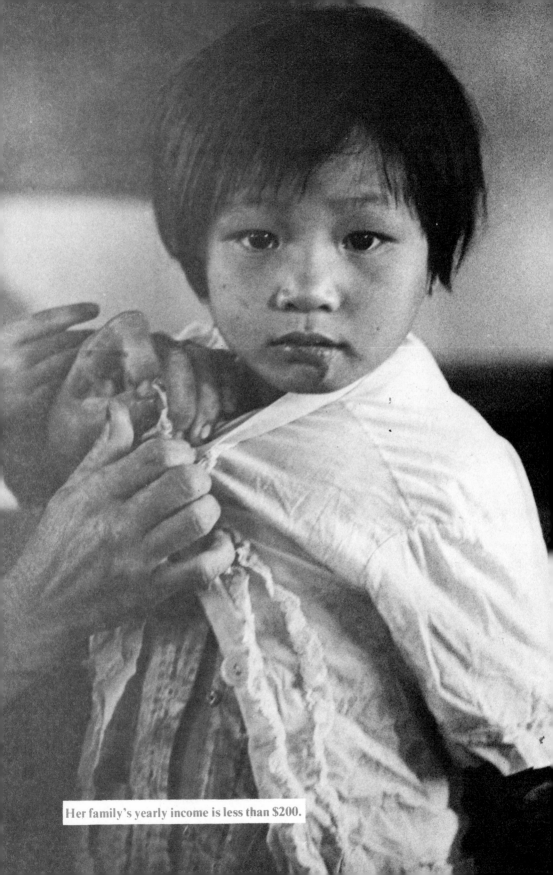

Her family's yearly income is less than $200.

The Story of People's Worship

Religion, broadly speaking, is the worship of a superior spiritual being. Many books have been written on how and why religion began but Catholic teaching has always held that the original primitive religion was a divinely revealed belief in one God.

The earliest humans who received this revelation from God passed it on to their children, and so it was handed down from generation to generation. As the human race grew and the great migrations began, the originally revealed religion was corrupted. Primitive man, savage and untutored, became full of superstitions based on ignorance and fear.

Without a continuing revelation, primitive man fell further and further away from the truth. He personalized the forces of nature over which he had no control. The next step was to perform acts that would propitiate those forces and keep them from harming him. Thus the elements became divine beings to be worshipped.

This corruption of divinely revealed religion became more complex the further man drifted away from original truth. It grew into religions like that of the Greeks who had to construct a big building to hold the images of all their gods.

As nations developed, religion played an increasingly important role. It inspired literature, painting and architecture. It served as a bond to hold people together.

While in the greater part of the world, religion developed naturally, God did not entirely desert man. He had a master plan that involved a certain people. He kept the true revelation alive among those people, visiting them when they seemed to stray away, sometimes punishing, sometimes rewarding. Those people were the Hebrews and for them God raised up leaders — Noah, Abraham, Moses, and others. It was the Hebrews who kept alive the original revelations in preparation for the day God would send His Son to earth to teach men.

31

Mangbetu girl of Zaire

How People Got Their Color

Because skin color was the most noticeable difference between people, the early European explorers thought it the most important. What color was Adam and Eve? No one knows for sure but the best scientific theory believes that our earliest ancestors were brown people—between white and black.

From somewhere in Asia, mankind began its great march—into Europe, down to the tip of Africa, across Siberia to the Americas. As people separated and lived apart, physical differences began to appear. People who settled near the equator developed a darker skin color. Those who went north into colder climates grew whiter and at the same time developed more hair because of the cold. As centuries passed and these people married within their own small groups, many of the traits developed by environment became fixed and permanent.

Today the darkest people in the world are to be found in equatorial West Africa. The lightest people are to be found in northwest Europe, particularly in the Scandinavian countries. Most of the rest of the people of the world (excluding emigrants from the above mentioned areas) are between the two extremes. These in-betweens are closer to the skin shade of our original ancestors.

Scientists know that skin color is determined by two chemicals, carotene and melanin. The former gives a yellow tinge, while the latter browns the skin. Every person has some of these chemicals in his or her skin, except for the albino who is wholly colorless. People who are browner than others simply have more melanin. Thus a negro is not completely different from a white man, he simply has greater amount of melanin in his skin. Indeed, there are members of the Caucasian race who have far darker skins than many persons classed as Negroes.

There are wide differences within a race. The Caucasian race, for example, inhabits Europe, the Near East and India. The extreme types within this group vary from the Nordic who is very light skinned, blonde, tall and blue-eyed, to the Indian of India who is dark skinned, with straight black hair and dark eyes.

It would be a good thing if people would not speak of races in terms of color. The use of the terms "black," "yellow" and "white" can be very confusing. It is better to use the words "Negroid," "Mongoloid" and "Caucasian."

The most important thing about human bodies is not that some bodies differ because of skin color but that the anatomy of all human bodies is the same. The human body is the best proof for the common origin of mankind. Each one of us has the same number of teeth. The human hand is composed of many bones and muscles, but everyone of us—Caucasian, Mongoloid and Negroid—have the same number and kind.

There's No Place

Everyone needs a roof overhead. A house gives shelter from rain and cold, a storage place for tools and personal possessions, and protection against enemies. A house answers a man's need for privacy and is a center for family gatherings. It is the first step in social living.

Man's earliest home was probably a natural rock shelter. Cave dwellings used by man have been found in many parts of the world. Some of them, like the Cro-Magnon caves of France and Spain, were beautifully decorated thousands of years ago with striking designs of men and animals.

Later people, like the prehistoric lake dwellers of Switzerland, built thatch-roofed houses on wooden stilts, near the shores. These people were as much at home on water as on land. Their villages could be easily defended against enemies,

Like Home

both animal and human. When they needed food, they had only to fish from their houses.

Over the years, houses developed. The richer and more important a person was, the greater became his house. The fashion in houses varies from region to region as the drawings on this pair of pages show. How many of these houses can you identify by their styles? Make a guess before reading the next lines. Starting at the lower left corner, and going up and around, you will find these homes: (1) Pueblo Indians; (2) Swiss chalet; (3) Cape Cod American; (4) Spanish; (5) Ona Indian of Tierra del Fuego; (6) French chateau; (7) Amazon Indian; (8) Bedouin; (9) African; (10) Mongolian Tartar; (11) Thailand; (12) New Zealand Maori. No matter what its shape or size, every man's home is his castle!

Why People Build Their

1. Material at hand. People build their homes out of the materials close at hand. The American Indians of our eastern seaboard made their huts out of birchbark, for birch trees grew all over their region. The Indians of the great plains lived in an area of few trees. However, they were in the midst of great animal herds—buffalo and antelope. As a result, they made their tepees from animal skins.

In the densely forested districts of Africa, huts of grass and broad leaves are common. The Pygmies of Zaire make use of the lush vegetation to build their houses. They show great skill in fashioning roofs out of layers of broad leaves. They stay dry even during the heavy downpours that drench the jungle.

Stone, twigs and thatch are other natural materials that have been used for building. The poorer Mam Indians of Guatemala build houses with sticks for walls and grass for roofs. Sometimes the sticks are woven together, other times merely set upright. Many European peas-

ant families live in wattle-and-daub (twig-and-plaster) houses. Here, too, thatch is the handy roofing material.

Mud is another handy material for construction. It is particularly suitable in lands where there is little rainfall. In our own Southwest many buildings are constructed of adobe which is mud mixed with straw. This type of construction is also used extensively in the Andes.

Most people are poor and that is why they must use available materials. When people are rich, they then tend to construct along better lines. A poor man must live in a log cabin but when he becomes rich, he builds a grand house of stone or wood with a slate roof imported from a great distance.

2. Weather and climate. Here are two more important factors that determine how houses must be built. A flat-roofed house in the Swiss Alps would collapse under the weight of snow, so roofs have a steep pitch there. Likewise in rainy lands, roofs must be sloping so that

Houses The Way They Do

water will drain off. In countries where the rainfall is heavy, roofs extend far beyond the walls of the houses so that there will be protective covering for people who move about outdoors.

When the Eskimo builds his snow house, or igloo, it is wind-proof and snug to protect him from the howling blizzards of the north. However, when an Indian in the Amazon jungle builds his shelter, very often the sides are left completely open. This is to give maximum ventilation against heat and humidity.

Even in our own civilization, weather and climate are important factors in architecture. A house designed for Florida or southern California can have lots of open areas, use plenty of glass, be flat-roofed and low and rambling. A house designed for Massachusetts, on the other hand, must be more compact and more closed in so that heating costs will be minimized.

3. Location. The places where people build their houses also help to decide the type of construction. Seminole Indians live in the swampy Everglades of Florida. Their houses are built on posts above the damp earth. The sides are left open so that breezes will keep their few belongings dry.

Sometimes the locations where people build their houses present problems from enemies. Such people

must either move away or build their homes so that they can be easily defended. Methods used to solve this problem are ingenious.

The Gaddang and Kalinga people of the Philippines build their dwellings high up in trees. Some of these houses are sixty feet from the ground. They are usually reached by ladders. One of the most unusual places for house building can be found in Southwestern United States in Arizona's Canyon de Chelly. There high in an opening in a cliff, Indians built a village of stone and adobe. This village could only be reached by very long ladders.

The main reason for a house is shelter. A house is built to provide protection from the weather. It has other ends, too. A house serves as a place of storage where food and personal property can be safely kept. A house answers a basic human craving for privacy. Finally, a house serves as a meeting place for family and friends. The house is one of man's greatest inventions.

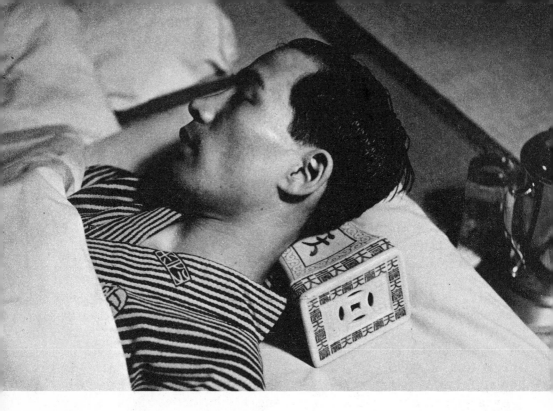

Sleeping Is an Art

Sleep is necessary for life. Scientists have shown that man can go longer without food and water than he can without sleep. Next to the air we breathe, sleep is the most important thing needed to preserve life. Most people require eight hours of sleep a day but the manner in which they take this rest varies from country to country.

Only in lands sharing the Western tradition (like North America and western Europe) do we find elaborate bedsteads, down pillows and soft blankets. In eastern Europe, for instance, unmarried men often sleep in haylofts during summer; but in winter all members of each family sleep on shelves built around the kitchen stove.

Eskimos crawl into fur sleeping bags, while the Chama Indians of the Amazon sleep exposed to the breezes on mats. In many warm areas of Latin America, the people sleep in net hammocks. In Persia, there are no beds as such. People just pile up a few richly colored rugs on the floor.

Pillows are another source of variety. Many people do not use pillows. Others, like most Americans, prefer a soft bump under the head. The Japanese rest their heads on wooden pillows.

Since earliest times, men have used the night for sleeping. In warm areas, most people use the noon hours for a siesta. Often they deduct the time spent in siesta from the night's sleep; in more advanced areas they dine and go to bed later.

The manner of sleeping is determined by custom and locale. Except in Western nations, few people sleep on beds as we in America know them. In Japan (opposite), the bed is made directly on the floor, and a wooden block is used as a pillow. Among poor Japanese families (below), the sleeping quarters are used for many purposes. The youngsters (above), successfully combat the torrid heat of Ghana by sleeping on a cool floor mat.

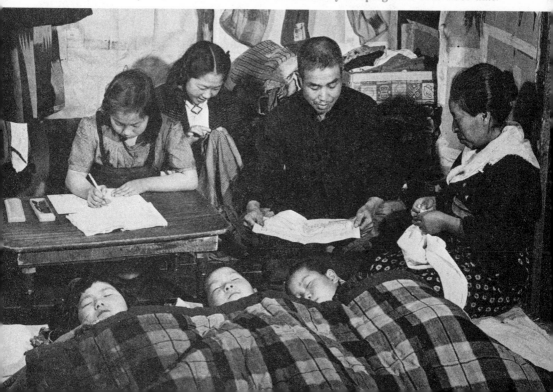

Cave Drawing

Mayan Glyphs

Egyptian Hieroglyphs

光
朗

Chinese Characters

Greek Letters

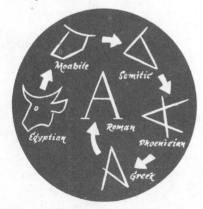

How Writing Began

Men first began to write with pictures. The cavemen knew how to tell a simple story in their vigorous drawings of men and animals.

At various times and places people have devised many systems of writing. We know, for instance, that the tax collectors of ancient Egypt kept records of their receipts by scratching pictures of containers—like a basket of grain—on the walls of their storehouses. Five baskets would indicate a payment of five times the normal measure. Eventually, pictures of objects were combined with sound symbols to form the hieroglyphics or characters of Egyptian writing. The Indians of Central America also used a system of hieroglyphic writing.

Pictures are the basis of the Chinese alphabet. But over centuries of use the original meaning of picture characters has become blurred. For example, the Chinese character for heaven is 天 (T'ien). It contains the picture of a man 大 raising his arms towards the sky. Chinese characters are symbols with no connection to sound; thus they can be understood all over China, even by persons speaking different dialects.

Our own alphabet is a handy system of indicating sounds by simple symbols. It was invented several thousands of years ago by Phoenician traders who spread it all over the Mediterranean world. The Greeks and Romans handed it on, through the Church, to our own civilization. Christian missioners have often adapted it to fit the needs of people with no writing system of their own.

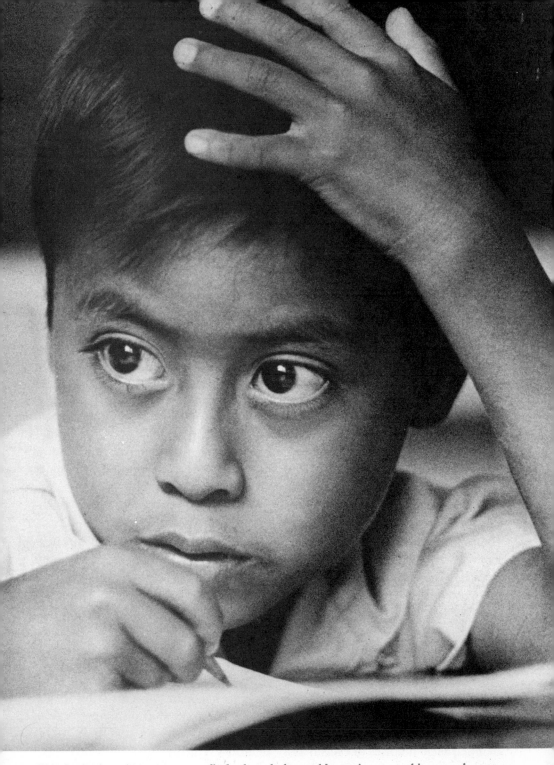

This Latin American youngster finds the whole world opening up to his grasp because he is at last able to read and write. Yet 60% of the people in the world are illiterate, unable to read or write. World education has a big job ahead of it to reach all.

What Catholics Must Believe About People

We are all brothers. There is a great equality among men. It makes no difference whether we are Eskimos, Americans or Hottentots, God loves all equally. Saint Paul said it this way: "No more Jew or Gentile, no more slave or freeman . . . You are all one person in Christ Jesus."

Some may have heard of Cardinal Stepinac, the martyr who defied Tito rather than yield the truth. This is what he said one day:

"We assert that every people and every race which has been formed on earth today has the right to life and to treatment worthy of man. All of them without distinction, be they members of the Gypsy race or of another, be they Negroes or Europeans, be they Jew or Aryans, all of them have equal right to say: 'Our Father, who art in heaven.'. . . Therefore the Catholic Church has always condemned every injustice and compulsion perpetrated in the name of social, racial and national theories."

Christian doctrine proclaims that all men are one because all men are made in the image and likeness of God, and all have been equally redeemed by Jesus Christ. Time and again Catholic popes have condemned false theories of racism as a denial of the oneness of mankind.

"How can we claim to love the divine Redeemer, if we hate those whom He has redeemed with His precious blood, so that He might make them members of His mystical body? For that reason the beloved disciple warns us: 'If any man say, "I love God," and hateth his brother, he is a liar.'"—Pope Pius XII, *The Mystical Body of Christ.*

Vatican Council II rejected racism in no uncertain terms. Pointing out that all men are created in God's image, the Fathers declared there can be no reason for distinctions among men. They added: "As a consequence, the Church repudiates, as foreign to the mind of Christ, any discrimination against men or harassment of them because of their race, color, condition of life, or religion."

What are the practical applications of the Church's teaching about people? They are these: (1) We must have a regard for all the peoples of the earth, our brothers in Christ. (2) Since we must love our neighbor, we must study who our neighbor is. (3) We must accept the responsibility to promote the welfare of all mankind according to Christian ideals. (4) We must share in some way in carrying Christ's teaching to all non-Catholics. (5) We must have devotion to the Church's task of carrying to all men Christ's life of charity.

42

Flathead Indian Woman

WHEN YOU SAY

Do You
Mean This?

my
~~Our~~ Father who art in heaven,

~~hallowed be Thy Name;~~

~~Thy Kingdom come; Thy will~~

~~be done on earth as it is~~

~~in heaven.~~ Give ~~us~~ *me* this day

~~our~~ *my* daily bread; and forgive ~~us~~ *me*

~~our~~ *my* trespasses ~~as we forgive~~

~~those who trespass against us;~~

and lead ~~us~~ *me* not into temptation,

but deliver ~~us~~ *me* from evil.

AMEN.

THE OUR FATHER

This is not the prayer of Christ
for all God's children. Instead...

You should say and think this!

Our Father	Father of every one of the world's 3.7 billion people.
who art in heaven, hallowed be Thy Name;	In my country and in the whole world.
Thy Kingdom come;	Among the billions of people who know You not.
Thy will be done on earth as it is in heaven.	I will do something in some way to help make Your will known to all men everywhere.
Give us this day our daily bread;	All of us. Those in Korea, and Mexico, and Africa, and everywhere.
and forgive us our trespasses as we forgive those who trespass against us;	Even my enemies and those who persecute Your Church.
and lead us not into temptation, but deliver us from evil. Amen.	Including the supreme evil of forgetting or ignoring Your commands.

How Well Do You Remember?

Here are some questions based on the pages you have just read. How many can you answer?

1. Is there such a thing as the English race? (p. 8)
2. Are more or fewer races appearing on the earth? (p. 9)
3. Why is the soul of every man infinitely precious? (p. 15)
4. Name three ways we depend on other people. (p. 12)
5. How many basic racial stocks are there? (p. 24)
6. Is it true that the blood of each race is different? (p. 27)
7. Where did the human race probably begin life? (p. 26)
8. What are the two main reasons for people moving? (p. 27)
9. Which reason is the more important? (p. 27)
10. Can you name two migrations of our own times? (p. 27)
11. How many words does the average American know? (p. 28)
12. How many languages are there in the world? (p. 28)
13. What people kept alive God's original revelation? (p. 31)
14. What probable color were Adam and Eve? (p. 33)
15. Can a dark-skinned native of India be a member of the Caucasian race? (p. 33)
16. What are the three things that determine how most people build their houses? (pp. 36-37)
17. What is the main reason for having a house? (p. 37)
18. Can man go longer without food and water or without sleep? (p. 38)
19. How did men first write? (p. 40)
20. Why must we study about our neighbors? (p. 42)
21. Why do we say "all men are one"? (p. 42)
22. How do we share in carrying Christ's teachings to non-Christians? (p. 42)
23. Must we forgive those who persecute the Church? (p. 45)
24. Why do you think this book was written? (p. 7)
25. Why are we sometimes suspicious of people? (p. 7)

Part 2

Looking At The World

Did you ever stop to think that if the 3.7 billion people of our earth walked past you at the rate of one per second, it would take 587 years, and that every other person who passed you would come from Asia?

Every year the population of the world increases by 30 million people. There are over five times as many people in the world today as there were in 1650. This is largely because modern science has been able to increase the life span of man. In the days of the Roman Empire a person could expect to live to be twenty-three. Even in the United States as late as 1850, a person could only expect to live to the age of thirty-nine. Today we can reasonably hope to live to be over seventy-one.

As a result, many areas of the world are becoming crowded. If all the people of the earth were evenly distributed there would be about 69 persons on each square mile of land. But in reality, some parts of the world are very crowded, while others have plenty of room. Java has more than 1,500 people per square mile, but Alaska has only one person for every *two* square miles.

In the following pages, you will meet many of these people closeup. You are sure to find them interesting!

Chapter 1

North America

YOU ARE one of 230 million North Americans. The term, North America, is usually used to cover all the territory from the Isthmus of Panama north together with the outlying islands. For convenience, however, we are considering North America as composed of Canada and the United States with their adjoining islands.

You are living on a very unusual continent. The people of no other continent are so mixed in race and nationality. In North America there are Indians, Eskimos, Africans, Asians and Europeans. The civilization of North America is very young, only about 450 years old. Today half the wealth of the world is possessed by North Americans, who represent only about a tenth of the world's population.

The oldest inhabitants of North America were Indians and Eskimos whose descendants today are engulfed in a new civilization. These original settlers represent only a very small part of the total population. They have adopted the American way of life which is a mixture of the customs of all the peoples who make up North America.

North Americans as a whole enjoy a higher standard of living than do the people of any other continent. They have a unity of purpose and a sense of destiny. North America is a Christian continent, divided between Catholics and Protestants. This belief in the doctrines of Christ has given the people of North America an interest in their neighbors around the world and has made the continent a storehouse of charity.

Americans of ancient heritage

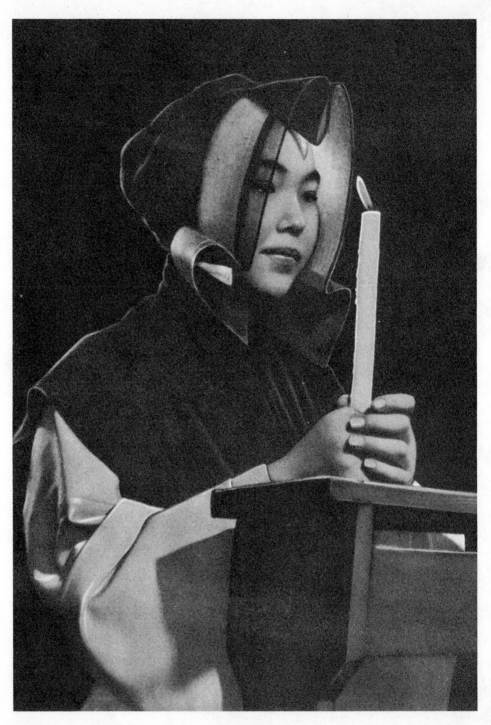

Sister Naya Pelagie is the first Eskimo girl to become a nun. She grew up in an igloo at Eskimo Point Village in Canada's north, where her father was a sorcerer.

Tomorrow Never Comes

ESKIMOS call themselves *Inuit,* which means *The People.* To the Eskimo their land is the center of the universe and their customs the only way of doing things. The rest of the world is out of step with them.

It was their cousin, the Indian, who contemptuously named them Eskimos, raw meat eaters. The Eskimos live under the flags of the United States, Canada, the Soviet Union, and Denmark, but none of these nations has made too great an impression on them. They range on both sides of the Arctic Circle from Greenland to the Asiatic mainland.

That the Eskimo has been able to survive in what is probably the most inhospitable territory on earth is an amazing tribute to his adaptability. He must exist without any agriculture whatsoever. He has no trees for building or wood for burning as fuel. He keeps no livestock other than his dogs, and thus gets no wool and no cloth for protecting himself against the most inclement climate. He lives in a region of great ice glare, where exposure can mean permanent blindness.

To solve these problems, the Eskimo has produced ingenious solutions. His diet is almost entirely meat and fish but instead of throwing away the internal organs as does his more civilized brother, he eats *everything.* In this way he obtains the necessary vitamins. To offset the lack of trees, he hunts for driftwood for building and when this cannot be found he builds with whale ribs or snow. From the seal and whale, he extracts oil for light and cooking. To replace cloth, he wears clothes of skins, carefully and expertly tailored. Needles for sewing are made from whalebone, and thread from strips of skin or the sinews of animals. To protect his eyes from the glare of the sun on ice and snow, he wears pieces of wood or bone over his eyes with small slits for seeing.

Where he comes into contact with the white man, he is ready to borrow whatever he wishes of the white man's culture without doing any essential harm to his own. He learns the usefulness of money and spends it for such things as Coca-Cola and bubble gum. When he can afford them, he buys whale bombs to use in place of the harpoon. These bombs explode inside the whale. He has no objection to replacing his kayak with a gasoline-powered boat or to use empty five-gallon cans as buoys and markers in place of inflated bladders. He sees no incongruity in carrying a thermos jug of coffee on the day's hunt or decorating the walls of his sod house with cheap alarm clocks.

He is even prepared to go further. Eskimos in Alaska have been elected to the State Legislature. Some Alaskan Eskimos have incorporated into a purchasing agency under the title Alaskan Native Industries Co-operative Association, and have established a headquarters in Seattle. Instead of killing off the aged infirm as was the custom a few years ago (and still is the custom in many areas), the Alaskan Eskimo now fills out government forms to acquire old age pensions. In place of hitching up a dog team to go visit his brother, he will make his way to the nearest airport. And when he lives near a mission, he is liable to become a Catholic and his daughter a nun as began some years back when the first Eskimo girl was professed.

For the most part, however, the Eskimos live in communities apart from a continuing influence of the white man. They lead a nomadic life, preserving as much as they can of the old ways. Their seasons are not a matter of temperature but daylight. Hunting to them is not a sport but a problem of life and death. Indeed, the rigors of daily life have given them a moral code and malformed conscience unlike that of any other people.

Take, for example, the Eskimo attitude towards homicide. Acts that to us would be revolting and criminal are to them perfectly acceptable. Infanticide, suicide, the killing of invalids and old folks are not only permitted but in the Eskimo mind are often necessarily good.

A N INFANT, for instance, is considered nonproductive to the community. Supposing that a mother is nursing one child when a second comes along. It is almost impossible for her to nurse two due to her need for ease in getting around and the tremendous work she must do. Father and mother will talk over the problem and offer the second child for adoption. If there are no takers, infanticide may follow with no blame attached.

Usually parents will go to greater lengths to preserve a boy because he is a potential food-getter. Girls are a poorer risk because they will be married off and be lost to the family. A boy on the other hand will remain in the family and thus becomes an investment for old age.

Putting to death old folks and invalids depends upon the Eskimo economy at the moment. When resources are scarce, old people and invalids become a threat to the continued existence of the entire community. Therefore, by Eskimo logic, they can be put to death without question or blame. Strangulation, stabbing and abandonment are the usual ways of causing death. However, in most communities the act must be performed by a close relative, otherwise it is considered murder. Often the deed is committed at the insistence of the aged one or invalid who insists on it as a right.

Cannibalism is also legally permitted by Eskimo custom in times of starvation. The Eskimo would prefer other food but when faced with a question of existence he has no scruples or moral reasons not to engage in the debased act, killing and eating the young, weak, and infirm. To him it is solely a matter of self-preservation and he is unable to comprehend white man's law that prohibits it.

The anthropologist, Knud Rasmussen, who is an authority on Eskimo culture, once spent a long period with a community of fifteen Musk Ox Eskimo families. He discovered that every adult male in the group had been involved in murder, and that in practically every instance the murder had been committed because of a woman. There is no community punishment for murder but blood revenge by kinsmen is expected. The revenge murder may be immediate or delayed over a long period, but the murderer knows that eventually he will meet the fate he gave out. Yet he does not appear concerned.

While single murder is left to settlement by blood revenge, repeated murder becomes a threat to the community. The multiple murderer is a social menace and as such is put to death by an agent appointed by the community. No blood revenge can be taken against the executioner since he is performing a community act. Usually a close kinsman is chosen to perform the killing.

Among many Eskimo groups, quarrels are settled by wrestling or fighting. Wrestling occurs in Siberia, Alaska, and Greenland. Fighting, or delivering alternate straight blows at one's opponent, is found among the central tribes from Hudson's Bay to Bering Strait. Victory in these contests goes always to the stronger man.

GREENLAND ESKIMOS have an unusual type of contest to settle grudges and disputes. The weapons used are words, usually in the form of songs. Song duels are carried on for months and even years. Usually by the time that the song duel is ended, the participants have received so much pleasure from the contest that the cause of the quarrel has long since been forgotten.

Among most Eskimo tribes, marriage and sex are not in any way synonymous. Marriage is necessary for the man, not for the fulfillment of basic instincts, but to have someone to look after him, prepare his food, and make his clothing. This often leads to unions between young men and old women. An unmarried adult male is an extreme rarity. A man marries for economic reasons, not for sex. The man's latter needs can be taken care of outside of marriage; in securing a partner marriage is not necessary. Marriage is regarded lightly. Partners are interchanged, and it is not unusual for a young man in his twenties to have had as many as a half-dozen marriages.

When children are born to a marriage, there is reason for more stability. But children are no guarantee of permanence. A wife is able to walk off and leave her husband at any time. It is not uncommon for a husband to come home from a hunt and find his wife "married" to another man. He has no redress other than personal revenge. The community ignores the whole affair and the best thing that the dispossessed hunter can do is take up with the wife of the man who replaced him.

NOT EVERY TRIBE is as loose morally as those described. The Nunivak Eskimos of the Bering Sea have a stricter and more conventional morality. Among these people marriages are arranged between families, usually when the boy is about twenty and the girl thirteen. The young man sends a gift of new clothing for the bride and she signifies her acceptance by carrying food to him. These two acts constitute the wedding ceremony. The Nunivak marriage is supposedly arranged between people in love. For the first few years of married life, the couple remain in the wife's home. Only when his family begins to increase does the husband establish a home of his own.

The Nunivaks have other customs that set them apart from their Eskimo neighbors. Like the Navajos, they practice a mother-in-law taboo. A man never looks at his mother-in-law and if he must speak to her, it is through a third party, usually his wife. On the other hand, while the wife is forbidden to look at her husband's parents, she can speak to her mother-in-law directly, provided her eyes are lowered.

In areas where the Eskimos live close to civilization, such as in Alaska, more and more couples are being legally married in religious or civil ceremonies. The reason in many cases is to establish legal inheritance rights. The Alaskan District Court appoints marriage commissioners, whose sole duty is to officiate at weddings in remote areas.

THE ESKIMO is by nature religious but like all primitive peoples his religion is a conglomeration of superstition governed by the shaman, or witch doctor.

Although the Eskimos are scattered over a wide area, religious beliefs are fairly constant. Eskimo religion is a complexity of spirits; indeed, everything seems to have a spirit from rocks, tools, and clothing to geographical features. Supreme control of the spirits rests in the Sea Goddess, or her husband, or the Moon Man, or the Spirit of the Air, depending on the area or group. The Eskimo believes in a human soul, and there appears to be some belief in reincarnation.

There does not seem to be any preoccupation with death or the position of the soul after death. The Eskimo leads a precarious existence and his thoughts are on the present. He has little idea of an afterworld, expecting punishment here and now for offense against taboos. His religion is intensely personal and there is little religious activity on the part of the community as such. Amulets and charms are necessary and part of his superstitious life.

In those areas where he does live close to whites, the Eskimo is continually discriminated against. He is exploited by the white merchant who will introduce him to alcohol and sell him useless knickknacks. We have introduced him to measles, tuberculosis, and chicken pox—diseases unknown before the white man came. We have changed his limited but healthy diet by giving him bread, coffee, and sugar, with a subsequent decline in health. In many areas, such as Point Barrow, we have given him work in defense projects with the consequent loss of his desire and ability to hunt. When the defense work ends, as it must some day, no one knows how the Eskimo will continue to exist.

In spite of the white man's "gifts" to the Eskimo, he remains strangely loyal—an extrovert worrying not about tomorrow but only about today.

All Men Are One

"For all peoples comprise a single community, and have a single origin, since God made the whole race of men dwell over the entire face of the earth (cf. Acts 17:26). One also is their final goal: God. His providence, His manifestations of goodness, and His saving designs extend to all men (cf. Wis. 8:1; Acts 14:17; Rom. 2:6-7; 1 Tim. 2:4) against the day when the elect will be united in that Holy City ablaze with the splendor of God, where the nations will walk in His light (cf. Apoc. 21:23 f.)." — VATICAN COUNCIL II, *Declaration on the Relationship of the Church to Non-Christian Religions*

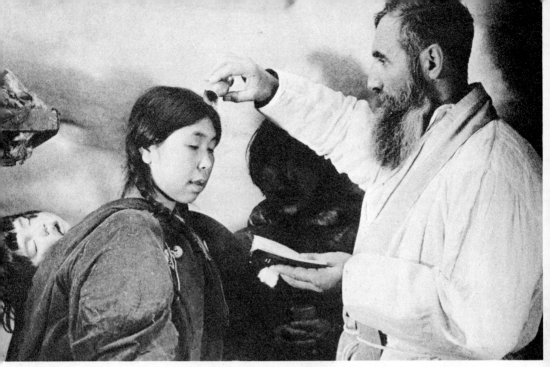

These Eskimos (see page 51) manage to make a successful blend of the old and new.

Alaskans are Americans. Alaskans live in America's last frontier, an area one-fifth the size of the United States. The name of the country means "great land" or "mainland" in the language of the Aleuts, one of Alaska's primitive peoples. While nearly a third of the territory lies within the Arctic Circle, most Alaskans live in the southern region where the climate is more temperate because of the warm currents of the Pacific Ocean.

Three-quarters of the people of Alaska belong to the white race. A few are descendants of the Russian fur traders who originally settled the country. Most are pioneers or children of pioneers who emigrated from the United States to the territory after it was purchased from Russia in 1866.

The original people of Alaska are split into three groups: the Eskimos, who live in the north; the gentle Aleuts, cousins to the Eskimos, who live in the chain of islands stretching westward; and some 14,000 Indians.

Alaskan Profile. Over three hundred thousand people in an area twice the size of Texas. There are about 33,000 Indians, Eskimos, and Aleuts; about 10 per cent of whom are Catholics. The religion of the white population is proportionately as in the United States. The people support themselves by fishing, lumbering, mining, and some farming.

Canada is like two countries. Canadians are our very good neighbors. Some 22 million of them live in a land larger than the whole United States; in fact, Canada is the third largest country on earth. The oldest

55

European settlers were French and today French-speaking Canadians make up one-fourth of the whole population. Their stronghold is the Province of Quebec. The five and one-half million French Canadians are good, hard-working citizens, justly proud of their Catholic Faith and French cultural traditions. French Canadians fought a long, bitter struggle in defense of their own religion and language. Eventually they won the right to live their own lives within the framework of Canada's fair, democratic system.

Canada's second tradition is British. Today about 50 per cent of Canadians are of English, Scotch, or Irish origin. In addition, about 18 per cent of the population represents the wave of immigrants who arrived in Canada during the past century, 2 million after World War II. The majority came from Germany, the Ukraine, Scandinavia, Poland, Italy and the Netherlands.

In Canada, the Catholic tradition is old and deep. It was established by pioneer Jesuit explorers, like Pere Marquette; it was nourished by the blood of many martyrs, like Saints Anthony Daniel and John de Brebeuf, who died gloriously as missioners among the Huron Indians. Today there are more than ten million Catholics, not quite half of the population.

Canadian Catholics, particularly those of French origin, are fervent supporters of the missions. Thanks to their efforts the Church is well established among the Eskimos and Indians of Canada's northern provinces, and in many lands around the world. Canada sends almost as many clergy to the foreign missions as does the United States.

Catholic Canadians are very proud of the world-famous co-operative experiments that were developed in Antigonish, Nova Scotia. The leaders who were trained at this Catholic school for both co-operatives and credit unions are now carrying on their social work all over the world. Two Catholic universities in Quebec Province—Laval University and the University of Montreal—have some twenty thousand students. The Catholic population is being increased by an influx of refugees to whom Canada has opened wide its doors because of a tremendous industrial boom. The GNP for 1972 passed the $100 billion annual rate.

Canadian Profile. A bilingual country where the government rewards parents for having children by granting a monthly allowance for each child. Since 1900, the people of Canada have seen their country undergo a rapid growth. The nation's population is up 400 per cent; farms number over 366 thousand; new mineral and oil discoveries have put export trade at over 18 billions. A new unity has come to French and English speaking Canadians, although a French separatist movement manages to make headlines.

This husky Quebec lumberjack traces his forebears to France but he is 100% American.

What Is an Indian?

Indians are a part of American life. Fred Harris became a senator from Oklahoma. Maria Tallchief was America's finest ballerina. Wayne Newton is one of the largest drawing names in Las Vegas. Dee Brown is a prominent author. All of these people have one thing in common: their American Indian heritage.

When Columbus reached America, he wrongly believed that he had found a westward route to the East Indies. So the inhabitants he discovered were called Indians.

Today more and more Indians are leaving their reservations and mixing with the white population. Sometimes it becomes difficult to tell who is an Indian and who is not. The Bureau of Census counts a person as an Indian if his neighbors recognize him as such. The United States Indian Service recognizes a person as an Indian if he has one-quarter Indian blood.

The American Indians belong to a branch of the great Mongoloid Race. About 20,000 years ago, their ancestors began to cross from Siberia to North America. Some scientists think that at that time there was a land bridge connecting Asia and Alaska. A great ice sheet extended from the North Pole to Wisconsin. When this ice sheet melted 10,000 years ago, say scientists, the water covered the bridge.

In time, the Mongoloid wanderers spread out over both Americas. At first they were all nomadic hunters. But gradually some tribes settled down and began cultivation. In some areas, like Peru and Mexico, great civilizations developed. But even by the time Columbus arrived, most Indians had not progressed far beyond the Stone Age. Their tools were primitive because they had no knowledge of iron. In 1492, there were about one million Indians in the United States; they were divided into about 2,000 tribes.

Once the white man arrived the life of the Indian began to change. Although brave in battle, the Indian was unable to resist the better-organized and equipped white settlers. War, the white man's diseases and the white man's liquor sapped Indian strength. Finally the Indians were forced onto reservations.

Today, better times have come to our original Americans. In 1924, Congress made citizens of all American Indians. In every state in the Union they have the vote.

Today there are 792,000 American Indians who represent about 300 tribes. One out of every three Indians is a Catholic. Indians are increasing in political action, following the lead of other minorities. Wounded Knee was an expression of unrest.

America's Indians have an inborn artistry. Those of the Southwest were skilled in ceramics and jewelry design. The Plains Indian created gorgeous feather costumes.

Man of the People

THE NAVAJO INDIANS, whose homeland encompasses some of the most rugged and barren territory to be found in New Mexico and Arizona, call themselves *Dineh*—the people. Ask a Navajo where he lives, and he will reply, *"Dineh twah"*—"Among the Navajo People."

The Navajos are great borrowers. Their language is closely related to Eskimo. Their religion comes from the Pueblo Indians. Their care of horses and sheep is a reminder of what they learned from the Spanish conquistadors. And on these ancient ways of life have been placed the marks of modern American civilization.

Many people think of American Indians as a dying and disappearing race. This is true of some tribes but not of the Navajos. Despite their incredible poverty and the many natural obstacles to existence, they are increasing at a rate almost double that of the rest of the country's population.

Typical of the modern Navajo is Tom Duran. This isn't his real name but it will serve to protect his desire for anonymity. Tom is a Navajo not easily forgotten. Taller than the average Indian, wiry, he impresses any observer with his restless energy. His dark eyes burn with the pride of his people. His full mouth shows determination. His mind is agile and sharp. When he gives one of his rare smiles, you note his even white teeth.

Educated in a Government school, Tom speaks perfect English as well as his native tongue. He served as a soldier in Korea. After the war he returned to New Mexico, and got a job helping to make atomic energy at Los Alamos. Combining the money made there with his wartime pay, he bought a pick-up truck and set himself up in business, hauling supplies and people over the rutted-dirt roads between Gallup and the Navajo Reservation. He is the type of man who could develop into a captain of industry; in fact, he has been offered good jobs outside the reservation but he prefers his own independence.

Tom, his wife, and two children live just inside the reservation area, north of Gallup. His father is a silversmith, and Tom learned the art but prefers not to follow it. His mother is a second wife; although polygamy is now proscribed by the Tribal Council, it still exists to some extent. Tom knows the comforts of the modern world and appreciates them but he chooses to remain amid the stark and naked beauty of his homeland.

Tom Duran lives in a stone hogan which he built himself. It stands out sharply against the black rocks and sage-covered plain. If one comes upon it early in the morning, with its thin wisp of powdery smoke climbing from its smokehole, it seems to have a sense of unreality and other worldliness. Inside, Tom's wife will

Dignity characterizes this Navajo elder.

be stirring up the smoldering fire made in a converted oil drum. Then while Tom sits on his sheepskin bed, enjoying an early morning cigarette, Mrs. Duran will roll balls of dough to be dropped into sizzling fat and become fried bread.

Although Tom could pass into the twentieth-century world, his wife could not. She is completely Indian, content to live in the manner of her ancestors. She dresses in Indian style—full, long skirt and purple velveteen blouse contrasting with her husband's work khaki. Her hair is pulled into a bun at the back of her head; her movements are marked by the tinkling of her bone-and-silver necklace.

While the family sits at the table for breakfast, eating tortillas and fried eggs and drinking black coffee, Mrs. Duran complains that her elder son should not be sent to school, but should be kept at home to look after the sheep. Tom, however, is insistent: his two sons will be educated. Then they will be able to choose their own ways of life. If they desire to leave the reservation and go to California to work, they will be equipped to follow their choice.

When asked why he himself remains in his parched, eroded homeland, Tom gives that peculiar Navajo smile, encompasses the whole desert with his gesture, and asks in turn, "Who would want to live anywhere else?"

What Tom is saying is that this land has been the home of his people for countless generations. It was not always a desert. Once there were much grass, plenty of game, room for rich living. Each canyon, mountain, rock, and cactus is part of him. The spirits gave the Navajos this land between the four holy mountains, and what man should wish for more?

Tom is content to have his life dictated by the customs of his people. When he first married, he thought of building a house like those found off the reservation. But when it came time to build, he followed Navajo construction.

His wife was chosen for him by his father, from outside his own clan. Both his father and his uncle (his mother's brother) carried on the negotiations, with his father making the final choice. Navajos reckon their blood lines only through their mother's families. That is why his maternal uncle was consulted. Actually, Tom married into a clan that was already united to his own through several previous marriages. His in-laws live close to his own hogan, a fact that gives an occasion to observe an unusual Navajo custom.

MANY NAVAJO TABOOS have disappeared with education and time, but one that still clings strongly is the mother-in-law taboo. From the time Tom became engaged, he has never spoken to his mother-in-law. In fact, both he and his mother-in-law take great pains so that they shall never meet or even see each other. Although his wife and sons spend much time with his mother-in-law, Tom never goes to her hogan. On several occasions, when Tom and his mother-in-law unknowingly found themselves in each other's presence, each looked away to avoid seeing the other and quickly departed.

It is difficult to gauge Tom's belief in these taboos. It is not clear whether he does them from custom and second nature, or from some logical conviction. Tom's participation in the religious ceremonies of his tribe—the Rain Ceremony, the Mountain Chant, the Night Chant, and others—seems to be that of sincere religious belief rather than that of mere fidelity to tradition. There is a distinct social aspect to all these ceremonies since they occur in inactive periods of the

Navajo woman—
change is slow.

year. But basically their function seems to be religious and for Tom they are acts of religion.

Another throwback to the past is the fact that Tom regularly travels a hundred miles out of his way to get salt from a Navajo sacred salt deposit rather than to purchase it from the store on one of his many trips to Gallup. It is not a question of expense, because Tom spends many times the cost of the salt in gasoline and depreciation on his truck. When asked about these trips Tom says he makes them "because that salt tastes better" than store salt. The real reason seems to be religious.

Actually, Christianity has not made the same headway among the Navajos as it has among the other tribes of the Southwest. This is due partly to the nomadic life of the Navajos, and partly to the barrier set up by his tribal language. Until recent years, few Navajos knew any English. Conversions among Navajos are largely among youths attending mission schools. Unfortunately, the faith of those young converts is sorely tried, and sometimes destroyed, when they return to hogan life.

THE EARLY SPANISH missioners attempted to convert the Navajos with little success. Today the burden is carried by the Franciscan Fathers, ably assisted by Blessed Sacrament Sisters, Franciscan Missionaries of Mary and Our Lady of Victory Missionary Sisters. Catholic missioners have been commended many times by the Government for their excellent work in behalf of the Navajos. St. Michael's Mission in Arizona is the center for work among these people. Modern mission efforts began in 1898 by the Franciscan Fathers and Sisters of the Blessed Sacrament — so the effort is only seventy-five years old.

In the raising of children, Navajos follow customs similar to those of Africans. The child is allowed to learn by experience, and its desires are indulged. Both of Tom's children were brought into the world by a midwife in his own hogan. As soon as Tom's wife was physically able, she took the babies, and from that time on they were always close to her and very, very seldom out of her sight. Navajo children are fed when hungry and allowed to eat whatever they wish.

In practice, Navajo child-rearing gives the youngster a sense of being wanted, a feeling of being loved, and a natural integration into community life.

Tom Duran is the product of two worlds. In his material life, he has adopted many of the ways of the white man. In nonmaterial things he clings to the path of his ancestors. The changes that have come to him are largely matters of externals. He lives in a proud loneliness rivaled only by the vast empty land that surrounds him. He dresses "white" and thinks Indian. He stops in a movie house in Gallup, and then returns to his hogan to partake in some religious ritual. In studying Tom Duran, it is difficult to know whether he is making his way into the new world or remaining in the old one.

Tom Duran is a man of "the People"—a people standing between yesterday and tomorrow. The Navajos have survived by making necessary adaptions. They have adapted from the Apaches, the Pueblo tribes, the Spaniards and now the white Americans. But everything they adapted came out with their own individual stamp of Navajo. And this, say the Navajos, is as it should be. For after all, they are "the People"

The Homelands of our Indian Tribes

There are eight great Indian families in the United States. 1) Algonquin. This family was spread from the Atlantic to the Pacific. Some of the tribes included: *Atlantic* —Delaware, Mohican, Massachusetts, Micmac; *Plains*—Arapaho, Blackfoot, Cheyenne; *Central*— Illinois, Miami, Shawnee; *Californians*—Wiyot. 2) Iroquois. To this family belonged the famous Six Nations of New York State and the Appalachian Cherokee. 3) Caddo. This family lived west of the Mississippi and included the Pawnee and Wichita. 4) Muskhogeans. This family was the elite of the aborigines. Tribes included the Creek, Choctaw, Seminole, and Natchez. 5) Siouan. Making their homes in Missouri and the Dakotas were the Crow, Dakota, Osage, Kansas, Iowa, Omaha, Biloxi, Winnebago, and Oto. 6) Dene. The majority of this people lived in Alaska and Canada but some members such as the Kiowa and Chiricahua Apache and Navajo found their way into the Southwest. 7) Uto-Aztecan. Represented in Middle America by the Maya and Aztec, this group built the most complex civilizations. In our own Southwest, tribes of this family numbered Hopi, Ute, Snake, Comanche, Taos, and other Pueblo peoples, and the Mission tribes of California. 8) Penutian. Scattered along the Pacific from Mexico to Canada were such tribes as Nez Perce, Chinook, and Wallawalla.

Today Indian ways have largely yielded to white civilization.

The United States is a Land Made up of Many People

The real wealth of America is her people. No nation, however rich in natural resources, can achieve greatness unless its citizens have the skills to exploit those resources and the wisdom to co-operate with one another for the common good. Despite big differences in our racial origins, religious beliefs, and local traditions, we Americans have succeeded for the most part in subordinating the wishes of individuals or special groups to the broad interests of the country as a whole.

Americans have their own language. Although English is the official language of the United States, the American people have wrought many changes in that tongue. Before the World Wars a tremendous gulf was growing between English as spoken in England, and English as spoken here. Since then, the gulf has narrowed, but only because the English have adopted many American expressions. In vocabulary alone there are important differences in the meanings of many words. Here are a few examples:

American	English
ashman	dustman
backyard	garden
billboard	hoarding

Main Foreign Settlements in the U. S. A.

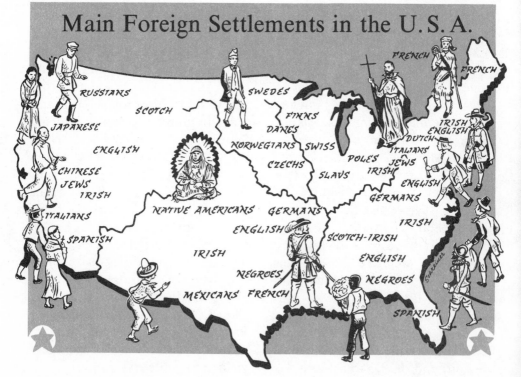

66

Americans have an ingrained respect for law and order. In some lands the uniform of a policeman is a sign of oppression and for fear. In the United States the policeman is a friend to whom we can turn in time of trouble or need. This is because our way of life guarantees us basic freedoms which are woven into our very Constitution.

checkers	draughts
cracker	biscuit
editorial	leader
elevator	lift
freight	goods
gasoline	petrol
hardware dealer	ironmonger
laborer	navy
orchestra seats	stalls
roast of meat	joint
shoe	boot
taxes	rates
undershirt	vest

America is an urbanized society where 73.5% of the people live on 1.5% of the land. In the United States today, out of every hundred people, eighty-seven are white, eleven are black, and the remaining two belong to other races.

Many Americans think that the first European settlers came on the *Mayflower* in 1620. Actually the Spanish were here a hundred years before that. French Huguenots settled in South Carolina in 1562. The Spanish founded the city of St. Augustine, Florida, in 1565; and in our Southwest, the city of Santa Fe was established in 1610.

After the explorers and missioners, traders came to America. Next came the settlers who established big plantations and imported Negro slaves from Africa. Most of those early settlers were adventurers seeking fortunes in the New World. However, thousands of people began pouring in to escape poverty, war, famine, and religious persecution in Europe. Such people were mostly poor or middle class.

They became our farmers and shopkeepers. On those people and their children, America was built.

England has had the most influence on America. While all nations have contributed to our greatness, the English have had the most influence. From the English, we received our national language, our respect for law, and our tradition of justice. From England, too, we received our system of education. Finally, from England we took the basis of our government; although of course, here as elsewhere, we made our own modifications. It was English law that told us to respect the dignity of all men. We took all of these things from England, adapted them to our own needs, and built a free and prosperous land.

America has a debt to the world. Since the contributions of other nations have given us our greatness, we must be prepared to give in return. This is only natural justice. As Catholics, we have a further obligation in charity. God expects us to share with others who are in need.

Americans cannot live in a corner by themselves. We have many things but we are not completely self-sufficient. We need the products of other countries. In the manufacture of your telephone, for example, forty-eight products from eighteen countries are needed. It was a European who discovered penicillin, the wonder drug that has saved many lives. We need other people. We are part of the human family.

Once a nation of rapid growth, the United States is at a zero growth.

David Ortega uses Spanish colonial art in his weaving for his New Mexico store.

Spanish Were Our First Settlers

America owes a great debt to Spain. Fray Angelico Chavez, the Franciscan poet from New Mexico, once wrote a charming little book called *La Conquistadora* It was written as the autobiography of an old statue of Our Lady that is still honored in Santa Fe. While telling her own history, the statue also tells the history of Santa Fe and the history of Father Chavez's own family, the first member of which arrived in New Mexico in 1625 to take up residence in a colony founded in 1598. The story is an interesting reminder that Spaniards pioneered many parts of our country at the price of their own lives.

Our Anglo-Saxon culture and language have influenced our thinking and even our history books. As a result, the part the Spanish played in developing our country is often forgotten or distorted. Actually, Spanish settlements began at the Atlantic Ocean and extended around the Gulf of Mexico, across Texas, to the Pacific Ocean. The Spanish names remain even to today—St. Augustine, Pensacola, San Antonio, Laredo, San Diego, San Francisco. It was a litany of saints that was strung across America from one ocean to another.

To the New World, the Spanish brought horses, Andalusian cattle, and seeds of every type. The Spanish started the fruit industry of California, the cattle business of Texas. They left behind a popular style of architecture. The American cowboy owes a big debt to the Spanish for they gave him his saddle, clothes, his *lingo*, and his way of handling cattle. *Rodeo* itself is a Spanish word.

Today there are about five million people of Spanish heritage in the United States. Many of these people have come from Mexico. They are found mainly in California and Texas although they are spread through the whole Southwest. Some of them are recent arrivals in the United States, others had ancestors here before the Pilgrims came. In recent years many Spanish-speaking people from Puerto Rico have emigrated to America. Most of these settled in New York City. Large numbers of Cubans fled to freedom in the United States.

Most Americans of Spanish heritage are Catholics. Some have been lost to the Church through marriage with non-Catholics. Others became Protestant when no Catholic instruction was available. The American hierarchy set up a special committee to take care of the Spanish-speaking. Many seminaries began Spanish courses and Mexican priests were brought to the United States. When persecution in Mexico closed seminaries, the American bishops opened a national seminary in New Mexico to train Mexicans. It is now closed.

Americans of Spanish ancestry dress for a pageant honoring Our Lady of Guadalupe.

Africa Also Contributed

Except for the English, no other people have given as much to our American culture as the Negro. Did you know that the pilot of one of Columbus' ships was a Negro, and that therefore the black man arrived in the New World at the same time as the white man? Did you know that Negroes were living in America before the Pilgrims arrived? Did you know that a Negro was killed in Boston during the first fighting that led to the Revolutionary War? The contribution of the Negro is woven into our whole history.

One out of every ten Americans is a Negro. Less than half of them live in the South, where most of them are engaged in farming. In recent years, their social progress has been tremendous, rising from unskilled to skilled occupations, many receiving recognition as teachers, doctors and lawyers.

The list of what Negroes have given to America is a long one. First, they have contributed labor to build our country. In the early days they developed cotton, rice, tobacco and sugar plantations in the South. Today they work in mills, mines and factories.

The second great contribution has been to our cultural life. What American has not been touched by the soulful words and melody of such spirituals as "Swing Low,

Sweet Chariot," or not had his feet set a-tapping by the syncopated melody of such songs as "The St. Louis Blues"? From the ranks of Negroes have come America's foremost entertainers. No other people have given so many great athletes to the American scene. In baseball, boxing, football, tennis, in almost every sport played, American Negroes have been at the top.

But the Negroes have not only contributed entertainment. The late Martin Luther King became a world symbol for human freedom. Thurgood Marshall was appointed to the Supreme Court. Dr. George Washington Carver discovered hundreds of uses for peanuts. Dr. Charles Drew set up the blood bank during World War II.

The main body of Negroes came to America as slaves. Even after the Civil War ended slavery, Negroes remained poor and uneducated. They were denied the vote and were kept in poor housing. It is only in the last two decades that they have found the opportunities given to all other Americans.

For the most part, Negro slaves followed the religion of their masters. In the West Indies most Negroes are Catholic. In the United States only 3 per cent are Catholic. Conversions, once vigorous, have slowed in recent years.

Her ancestors came to America in a slave ship but she was born to rightful freedom.

The Orient in America

Orientals are few among us. It is a surprise to many Americans to learn that the most decorated unit in our Army in World War II was the 100th Battalion, composed entirely of boys of Japanese ancestry. Of the battalion's 1,300 men, more than a thousand were wounded in action and awarded the Purple Heart. The unit was cited time and time again by commanding officers. No other unit in our Army boasted of more Distinguished Service Crosses, Silver Stars, Bronze Stars, and Legion of Merit Medals. Forty per cent of the men in the battalion were killed fighting up the Italian peninsula. During the war, the battalion had not a single case of desertion or absence without leave.

The amazing thing when the record of the 100th Battalion is considered is that at the same time its youths were bleeding and dying, the soldiers' relatives were being persecuted by other Americans because of their ancestry. Under governmental order every Japanese was excluded from the West Coast. Those who lived there were forcibly removed from their homes and put in concentration camps.

Of all the Orientals who came to America, none were made to suffer as much as the Japanese. The Chinese were laughed at and teased, but the Japanese were abused and persecuted. As early as 1905, the San Francisco *Chronicle* opened a campaign against the Japanese as the "little yellow man" whose characteristics were "treacherous, sneaking, insidious, a perfidious and betraying nature." The reason for the feeling against the Japanese, and to a lesser degree the Chinese, was because when the Japanese or Chinese came into competition with white Americans, they usually won out because they worked harder and lived more frugally.

The Chinese and Japanese began to arrive in the United States in the middle of the nineteenth century. They came to escape overcrowding and poverty at home. The Chinese arrived first, about the time of the

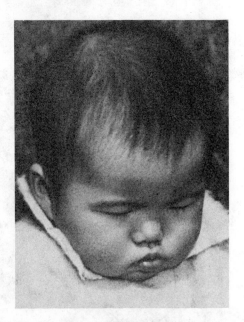

His features are Chinese, but he's as truly American as is an Iowa farmer.

74

Japanese immigrants have enriched our culture by their love for the things of nature.

California Gold Rush. They found employment as cooks and handymen in California's boom towns. Later they did a major share of the labor in building our transcontinental railroads. Meanwhile, the Japanese were arriving on the West Coast, showing great skills as gardeners and fishermen.

Today there are three quarters of a million American citizens of Oriental ancestry. These people proved themselves an asset to our American way of life. They never become burdens on the community, crime and juvenile delinquency are almost unknown among them, and they have turned arid deserts into green farms. In our big cities, they give us colorful Oriental quarters. Unfortunately only a minority are Catholics.

West Point Cadet

Circus clown

Chapter 2

Middle America

Propertly speaking, Mexico belongs to North America and not to Central America. To join the Mexican people to their neighbors with whom they have so much in common, geographers coined a new term, "Middle America." This comprises all the area between the United States and South America, including in addition to the mainland the islands of the Caribbean.

In this chapter, we are going to talk about the peoples of Middle America. Here we shall find people belonging to the oldest civilization of the Western Hemisphere, people whose ancestors were the first white settlers in the New World, people who belong to the world's first Negro republic. We shall meet highly civilized men and women and also primitive Indian folk. We will visit with the rich and the poor, the city dweller and the mountain farmer. In short, you will meet more than seventy million fellow Americans.

For the most part, the peoples we will visit live in the midst of an ancient Catholic culture. Unfortunately, many have long been out of touch with the Church because of lack of priests to instruct them. Things are brighter now, in the lands south of the Rio Grande, than they have been for many years, but there is a long way to go before the people there will have anything like the spiritual care that we get here in the United States.

The Peoples of Middle America

The Long March. The Kickapoo Indian tribe first appeared in history when it was discovered in northern Wisconsin. A few years later, the Kickapoos had moved into the area now around Milwaukee. By 1812, the Kickapoos extended from Illinois into the prairies. Forty years later the tribe was living in Texas, and within a few years crossed the border into Mexico. Today the Kickapoos are found in the Santa Rosa Mountains, in Chihuahua, Mexico.

The travels of the Kickapoos are interesting because their migrations give us a picture of how our continent was populated. Indians moved out of Siberia; across Alaska, Canada, and the United States; down through Central and South America, to the tip of Chile. It was a long walk that took thousands of years for completion. The Kickapoos give us an example of how it was done.

A study of the American Indians provides insights into the Indian tribes to the south of us. We can better understand the fierce opposition of the Mayas and Aztecs to the Spanish advance when we realize that they belonged to the same family as the Comanches of the United States. Our own history tells much of how the Comanches resisted white settlers.

Middle America is a mixture of races. In the United States, some of the early trappers married Indians, and most of us have read about "half-breeds" and "squaw men." But these cases were the exception, rather than the rule. This was not true in many parts of Latin America. In Mexico, for example, more than half the population is of mixed blood. Mixing also took place in the West Indies, although in those islands it was of black and white. Today, Haiti is predominantly black; Guatemala is predominantly red; Panama is predominantly white; Nicaragua is predominantly mestizo, or mixed.

Many nations have played roles in the building of Middle America. However, the major parts belonged to Spain and England. On the mainland, Spain had the greater influence. On the islands of the Caribbean, the influence was divided between Spain and England; although in places the French, the Dutch, and even the Danes ruled at one time or another.

The people of Middle America live in a civilization that is older than that of the United States. The Cathedral of St. John the Baptist in San Juan, Puerto Rico, was built in 1527. In the Dominican Republic, not far from the cathedral where the remains of Columbus were laid to rest, one can visit the University of St. Thomas Aquinas, the oldest university in the Western Hemisphere. When the United States was just beginning its colonial life, a great city of the Caribbean had already disappeared. In 1692, the wealthy and riotous city of Port Royal, Jamaica, vanished into the sea during one terrible, stormy night, and was lost forever.

Middle Americans live in varied climates. It is difficult to generalize about the climate in which the peoples of Middle America live because it varies so widely. The author has sweltered in the enervating heat of Yucatan; then farther south, close to the Equator, he has had to break ice in a Guatemalan fountain in order to get water for washing. The explanation is in altitude. In Middle America, you can take the climate you like— hot or cold, rainy or dry.

This Seri Indian woman, near Sonora, belongs to an almost extinct tribe.

Chains in Mayaland

AWN WAS JUST BREAKING when the little wood-burning train pulled into the station at Tekax, Yucatan, and I alighted. I looked around for Padre Zapata, the Mexican priest who had invited me to see his parish, but he was nowhere in sight. Just then an old man approached. He was a taxi driver whom the Padre had sent to meet me. As we drove through narrow streets, the man explained that the Padre was busy with Mass and many weddings.

The ramshackle taxi left me at the door of the church—a building so huge that it seemed definitely out of place in this small Mayan village. Later I learned that Tekax (pronounced Taykash) had formerly been a very populated section but the Indian war and hard times had driven many people away. It took me some moments to adjust to the darkness inside the church. Then at an altar lighted only by candles, I made out the figure of Padre Zapata celebrating Mass. Before the altar knelt a half dozen couples who were being married.

The wedding couples were all dressed identically. The men wore sandals, white trousers and white shirts. The women wore the traditional Mayan hupil—a white alb-like garment, squared at the neck and shoulder, embroidered with red flowers about the neck and hem. Several of the women wore earrings, all had gold chains about their necks. They were all barefooted. Each woman had a dark shawl covering her head.

The ages of the couples varied. A number of them must have been living in wedlock for many years before getting the blessing of the church on their marriages. One couple, however, had the freshness of youth. The girl was radiantly beautiful, her brown skin soft and shining. The boy's features were even and neat, his face longer than that of the typical Mayan man whose tribal characteristic is his rounded, moon shaped face. Each of them held a bouquet of flowers. Later over breakfast, I asked Padre Zapata about the young couple.

The boy's name was Diego. He was the seventeen-year-old son of a headman in an outlying village. The young bride was named Maria. She was fifteen. The manner in which the marriage was arranged and accomplished is typical of Mayan customs.

One day a group of young blades was sitting around talking. The conversation veered to girls and marriage. One of the boys turned to Diego, who was in the group, and asked him when he was going to be married.

"Soon," replied Diego, who up to that moment had had no plans.

"Who is the girl?" asked another of the group.

"That's a secret," answered Diego, evasively.

"What does your father say?" asked another.

"I haven't told him yet," replied Diego truthfully.

"Then he may have other ideas for your wife," said the boy who had asked the name of the girl. "You had better steal your bride to be sure." The term "stealing the bride" referred to a practice of taking the girl of one's choice to the home of a relative or friend and presenting the parents with an accomplished fact.

"No," replied Diego. "I will be married by the Padre."

The conversation remained in Diego's mind all that day and finally he decided that it was time for him to get married For some months he had been watching a village girl named Maria and he liked what he saw. He decided on bold action. One afternoon he arranged to be on the path from the village water hole when Maria was returning. Maria came along the path with her jar of water gracefully balanced on her head.

"May I have a drink of water?" asked Diego when the girl was opposite him.

Maria looked at the boy. It is against custom for young people to speak or be together without a chaperon. Maria, however, hesitated only a moment and then passed the jar to Diego. He drank silently and returned the jar to the girl who then went on her way. The fact that she had given him a drink of water told Diego that he had found favor in her eyes, otherwise she would have rebuffed him. That night Diego went to his father and told him that he wanted to get married. He mentioned Maria's name and said that she was the girl of his choice. Diego's father grunted something to the effect that it was the right of the parents to choose the bride for their son but Diego could tell from the reply that his father would consider the son's wishes.

NEXT DAY Diego's father approached Don Hector, an elderly man who was respected by everyone in the village and who often served as go-between in marriage arrangements. Don Hector agreed to make the first approach and Diego's father gave the old man a package containing rum, cigarettes and chocolate as gifts to the girl's family. In return for the service, Diego's father promised that he and his sons would help the old man in his cornfields when the next planting time came around.

That night Don Hector casually dropped into Maria's home. Her parents suspected from his reputation what he had come about but wondered whom he represented. However, there was an hour of casual conversation about all sorts of topics before Don Hector slipped into the conversation the fact that he had been asked to call by Diego's father. He handed Maria's father the rum and other gifts. The chocolate was passed to the women, the men lighted up gift cigarettes and sat back to enjoy the free rum. No more was said about the proposed marriage except that a date was made for two weeks hence when Don Hector would call again, this time accompanied by Diego's father. The fact that an appointment was set indicated that Diego was considered a suitable suitor for Maria's hand.

Two weeks later Don Hector and Diego's father went to Maria's home. The girl was not present but her parents and other relatives were. Again there was a present of rum, cigarettes, and chocolate. Again there was casual conversation. Just before leaving, Diego's father mentioned that he thought it would be appropriate to unite the two families by having Diego and Maria married. Maria's mother said that her daughter wasn't worthy to marry into the family of the headman. Maria's father said that his daughter was lazy and would make a poor housewife. Diego's father had investigated the girl and knew this to be untrue. Everyone spoke very highly of her but he knew that custom demanded that the parents not seem anxious to be rid of their daughter. Maria's father suggested another meeting in two weeks and Diego's father agreed, knowing from the invitation that his proposal was being favorably considered.

ON THE NEXT VISIT, Diego's father and mother and Don Hector made up the party of envoys. There was the usual gift and small talk, although this time the casual conversation was quite short. Maria's mother was the one who brought the subject up.

"My husband and I have talked about a marriage between your son and our daughter. We feel it can be arranged provided the *muhul* is right." The muhul is the bride-price or gift that must be made to the girl's family.

"And what muhul is sought?" asked Diego's mother.

"A gold chain, two gold rings, three hair ribbons, an embroidered handkerchief, five yards of cotton cloth, four bottles of rum, a new dress and shawl for the bride, rum and bread for the wedding feast, half of the expenses of the wedding feast, and one hundred pesos from your son."

Diego's father paused for effect, pretending to consider the well-memorized list. He knew that the demands were fair and that he would not have to bargain but he did not wish to seem too hasty. Finally, he agreed and another meeting was arranged for two weeks later.

At the next and final meeting many relatives and friends were present, including the godparents of the bride and bridegroom. Diego was there but not Maria. With a flourish, Diego's father deposited the requested gifts on a table which had been placed in the center of the room. Everyone exclaimed on the fine quality of the gifts with the loudest praise reserved for the gold chain, the most important gift. Besides the purpose of adornment, gold chains represent family wealth in Mayaland, like cows in Africa or dollars in the bank in America. The more chains a woman wears, the greater her family's financial status.

DON HECTOR MADE the formal presentation of the gifts, composing a short speech as he did so. "It was Our Lord God who said that every man should marry," declared the old Indian. "Therefore, in joy at the union that is to take place, the *compadres* of the boy offer you these gifts. May you accept them in satisfaction."

"I thank you for myself and for my wife," replied Maria's father. Then turning to the father of the prospective groom, he added, "May the Lord God give back to you what you have spent on these gifts."

With this acceptance, the formal betrothal took place. Don Hector was commissioned to go to Tekax and see Padre Zapata about a date for the wedding. Several days later the old man had fulfilled his task. He reported that Diego and Maria would be married at a ceremony in which several other couples then under instruction by the Padre would also be wed. He also arranged for a civil ceremony to take place the same morning.

Three weeks before the date of the wedding, Maria and Diego, their parents

Mayan woman

and friends journeyed into Tekax and went immediately to the Padre. He in turn led them into church. Kneeling before the altar each one swore that Diego and Maria were not prevented by any impediments from being wed to each other. The Padre gave a short lecture on the obligations of the marriage state and dismissed them.

The day before the wedding they were all back in town again to stay at the homes of friends. Diego went to church with his godfather and made his confession. Maria did the same accompanied by her godmother. There was a small party in the evening that broke up early. Long before dawn the bridal party was up. Maria dressed in her fine new *hupil* and shawl while Diego put on new clothes. The parents spoke to their respective child and gave a blessing. Then the party went off to church joined by relatives and friends, and the *padrinos* or marriage godparents. These latter godparents furnish things connected with the wedding. One pair gave the thirteen silver coins used in the Toledo rite of matrimony. Another pair furnished the silver chain also used in the ceremony. The third pair supplied two bouquets of flowers, one for the bride and one for the groom.

At the church they joined the other bridal parties. The couples to be married were met at the door by the Padre. He blessed the rings, one for the bride and one for the groom. Then Diego took the silver coins and let them slip one by one through his hands into the hands of Maria, thus signifying that he would always support her. The silver chain was placed over the shoulders of the bride and groom signifying that they were joined for life. After the actual wedding was concluded the couples followed the Padre to the altar where they knelt together, still joined by the chain, and heard Mass. They were thus when I found them.

LATER THAT MORNING Diego and Maria went through a brief civil ceremony in the municipal building in Tekax. Often this ceremony is ignored by the Indians but since Diego's father was the alcalde or headman of his village the ceremony was deemed advisable. After the civil ceremony the entire bridal party returned to the couple's village where a big party was held.

Padre Zapata told me that Diego and Maria will live with Maria's parents.

"Diego must live in his father-in-law's house for about a year," said the Padre. "When the bridal gift was made everything was there but the hundred pesos. This must be paid by Diego himself. He pays by working for his father-in-law. In about a year the debt will be finished, then they will go off and start their own home. By that time the new family should number three."

Thus does family life begin in Mexico's Mayaland where the people cherish the past. And what sensible man will dispute with them?

The Family Answers to God

"Since the Creator of all things has established the conjugal partnership as the beginning and basis of human society . . . the apostolate of married persons and families is of unique importance for the Church and civil society. . . . The family has received from God its mission to be the first and vital cell of society." — **Vatican Council II, Decree on the Laity.**

While this Todos Santos Indian of Guatemala wears the distinctive clothing of his tribe, he is gradually adopting ways of the outside world and modernizing.

Maria Trinidad, 80 years old, a Mayan woman of Mexico, is active in her parish.

The heart of Mexico is in its country villages where life centers around old colonial churches. For many years persecution deprived the people of priests but now religion is on the upswing with Maryknoll missioners like Father John McGuire (below) aiding.

Mexicans are a very Catholic people. The key to the understanding of Mexico and her people lies at the base of the hill of Tepeyac some three miles northeast of Mexico City. There one winter morning, just ten years after Cortes had conquered Mexico City and the surrounding territory, an Aztec Indian, Juan Diego, was on his way to Mass. As he descended a path on the hill of Tepeyac, he met a beautiful lady who spoke to him in his own language.

The lady told Juan Diego that she was the Virgin Mary, that she had a special love for his people, and that she wished a chapel built on that hillside. She instructed Juan Diego to carry her message to Bishop Zumarraga. Old Juan Diego did as he was bid. The bishop received him kindly and then dismissed him, attributing the message to the Indian's imagination. On his way home that evening Juan Diego met the lady again. She asked him to return to the bishop the next day.

After Mass the next day, Juan Diego went back to the bishop. This time the kindly Franciscan was impressed. Could Juan Diego bring him proof, some sign of the lady's visit? Juan promised to try. When Juan Diego returned to the lady she promised him a sign.

But on the next day, Juan Diego forgot all about the lady. His uncle had fallen ill, and Juan Diego spent the day nursing the old man and looking for an herb doctor. The uncle grew worse and on the following day sent his nephew to fetch a priest to prepare him for death.

Juan Diego hurried off. He decided to skirt the hill of Tepeyac so that he would not meet the lady and be delayed on his mission of mercy. But it was to no avail. Just as he made the last turn, there was the lady waiting for him!

Juan Diego explained that the uncle who was like a father to him lay dying and that he was in a hurry to get a priest. The lady told Juan Diego not to worry. His uncle was cured—for had she not told him of her love for his people? She instructed the Indian to climb the hill and fill his *tilma*—a long, bib-like cloth worn by the Aztecs—with roses. Juan Diego knew that roses did not grow in December, and that on rocky Tepeyac no roses ever grew! But he went as he was told and to his surprise found the hilltop blooming with sweet-smelling, Castile roses. He filled his tilma and trotted off to the bishop.

After some trouble with secretaries and clerks, Juan Diego finally reached the bishop. He announced that he had brought the sign, opened his tilma, and let the roses spill out on the floor. The bishop sank to his knees, for more miraculous than the roses was a picture of Mary Immaculate that appeared on the cloth.

To make a long story short, the bishop believed. Juan Diego's uncle had been cured when the lady appeared to him and told him her name which to the Spaniards sounded like "Our Lady of Guadalupe," a famous shrine in Spain. Later scholars said that since she was speaking in Aztec, she probably

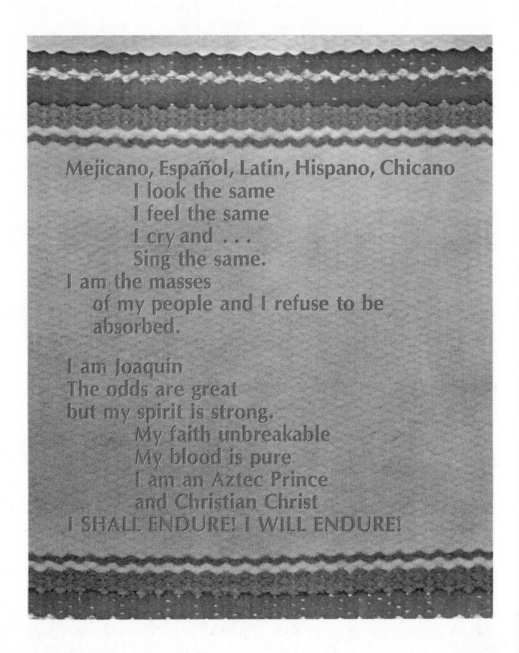

Mejicano, Español, Latin, Hispano, Chicano
      I look the same
      I feel the same
      I cry and . . .
      Sing the same.
I am the masses
   of my people and I refuse to be
   absorbed.

I am Joaquín
The odds are great
but my spirit is strong.
      My faith unbreakable
      My blood is pure
      I am an Aztec Prince
      and Christian Christ
I SHALL ENDURE! I WILL ENDURE!

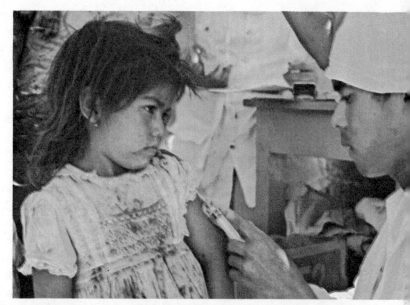

Middle America lies in an earthquake zone. Both Mexico and Nicaragua have suffered severe tremors in recent years which caused much damage and many deaths.

said "Our Lady of Tecuatalope"—which means "she who appeared among the rocks" or "she who drove away those devouring us." Either title would have been accurate for she did appear on a rocky slope and through her miracle finished forever the Aztec gods who demanded human sacrifice. Today on the spot of the apparition a great basilica stands and inside one can see the miraculous painting given to Juan Diego.

Mexico's whole life and history are tied up with Our Lady of Guadalupe. Every revolution was fought under her banner. Her picture is in almost every home. Taxis and busses have little shrines in her honor. The Tepeyac basilica is always crowded with her devotees.

During the persecutions when an atheistic government closed every other church in Mexico, the basilica remained open. Once when it was rumored that the basilica was to be closed, a hundred thousand Indians poured out of the hills overnight. The next morning, when soldiers arrived, they found the basilica surrounded, and they prudently withdrew. On another occasion when a fanatic planted a bomb, the explosion wrecked the main altar, twisting a giant metal crucifix like a corkscrew but not even cracking the glass of the miraculous painting behind it.

Mexicans live in a land of contrasts. Walk down a street in Mexico City, and you will see stately old colonial buildings flanked by the most modern office and apartment buildings. On country roads, Cadillacs wend through a team of pack burros.

There are 50 million people living in 29 states and two territories that make up the United States of Mexico. One out of every ten Mexicans is pure white. Three out of ten Mexicans are pure Indian. The remaining six Mexicans are mestizos—a blend of white and Indian.

Most of the Indians are rural people who live in small adobe homes. They haul their water from public fountains and cook over tiny charcoal braziers. They sleep on fiber mats, and wear heavy woolen serapes to keep them warm. Their diet is largely beans and corn.

The Indians are proud people whose first loyalty is to their villages and not their country. They speak over fifty dialects, although today the majority also know Spanish. Most of the Indians are peons, who work as subsistence farmers, miners, or other laborers.

The white Mexicans are found mostly in the cities. Upper-class Mexican society is very exclusive and modernizing. Family life is very close. Mexicans are great individualists, and they do not like the mass production and standardization of the United States.

Mexico, like all of Latin America, needs priests, although it is not as badly off as some other countries. Because of the persecutions and priest shortage, many of the people lack instruction but Our Lady of Guadalupe has kept the faith alive.

Superstition in the Mountains

MARTIN RAYMUNDO and his wife, Maria Vicente, live in a new little adobe house deep in the Cuchamatanes Mountains of Guatemala—a remote area seldom penetrated by outsiders. Although neither of them is yet twenty years old, they have been married almost four years, and have two children—a boy and a girl. A third child died almost immediately after birth.

Up until a few months ago, Martin and his family lived in the home of his father. But after the birth of the second surviving baby, it was decided that more room was needed. With the help of his father, a brother, and some friends, Martin built his house a short distance away from that of his father but on his father's land.

The house has only one room. It boasts two windows—one on either side of the door. The floor is of packed earth; the roof is high-peaked and covered with thatch. The furnishings of the house are simple—a small table, one chair, several stools, a raised platform covered with mats for sleeping, an open fireplace on the floor for cooking, and a chest in which valuables such as clothing and trinkets are stored. Hung in the rafters of the house are a spinning wheel, several baskets, a box containing seed corn, and some simple farming implements.

To see Martin and Maria at their best is to visit them when they are making their weekly trip to the Sunday market at Soloma or to a festival in Santa Eulalia. Then they are dressed in their finest clothes. There is no individuality in their style of dress, since everyone else in the area is similarly clad. Indeed, a person familiar with Guatemala can tell a person's village simply by looking at the mode of dress. Every village has its own costume.

Martin wears brown chino trousers of foreign make, and a white cotton shirt that is buttoned at the neck. Over the shirt he slips a distinctive waist-length garment made of heavy dark brown wool. There is a V-line to the neck; the sleeves are elbow length, flowing, and slit underneath. A simple design is embroidered about the hem and neck. He wears a Guatemalan-made straw hat. On his feet are simple sandals—leather soles with thongs strapped about the ankles.

Maria's dress is a white, loose-fitting gown. The foot-wide collar is embroidered with chain-like designs in black, with yellow and red stripes in between. The dress has wrist-length sleeves and has about as much of a contour cut as an alb or Mother Hubbard dress. Maria's long, dark hair is tied and banded with a bright red ribbon. She is barefooted. About her neck she wears gold beads.

The dress has one unique feature. Maria carries her youngest baby under her dress. She straps the baby to her right side with a broad woolen sash, then slips on the dress. When she wants to get at baby, she simply lifts the wide collar of the dress and there is baby's head appearing through a slit in the dress. Keeping the baby covered this way protects it from the elements and the "evil eye." Baby is also kept warm by his mother's body, is able to feed at will, and mother's hands are left free for whatever task may present itself.

Martin and Maria belong to the Mam nation, a Mayan tribe that goes back to pre-Columban times. The Mams were one of the earliest peoples in Guatemala and their name means Old Men. One explanation given for this title is the fact that they were in Guatemala before the more populous Quiche tribe. Another is that they stuttered like old people when they tried to pronounce the difficult names of the Quiche enemies.

The nearest parish for Martin and Maria is in Soloma, a day's journey away. They have never been to church there and do not know the American priest. Although they lack any sort of a religious education, they are both very religious. They consider themselves *Catholicos* yet they also practice *costumbre*—a superstitious way of life from Mayan times, guiding actions from birth to death.

"God is everywhere," Martin will tell you. "He is in the trees, in the rocks, in the air, in the water."

Even in their religious symbolism, Martin and Maria carry over confusion between past and present. Regularly Maria prays before a cross erected on a mountainside behind her home. An American seeing her kneeling in prayer or burning copal incense before the cross would consider her a devout Christian woman.

Yet to her the Cross represents more than the instrument on which Chist died. It is a symbol from the old Mayan religion that was used before the coming of the white man. It means the four winds of heaven and symbolizes everlasting life.

EACH YEAR, Martin and Maria go on a journey of many days to take part in the Chiantla fiesta, honoring the Silver Virgin who has worked many miracles. Each of their children was baptized during a fiesta at Chiantla because like every other Indian the young parents believe that if a child dies without baptism its soul will forever be cut off from its parents and ancestors.

Yet at the birth of each of Martin's babies, the local *cheman,* or pagan priest, was also called to assure that each child would have good health and protection from the evil eye. This feat is accomplished by making a cross over the head of the child with a burning candle and burying some hairs from the head of the child under a stone.

Each time Maria has gone to Chiantla, she first prays outside the church to the pagan gods. Then she enters and prays to the statues of the saints. When she was expecting her first baby, she poured a little *aguardiente* over the feet of one of the *santos* as an offering. The priest saw her and reprimanded her. She could not understand why the priest was displeased that she had offered the saint the alcoholic beverage.

Both Martin and Maria think of the saints as real and present in their statues. They speak out to the statues directly in a loud voice, unmindful of others around them. Martin's conversation (one-sided) might go like this:

"Virgin Mary, the last time I was here I burned a big candle to you. All I asked was that I would have a good harvest. Well, the harvest wasn't very good. You let worms get into my corn. That wasn't very nice after I spent my money for a big candle. I'll give you another chance. This time we need rain for our corn. If you don't send the rain, you can be sure I won't burn any more candles."

Then not to take any chances, Martin will return home and hire the local cheman to bless his fields. This ceremony consists of burning copal incense in the fields and spilling aguardiente on the ground as a sacrifice, and placing lighted candles in the shape of a cross in the fields.

The chemans are used for more than blessings and spells, however. They have a detailed knowledge of the medical properties of herbs and roots. There is the algalia plant, for example, whose seeds are mashed and the oil extracted for curing malaria and snake bite. From the ixbut plant, the cheman makes a preparation that increases the flow of milk. Each cheman has medical secrets passed down from generation to generation.

MARTIN AND MARIA lead a simple life at home. They are up at dawn each morning. Maria grinds the corn for tortillas and boils the water for breakfast. After breakfast, Martin goes off to his fields to tend the corn. When the corn is planted and growing, he remains at home to card and spin wool, as he owns some sheep.

Maria takes care of the babies, prepares the meals, hauls water and wood, searches the hillsides for weeds that can serve as vegetables, and weaves woolen cloth that will be sold in the market.

Sometimes when things are slack at home, Martin hires himself out as a porter. The only manner in which supplies can be brought into the mountains are on men's backs. He will carry almost a hundred pounds all day and be satisfied with thirty or forty cents in pay. Between this work, the woolen cloth and farm produce, he manages to get a cash income each year of about fifty dollars.

While many highland weavers are now using manufactured dyes, Maria prefers the natural colorings her mother taught her. She gets blue dye from the boiled pulp of the campeche tree. Brown dye is obtained by boiling the cloth in a lime solution and then immersing it in an extract from the bark of the aliso tree. Red color is given when lemons are boiled over a slow fire (thirty lemons to a pound of cloth) and then adding a plant called *chin-chinegrito*.

ALTHOUGH MARTIN had two years of schooling, he learned very little because the teacher spoke only Spanish, although governmental regulations call for classes in both Spanish and Indian dialect. He can write his name but no more. He cannot read. Maria, having had no schooling, cannot read or write. While Martin knows a smattering of spoken Spanish, Maria knows none.

Likewise, while a year's military service is required of every male after he reaches the age of eighteen, Martin for some reason has never been called up. The reason is probably that Martin and his family live quite removed from any municipal center, in a ravine far back in the hills. It is quite possible that bureaucracy doesn't know he exists. He has never paid any taxes although a municipal tax and road tax are supposed to be levied on everyone.

Martin and Maria were married according to Indian custom. The marriage has not been blessed by the Church. When Martin was just turning seventeen, his father, Raymundo, decided that the time had come to get the boy a bride. He consulted some of his friends and finally chose three girls in the area who were of marriageable age. He then went to the cheman and gave the man the three names. The witch doctor (for the fee of a chicken) studied the names, consulted his oracles, and decided that Maria Vicente would make the best wife.

Raymundo then went to the village elders and told them of developments. That evening the cheman, Raymundo and a committee of village elders went to call on Vicente, Maria's father. When the house was reached, the cheman who was carrying a thurible of burning incense entered the house alone. He broke an egg over the burning incense, meanwhile uttering incantations and prayers. The delegation then entered and joined the cheman in prayers. When this was done, the cheman announced the purpose of the visit.

Raymundo then asked for a glass and poured a drink of aguardiente from a bottle he brought. He offered this to Vicente. Maria's father hesitated a moment before accepting the drink. He considered the pros and cons of the marriage. Then with a smile he reached out and accepted the glass, quaffing the liquid fire in a single gulp. It was his way of accepting the proposal—subject of course to future negotiations.

IT TOOK TWO WEEKS to settle the terms for the wedding. It was finally agreed that Raymundo would pay twenty-five dollars, 300 pounds of corn, ten chickens, three sheep, and that Martin would give two months' work to his new father-in-law.

Once the terms were agreed on, Raymundo, Vicente, the cheman and the village elders met anew. A rooster was sacrificed and toasts were drunk in aguardiente. Raymundo and Vicente became very buddy-buddy over the drinks. When the party broke up and all returned to their respective homes, each was well the worse for wear. Martin, who had no part in any of the negotiations, was eagerly waiting for his father's return.

"It is all done," said the old man.

Martin immediately went to Maria's house and brought the girl home with him. Married life began as simply as that. No rings were exchanged, no promises given. It was understood that if after the first few days Maria didn't like her new home or husband, she would be free to return home. In that case Vicente would have to return the bridal price. There are some cases of polygamy in the mountains but these usually occur because the first wife is unable to bear children. For this lack, the husband can return his wife to her father and collect the bridal price.

The life of the mountain Indian is a simple one. He is far removed from the complexities and luxuries of modern civilization. He lives close to nature and close to God. Without proper religious instruction he often confuses nature and God. Where priests are available, superstition dies. The mountain Indian then has a faith equal to that of any people in the world. Some day soon a catechist will arrive in Martin's village to prepare the way for a priest. When that time comes Martin and Maria will learn to separate truth from superstition.

Central Americans. Someone once described Central America as a place where rivers flow backwards, bananas grow upside down, and people say *"Como no"* when they mean "yes." Actually, the people of Central America live in six Spanish-speaking republics—Guatemala, El Salvador, Honduras, Nicaragua, Costa Rica, and Panama—and one English-speaking colony, Belize of British Honduras. Central America begins in a jungle at the Mexican border and ends in another at the Colombian border. In between we find Indians, Whites, and Negroes living amidst spectacular scenery—smoking volcanoes, sparkling azure lakes, and the bluest of blue skies.

Guatemala is an Indian world. Here four and a half million people live in an area the size of Ohio. Coffee, banana, and chicle prices determine how the people live. The country was once a center of the Mayan empire, and later became a Christian mission center.

Nicaraguans live in the largest (about the size of Michigan) country in Central America but the most sparsely (less than two million people) populated. Most Nicaraguans live in the volcanic-rich western part of their country. On the rainy eastern coast are the banana plantations and the Mosquito Indians.

Coffee-growing El Salvador is the smallest Central American country. The main body of its citizens are mixed Spanish, Indian, and Negro. They are mostly farmers and are more prosperous than most Central Americans. One out of ten Salvadorians is Indian, belonging to the Panchi tribe. Three and a half million Salvadorians live in an area as large as Massachusetts.

Costa Rica is a white man's country. The Costa Ricans are one of the most prosperous and progressive peoples in all Latin America. Coffee, bananas, gold, oil, and fine woods give them their

These Nicaraguan altar boys live in a gold-mining camp operated by Canadian engineers.

Man in Honduras with a banana seed

wealth. Eight out of ten Costa Ricans are farmers who have their own small land holdings and who live in neat red brick homes. Nearly all have some education and they are noted for their orderly democratic and political ways. There are 1,337,000 Costa Ricans.

British Honduras is a black man's country. Only a half of one per cent of the populace are white; 80 per cent are Negroes; the remainder mostly Asiatics. The people live on the border line of starvation, eking out an existence from chicle and hard woods. There are 120,000 people in an area equal to New Jersey.

The people of Honduras live in a country dependent on banana prices. In the early days of colonization (1527), missioners introduced the banana plant to Honduras. Today the country is one of the leading banana pro-

ducers in the world. The majority of the people of Honduras are a mixture of Indian and white. Ten per cent are Indian and 2 per cent are white. Honduras has the worst proportion of priests to people in all Latin America. The almost two million people occupying an area slightly larger than Kentucky live in the flavor of colonial isolation.

Panamanians are the orphans of Central America. Geographically speaking, the isthmus of Panama belongs neither to Central nor South America. Once Panama belonged to Colombia but since 1903 has been independent. Panamanians live in a mixed culture. The big cities are *ersatz*—a mixture of hot dog stands, Navy bars, and East Indian bazaars. In Panama, one can find the gentility of the old colonial way of life and also some of the most primitive Indian life.

The people of Panama are diverse. Because the Isthmus has been a crossroads for the world since colonial times, men of many nations and colors came to live there. The majority of the people are of mixed Spanish, Indian, and Negro stock; but there are also Indians, East Indians, and Chinese. The San Blas Indians live on a group of islands east of the Canal. On the west side of the Isthmus live the forest-dwelling Darien Indians in their homes built on stilts.

There are two million people in Panama, living in an area equal to West Virginia. Panamanians live in poverty both in body and soul.

The people of the Caribbean are a product of many nationalities and cultures. Civilization first came to the New World through the islands of the Caribbean. It was here that Columbus first sighted land and it was here that the first settlements were made. The islands played an important role in the struggle among the Spanish, English and French.

Cubans are as sociable and friendly as the sparkling sunshine of their homeland. The original inhabitants of Cuba were the Carib and Arawak Indians who fled to other islands with the coming of the Spanish. Later, Negro slaves were imported to work the large sugar plantations. Today, one fourth of the eight and a half million Cubans are pure Negro, while the majority of the people are a mixture of white and black. There is little distinction because of race.

Under the dictatorship of Fidel Castro some social progress has been made, particularly in literacy and health services but it has been done at the cost of individual liberty. Cubans must live frugally on an economy based entirely on the Soviet bloc. The country has a serious lack of professional people since most of this class fled to the United States as refugees. Despite their poverty and lack of freedom, Cubans are gay and volatile by nature. They love bright colors and are happy when they can dance to the music of guitars. They are overwhelmingly Roman Catholic in an atheistic environment.

His name is Pizarro, and the blood of Spain and Africa flows in his veins.

Haitians live in the only Negro republic in the Western Hemisphere. When Columbus discovered Haiti in 1492, the island was inhabited by the Arawak and Ciboney Indians. Many Indians fled the Spanish, and as a result Negro slaves were brought in to work mines and fields. Because Haiti was controlled by France, the people there speak a patois French called Creole. They claim to be Catholics but practice a superstitious religion called voodoo. They are a poor people without education, depending on sugar prices and tourist business for income. They share the island of Hispaniola with the Dominican Republic, their eastern neighbor.

For most poor children, shining shoes is the way to supplement the family income.

"Christmas in Puerto Rico" by Rafael Tufino, one of the island's leading artists.

Living on an island, this young Puerto Rican is raised in the traditions of the sea.

Dominicans live in the first permanent white settlement in the New World. The Dominican Republic, formerly San Domingo and before that Hispaniola, marks the spot where Columbus landed in the New World. The people of the Dominican Republic live in palm-thatched huts in small villages. They are poor, working small plots of ground for themselves or working for low wages on sugar estates. Sixty per cent of the Dominicans are mulattoes (white and Negro); 28 per cent are white; and 12 per cent are Negro.

Puerto Ricans have pulled themselves up by their own bootstraps. Not too many years ago, Puerto Rico was a languid, backward place where the people lived in great poverty. Today, Puerto Rico is as modern and hustling as any place in the United States. In Puerto Rico you will find towering skyscrapers, modern airports, new schools and office buildings; and alongside them will be graceful old colonial churches or pastel-tinted Spanish-style houses.

To meet Puerto Ricans you need only visit any large city in the United States. But to understand these gay, friendly people, you must see them on their own enchanted island—a region about half the size of Connecticut. Puerto Ricans are white, Negro, and mulatto. Ninety per cent are baptized Catholics but for many years there has been a shortage of priests. The language of the 2.7 million people of Puerto Rico is Spanish although now many are also able to speak English.

Virgin Islands. These possessions of the United States lie directly east of Miami, Florida. They have been under Dutch, British, and Danish rule. The majority of the people are Negroes and are quite poor. In recent years, Continentals (whites from the United States) have gone to the Virgin Islands to live.

Other peoples of the island world. There are many islands in the Caribbean area and it would take a disproportionate amount of space to describe all of them. However, a few of them are large enough for attention. North of Cuba live the Bahamians, inhabitants of the Bahama Islands, recently independent. Eighty-seven per cent of the people are Negroes, 20 per cent of whom are Catholics. Directly east from North Carolina is Bermuda, the oldest self-governing British colony. One-third of the people are white, the remainder Negro.

Lesser Antilles. The chain of islands extending south from Cuba and Puerto Rico is known as the Lesser Antilles. The majority of people in these islands are of Negro origin. These islands are Dutch, British, and French possessions. They include such places as St. Kitts, Martinique, Curacao, Barbados (independent), Granada, and Guadeloupe.

Trinidad and Tobago. Islands off the coast of Venezuela have many religions and peoples. The population is a mixture of Chinese, Negro, East Indian, British, French, and Portuguese. Trinidadians have made their island famous for calypso music. There are a million inhabitants—one third are Catholic, one third Protestant, and one third Hindu or Moslem.

Jamaica. Almost two million people here live in crude simplicity. Most of them are Negro, many emigrate to the United States. Catholics are in a minority.

Haitians live in repressive poverty under a family dictatorship of great cruelty.

The youth of Latin America
hunger for knowledge.
in recent years many volunteers
have given assistance.

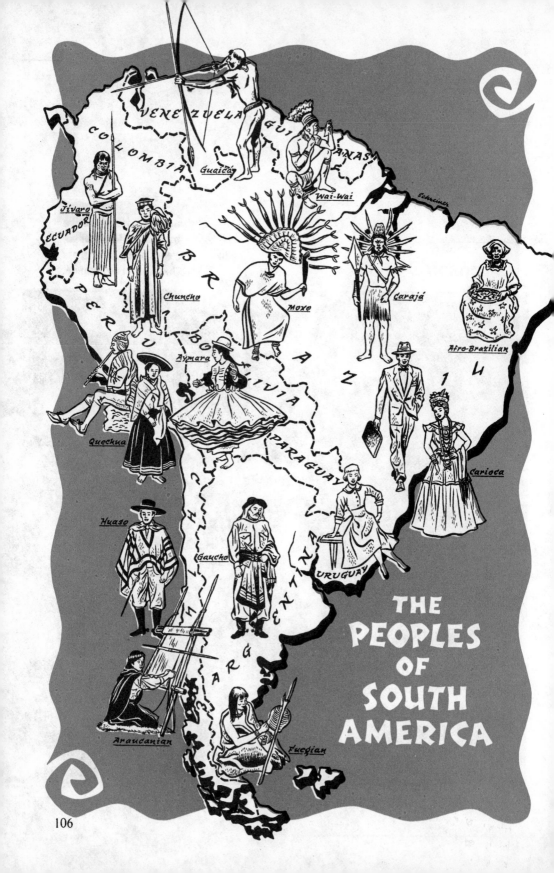

THE PEOPLES OF SOUTH AMERICA

106

Chapter 3

South America

THE PEOPLE of South America live in eleven countries and two dependencies, extending from the tropics to the southern polar regions. They represent many lands and many races—Europe, Africa, Asia, and some eight hundred tribes of Indians. The first Indians reached North America from Siberia about 20,000 years ago and eventually spread southward with the final influx reaching Tierra del Fuego about three to four thousand years ago. Europeans began arriving in numbers in the sixteenth century. Today there are 190 million South Americans.

The vast majority of the people of South America belong to the Catholic Church. In fact, with the other countries of Latin America, 35 per cent of the Catholics of the world are found in this area. Yet the spiritual poverty of the people can be imagined when we realize that only 9 per cent of the priests of the world are in Latin America and half of these are engaged in nonparochial work.

South Americans live in a land of great contrasts. They live in tremendous cities of skyscrapers and bustle and they live in areas that have not yet been explored and mapped. People who live in the most wretched of huts that lack sanitation, electricity, or running water can window shop and see the most modern refrigerators and television sets. While untold millions of South Americans can neither read nor write, other South Americans lead the world in the arts and sciences. The one thing certain about the people of South America is that it is impossible to generalize about them.

Quechua and Aymara Indians
are the great Indian
tribes of the Andean highlands.

The Andean Indian has great devotion to the Virgin but often superstition enters.

The Great Builders

LONG, LONG AGO, says an Andean legend, the sun and moon had two children, born on an island in Lake Titicaca. One was a boy named Manco Capac, and the other was a girl called Mama Ocllo. In due time, these children married. One day the sun god gave Manco Capac a golden staff and told the young man to take his wife and leave the island. In that spot on the mainland where the golden staff would sink into the ground, there a great city should be built.

Manco Capac obeyed the command. When he and his wife reached the mainland, they stopped while he tried to plunge the golden staff into the earth—but it would not enter. Along the shore, over the mountains, through the valleys, the young couple went. Finally they reached a hilltop overlooking a deep valley.

Manco Capac and his wife went down into the valley. He placed his staff upon the earth—and it disappeared from sight. The couple knew that this was the place where their father, the sun god, wanted them to settle. Thus the city of Cuzco, Peru, was born. Manco Capac taught the men of the valley how to cultivate the land. His wife taught the women to weave and to cook. In this manner, the great Inca race was born.

While the legend has the sound of fantasy, the fact is that the Inca tribe did have its beginning in the

Amid ruins of past greatness, an elderly Peruvian shepherd serenades his stately llamas.

valley of Cuzco. They conquered the surrounding tribes until at last they ruled over all the land that is now known as Ecuador, Peru, and Bolivia. They conquered parts of Chile and Argentina as well.

The Incas were great builders, and they built like the mountains that surrounded them—massively and to last. They built roads to all parts of their empire. They threw bridges across mountain chasms. They had walls and terraces constructed so that crops could be grown on every bit of available land. They built cities of stone of which Cuzco was their masterpiece.

In Cuzco were the finest of the Inca's buildings. Most beautiful of all were the palace of the emperor and the Temple of the Sun. On one whole side of the Temple was a huge golden sun, set in rays of gold that threw light in every direction.

The most amazing of the Incas' accomplishments was their skill in handling stone. The fortress of Sacsahuaman above Cuzco is an excellent example of their massive construction. Some of the stone blocks used are twenty feet high and twelve feet thick. Many of these stones are cut in intricate patterns and fit together so tightly that not even a razor blade can be slipped between them.

The mystery is how the stones were moved since they were brought long distances and up mountains. The Incas did not have horses or mules. They did not know the secret of the wheel. They did not have cranes or pulleys. They

This Bolivian has royal Incan blood.

didn't even have iron tools for cutting. Yet in grandiose construction, the Inca surpassed any other tribe in the New World.

However, in other ways the Incas were very backward. They had no system for writing; they did not have the refinement of art found among the Maya; they had no money and were able to record numbers only on knotted strings. They were also very cruel, subjugating people under a reign of terror. One Inca ruler not only killed his own two hundred brothers but also his nephews, uncles, and cousins. All of these relatives were put to death by slow torture so that the chief could enjoy their suffering.

A young descendant of the Incas sits above Cuzco, the great capital of the Incas.

The grim reminder
of an earthquake slide
in a Peruvian valley.

In many areas of South America, particularly Chile and Peru, water is precious.

A Free, Happy Life

THE GREEN WORLD of Antonio Plaza fills the heart of a continent. This is the vast South American rain forest where the only highways are rivers.

Except for the polar regions and a few desert areas, the Amazon jungle is the most sparsely inhabited region in the world. Large sections of it have never been explored, great areas have never been mapped. It could swallow up the whole United States with plenty of room to spare. It is a harsh, cruel world that is sometimes prodigal but always demanding.

There are not many Americans who understand the jungle. Too often this matted, tortuous forest is viewed with eyes colored by the romance of Hudson's "Green Mansions" or by the adventure of the Tarzan stories or by the sensual disillusionment of Somerset Maugham's tales. Those veterans who had to fight their way through the jungles of the Pacific will appreciate Antonio Plaza's world. But for most of our citizens, it is truly a *terra incognita*—an unknown land that must be experienced to be believed.

It is a world of contrasts. Mention the word "jungle" and there comes to mind stifling heat; yet, when the *sur* is blowing the Plaza family shivers from the cold. There is beauty in the jungle—orchids and flowering shrubs in profusion, an unending dancing pattern of sunlight and shadow. But this beauty is hard to enjoy because of the swarms of insects that attack every visitor—*niguas* that drill their way under the skin to rot and fester, mosquitoes whose sting leaves behind the chills and fever of malaria. These are dangers far more deadly and present than the bone crushing anacondas or man-eating alligators or treacherous jaguars of the travel writers.

Antonio Plaza, his wife and three children dwell among the headwaters of the Amazon river. Indeed, they live on the bank of one of the numerous streams that snake through the area, eventually to reach the distant Atlantic. These rivers are the only contact of the jungle folk with civilization—a contact that is seldom made except when a trading boat comes upstream in search of rubber or bananas or Brazil nuts. These are the crops that bring a little cash to the Plaza family—cash that does not go very far when the family makes its annual buying trip downriver to the nearest jungle town about a week away.

The Plaza family lives in a little one-room house that Antonio himself built. Poles form the walls of the house, and layer upon layer of palm leaves make up the roof. The floor is of packed earth. Furniture is almost non-existent. A battered table, one stool, a few boxes to serve as chairs, a chest for holding clothing, five hammocks. Behind the house are two covered sheds, open on all sides. One is used for cooking, the other for smoking rubber and doing other odd jobs on rainy days. Sometimes in hot weather the hammocks are strung under this second shed, and the family sleeps outdoors.

There is an air of impermanence about the Plaza house, and justly so. Termite ants are forever eating into the wall poles, causing a constant threat of collapse. The palm roof in the dry season becomes dangerous because a single spark from the fires can set it ablaze. In the wet season, dampness causes the leaves to rot.

SURROUNDING THE HOUSE is a small clearing where there is a garden containing vegetables and some orange and lemon trees. Beyond are the banana plants—an important staple in the Plaza diet. Some of the plants produce bananas that can be eaten raw; others give fruit that becomes tasteful only after cooking. Mrs. Plaza prepares bananas in many ways. Many are fried in oil, others baked, and some even boiled. Bananas and yucca are the family's staff of life. Meat is a great luxury and is had only when some animal is shot in the jungle. Fish is more common since the river is right at the door. Occasionally there is duck but only when Antonio's homemade shotgun shells are accurate.

The life of the Plaza family falls into an unchanging pattern. The Plazas know only two seasons—rainy and dry. Just before the rainy season starts in October, crops are planted. Rubber is collected until the rains turn the jungle into a treacherous morass. This is the time of starvation. In December, corn is harvested and if the jungle is not too badly flooded, the Plazas hunt for Brazil nuts.

January is the height of the rainy season. The rivers rise to fantastic levels and spread out into the jungle. Four times the Plazas have lost their home in the floods and once a four-year-old Plaza child was carried away to his death in the swirling, muddy waters. Fishing is impossible in this season but hunting is good because the animals are crowded on high, dry ground, and can be hunted from a canoe. Once the jungle begins to flood Brazil nut collecting must be abandoned. In February, the small Plaza rice patch is harvested.

The rains slacken in March and the floods recede from the jungle. Rubber collecting is started again to continue until August. April and May are cold months, and frigid winds blowing up from the distant Antarctic leave everyone miserable. When the *surs* stop blowing, the dry season starts. The rivers are low, with sandbars and protruding logs making navigation treacherous.

AUGUST IS THE TIME of *suspension*, or rest. During this period no rubber is collected. The trees are allowed to heal over and regain strength. In September, watermelons and pineapples ripen. Vegetation becomes very dry from lack of rain and there is danger of fire because in this period farm land is burned off in preparation for new planting. Over every jungle clearing there hangs a pall of smoke. Care must be taken lest the jungle be set ablaze.

Thus jungle life passes in a monotonous and unchanging cycle. Occasionally, a friend or relative traveling on the river stops in for a visit. Twice a year an American padre calls at the clearing as he travels about his extensive river parish. It was this priestly visitor who fixed up Antonio's marriage. All of the Plaza children have been baptized but they know little about their Faith. The padre tries to teach them when he stops overnight but the time is too short and the space between visits too long for much to be accomplished.

If there is a monotony in the seasons, there is also a sameness in the daily routine. At four every morning, the whole family arises. While Antonio's wife stirs the fire to make breakfast, Antonio and his eldest son, 13-year-old Pepe, get ready their tools and equipment. Breakfast is always the fried bananas and yucca gruel. If meat is available, it is mixed with the yucca. As soon as breakfast is finished, Antonio and Pepe are off into the jungle until late in the afternoon.

While the men are away in the jungle, Antonio's wife, Maria, and his 10-year-old daughter, Rosa, are busy about the house. Three-year-old Juanito is allowed to amuse himself. There is always laundry to be done since white clothes dirty easily in the jungle. Clothing must also be made—shirts, trousers and dresses. Ready-made clothes are a luxury that cannot be afforded. Wood must be hauled for the fire, and water brought up from the river. The garden needs constant weeding otherwise jungle growth would quickly smother the vegetable plants. Maria and Rosa must also care for the fruit trees. The banana plants need much attention. A banana plant grows for seven years before bearing fruit, and then produces only one bunch of bananas. Old plants have to be cut down and new ones set out.

When the river starts to drop, Maria and her two younger children walk up and down the sandy shores searching for turtle eggs. Juanito makes a game out of the hunt. When he finds a turtle track in the sand, he alerts his mother with a howl. The tracks are followed until they come to an end. Rosa sinks a stick into the sand. In the spot where the stick enters with little resistance, she, her mother and Juanito dig out the eggs. Discovering a cache is a happy moment because turtle eggs are a great delicacy and a welcome change in diet.

MEANWHILE, ANTONIO and Pepe are hard at labor. They do not work together but divide the area to be covered between them. The rubber trees are quite scattered, seldom more than three or four to an acre. The father and son follow narrow trails from tree to tree. Each walks close to 20 miles a day to cover 80 to 100 trees. Father and son work as quickly as possible because in the early morning the rubber sap flows most freely.

On the way into the jungle, Antonio and Pepe stop at each rubber tree. They pull away the thin strip of dried latex from the previous day. Then with a sharp knife each slices a thin cut just below the old one, extending the cut about half-way around the tree, and being careful not to cut too deeply lest the tree be killed. At the bottom of the diagonal groove, each attaches a small cup into which the milky white latex drips. Then each goes on to the next tree.

The Amazon valley is the region where all the world's natural rubber originated. Indians knew of this magic liquid long before the arrival of Columbus. They called the tree *cauutchou*, "the tree that weeps". When the early explorers came, they took samples of the strange substance back to Spain but little use could be found for it. In 1839 Charles Goodyear discovered that by treating rubber with sulphur and heat, it would remain constant in both hot and cold weather. Thus the modern rubber industry was born.

116

After Antonio and Pepe have tapped all of their rubber trees, their job is half finished. They then retrace their steps, stopping at each tree to collect a cup of latex. Late in the afternoon they arrive home. Before they have supper, they must take care of the latex. They prepare a fire that gives off much smoke. A paddle is dipped into the white liquid and held over the fire until the latex turns hard and black. Over and over this is repeated until a "biscuit" weighing almost 100 pounds is on the paddle. This then is put aside to be taken to a merchant in town, or sold to a river trader.

Father and son collect about 20 pounds of rubber a day. With rubber selling for about $100 a ton, this means that father and son make approximately a dollar a day, or 50 cents each. For this amount, they work from dawn to dusk, walk countless miles of jungle trails, face many dangers, and are often caught in drenching storms. In a good year, Antonio and his son will gather a half ton of rubber, thus making about $50.

THE OTHER CASH CROP of the family is Brazil nuts. When the jungle is not flooded too early in the rainy season, they can harvest almost a ton of these delicacies. However, miles and miles of jungle trails must be scoured to get this many nuts. Brazil nuts grow at the top of the highest trees in the forest. They can only be harvested when they fall to the ground. The nuts are formed inside a pod as big as a large grapefruit. When this pod falls from a tree, it can fracture the skull of anyone unlucky enough to be underneath.

For every 300 pounds of nuts Antonio sells, he receives two dollars. Since he and his family collect a half ton, they will get less than seven dollars—poor pay for this dangerous, exhausting work. By the time transportation and the charges of the middlemen are added to the nuts, the American housewife will pay almost $500 for Antonio's nuts—70 times what he gets for harvesting them!

A few bananas are also sold to bolster the family income. These are mostly sold to passengers and crews on passing boats. Altogether the cash income for Antonio's family averages about $60 in a good year. This magnificent sum is spent in one visit to Riberalta, the nearest town. Cloth, gunpowder, salt, sugar and other such necessities quickly devour the income because jungle prices are high—gasoline a dollar a gallon, cornflakes a dollar and a half a box, and so on. Antonio and his family know no luxuries and even little of the necessities of life.

DESPITE POVERTY, Antonio figures that he is better off than many of his jungle neighbors. He owns and works his own land. Many jungle people live on the property of one of the large jungle holding companies. They live in practical serfdom, never getting out of debt, laboring under a *patron* who often holds the power of life and death over his subjects.

Antonio is poor but he is independent. It is this desire to be free that keeps him living apart from civilization. For it, he sacrifices many comforts and opportunities. Medical care is not available for him and his family. There is no education for his children. Even opportunities to exercise his religious beliefs are scarce. All of this is a high price to pay for independence. Americans born to freedom will not very readily understand.

Bora Indian chief of Peru

Indians of the Great Rain Forest. While the Indians of the Andes came into conflict with the white civilization of the Spanish, the jungle Indians were able to preserve their own way of life until recent times. In fact, many isolated tribes still live apart from the influences of white culture. The jungle Indians lived in the Stone Age. They had loom weaving, ceramics, and basketry. They did not practice the idol cult of the Andean Indian.

Today they are much the same. They live in thatched frame houses; wear scant clothing, usually made from bark cloth; hunt with blowguns, and bows and arrows; put poisons on the tips of their weapons; and use tobacco.

The existing Indian tribes are very numerous. Brazil has over three hundred, of which the best known are the Arawak, Carib, Chavante, Shipibo, and Tupi. Colombia and Peru have over a hundred different tribes, while Bolivia, Ecuador, and Venezuela have about fifty each.

Many of these tribes have not yet been reached by Christianity. It is only in recent years that contact has been made with such tribes as the head-hunting Jivaro of Ecuador, the unsociable Chavante of Brazil, and the unfriendly Motilone of Peru. In fact, it is believed that there are groups of Indians living in the vast rain forest who have never seen white men.

An interesting sidelight on the jungle Indian is his or her love of ornamentation. Although most

This Cunibo boy wears silver balls.

Cunibo chiefs off for a jungle hunt.

119

tribes wear little in the way of actual clothing, the members like to deck themselves out in ornamentation, even to the children. For example, among the artistic Caraja Indians of Brazil, boys are dressed in the finest ornaments. Their faces are painted red, and they wear elaborate bracelets and long black streamers from their arms. Their ears are adorned with "flowers" made from feathers with mother of pearl centers. They have a few strings of beads about their necks, and anklets. Nothing else is worn.

The Campa Indians of Peru have only recently come into contact with white civilization. The men of this tribe decorate their faces with red paint. On his head, each Campa wears a woven bamboo crown that flares out at the top. Under the crown, he wears a hand-woven cotton hood trimmed with parrot feathers.

The days of the forest Indian are numbered. All the forces of civilization operate against his continued existence. His domain has been invaded by outsiders seeking oil, minerals and other natural wealth. Where he tries to resist, he is exterminated. Marriage with other Indians and with whites, education, modern communications, all of these work together to have him conform to the dominant civilization. His way of life is doomed.

For a world that accepts him as an equal, the Indian has much to give. His latent artistic skills, his knowledge of herbs and roots, and his love of the earth can all be used. In return, he can be told of the God who made and redeemed him. Thus he who is religious by nature will no longer have to worship the spirit and forces of the forest in a vast pantheism that keeps him in daily bondage.

The Shipibo Indian women of Peru artistically create huge earthenware pots and vessels.

Yagua Indian making darts

Colombia's Chibcha Indians once had a high civilization allied to that of Peru's Incas.

Venezuelans have made the most rapid economic advances of any country in South America. A generation ago, Caracas, the capital of Venezuela, was a sleepy, small, provincial city. Today it is a spectacular, traffic-jammed metropolis of over two million people. The secret behind the change has been royalties received from oil leases.

However, the prosperity that has come about because of oil royalties benefits the upper class far more than the laborers who must struggle to keep their families together in the face of ever-rising prices. In Caracas, a "white-collar" class has come into existence.

Religious progress in Venezuela has not kept pace with material ad-vances. Indifference to religion on the whole increases in proportion to material prosperity. It is the poor who are the most devoted to the Church. In Caracas, it is estimated that less than 7 per cent of the Catholics attend Sunday Mass.

Today Spanish missioners are working in the country but their numbers are inadequate. The Venezuelan clergy is zealous and dedicated but the task facing them is tremendous. Spanish nuns of the *Opus Dei* group and various Catholic Action organizations are at work. But the voices of these hard-working apostles are drowned out by the gushing of wealth that pours from the oil fields. Ten million Venezuelans stand at a crossroads.

122

Colombians live by an economy based largely on coffee. When the Spanish first entered the country now known as Colombia they found the region inhabited by many Indian tribes. Today only 7 per cent of the population is pure-blooded Indian, and most of these inhabit the jungle wilderness east of the Andes. However, 70 per cent of the people of Colombia are of mixed Spanish-Indian blood. Bogota, the capital, is built on the site of the Chibcha Indian capital.

Along the tropical Caribbean coast line live most of the country's Negro population (about 5 per cent out of the total eighteen million). Their ancestors were brought from Africa as slaves, and the present day descendants are not much better off. They are wretchedly poor, suffer from tropical anemia, and have little religious care.

The main bulk of Colombia's population are the mestizos. They are mostly highland farmers, living on mountainsides and on high plateaus where the soil is fertile and the climate invigorating. Here they have their small farms, raise food and livestock. Here, too, are the coffee plantations on which the economy of the country depends.

From the religious viewpoint, Colombia is the best off of all South American countries. Vocations exist and Colombian priests promote the social doctrines of the Church.

The center of Catholic life is found high in the mountains northwest of Bogota, in the region known as Antioquia, where the people are Basques in origin. They produce excellent coffee on neat, individually owned farms. They raise fat cattle. More than half of Colombia's gold is mined in this region.

But the chief glory of this area is the glowing religious example it gives the rest of the country. Vocations to the priesthood are numerous. Sunday Mass attendance is the best in all Latin America. Many people are daily communicants. All children receive religious instruction. Antioquia is an island of faith in a sea of indifference.

A Venezuelan country schoolroom.

Education for the Millions

TWO AMERICAN oil prospectors recently were traveling by horseback along a dusty road some hundred miles north of Bogota, Colombia's capital city.

As they reached a junction in the trail, they heard a radio blaring forth from behind some bushes. Almost simultaneously, each man in amazement halted his horse, for the sound of a radio in this remote and backward mountain region was most unusual. Curious, the men dismounted to investigate. When they had walked around the bushes, they saw a score of people—men, women and children—squatting Indian-style in a field listening to a battery radio which brought them simple instructions on how to read and write. So intent were the peasants on their lesson, that none noticed the intrusion of the strangers.

One of the prospectors, now back in New York City, was asked the other day what had impressed him most during his journeyings South of the Border. His answer was not in the places he had seen—the great modern cities of our neighbors to the south, the awesome Inca ruins, the mighty Andes, or the hundreds of gems of colonial architecture. But his reply was the incident related above, and he told it with the fervor of a new disciple.

"The desire of these simple farming people to learn to read and write, and the unusual way in which they were doing it," he concluded, "was the most impressive thing I saw in the many thousands of miles I traveled."

The strange sight, so vividly recalled by the oil man, is part of an extraordinary chain of schools which have been set up by a young Colombian priest to combat his nation's high rate of illiteracy.

The man responsible for this modern revolution in Colombia is Monsignor Joaquin Salcedo, who was ordained in 1947. A tall, angular, sharp-featured man with the eyes of a dreamer and the dynamic drive of a practical executive, Monsignor Salcedo began in the space of months what the Colombian government had been trying to do for decades.

"Illiteracy has always been a major problem in South America, and Colombia is no exception," declares a high ranking member of the Colombian Commission of Inter-American Development. "The upper classes of my country are well-educated and have produced many of the foremost cultural and artistic leaders of the continent. But the poor, which compose the vast majority of our population, must face a life of blindness."

Since 1931 the Colombian government has been waging a vigorous campaign to overcome illiteracy. In 1934 a law was passed stating that 10% of the national budget had to be used for education. In the next ten years this appropriation was increased 500%. Young women were given special training, and then offered one peso for every person between seven and twenty years of age whom they taught to read and write. In 1942, alone, the Government opened 208 new schools. Yet despite this increased activity almost fifty per cent of the population were still illiterate in 1947.

The government had made good educational progress in the cities where the compulsory education law was possible to enforce. But Colombia is a vast country (the third most populous in South America, and twice the area of our state of Texas). Four-fifths of its people live in the rugged hinterland—on high plains or savannas, and in mountain valleys separated from each other by ranges and spurs that make communication between them extremely difficult. Three parallel mountain chains, rising to a height of 19,000 feet, divide the country into four parts. Travel is rigorous, and the few roads and railroads that run down to the Pacific or Caribbean lowlands are cited as major engineering feats. To reach and educate the people in the upland plateaus, in the mountain valleys, and in the tropical jungles was a task which engaged some of the best brains in the nation. Colombia, moreover, is a unitary rather than a federal republic. There are fourteen Departments, or States, which elect local legislatures, and enjoy partial autonomy. Some of these Departments did not give their full cooperation to national educational plans.

One high official addressing a national educational congress in Bogota, declared, "To reach successfully the great mass of our people will take a century."

BUT THE LEGISLATORS and administrators were reckoning without Monsignor Salcedo. In May, 1947, young Joaquin Salcedo was ordained to the priesthood by Bishop Crisanto Luque, of Tunja. In August, the Bishop called this mild-mannered, affable, but high-strung young man into his study.

"Father," said the Bishop, "I am assigning you to Sutatenza. It is a difficult parish because your people will be so widely scattered. Out of a parish of 9,000 souls, only 195 live in the vicinity of your church. You must work diligently to bring the blessings of God to all your flock. I expect you to do this as effectively as you know how."

Thus newly-ordained Father Salcedo gathered together his few belongings and set off for his first parish with his Bishop's charge ringing in his ears. Being a native of the diocese, he knew the difficulties that lay before him. Travel in this mountainous territory would be slow and difficult, but he had been instructed to reach all his people as effectively as possible. Travel by horseback would not be effective—there would be long hours in the saddle, too much time wasted. No, he had to get to his people quickly. If he could only travel on a bolt of lightning. Electricity, he recalled from his physics course, moved at a speed of 187,000 miles a second. He needed electricity. And the child of electricity—the radio.

By the time Father Salcedo reached his new parish, a plan was beginning to form in his mind. He had experimented with radio as a boy and as a seminarian, and was familiar with its workings. If he could set up a radio station at Sutatenza and provide his people with receiving sets, he could talk to them whenever he wished. It was as simple as that! The problem of money and obtaining the sets would be met when the time came.

At first Father Salcedo thought only of reaching his people in spiritual matters, but as he meditated more deeply on his idea, he was convinced of the vast possibilities it presented. Through the radio he could teach his people to read and write. He could give them lessons in the history of their country, in agriculture, in sanitation, in the hundred and one things that would help them to a better living. He could even go beyond his own parish, reaching out into the neighboring countryside, and perhaps even into the whole country.

In Sutatenza, Father Salcedo found his first ally and assistant in Enrique Parra, the village schoolmaster. Alert, and aggressive young Parra was one of those idealistic men who had decided to devote his life to the poor-paying and often thankless job of trying to educate the back-country children. The first time he heard Father Salcedo speak of what the priest called his "radiophonic schools" was like a dream come true. Parra enthusiastically threw in his lot with his new pastor, and in the ensuing months the two men put the plan into working order. When all the details were on paper, Father Salcedo rode off to see Bishop Luque.

The Bishop listened carefully, and when Father Salcedo had finished, said, "The idea is well formulated. It has my blessing. But from where will the money come to finance your project?"

"From the people themselves," Father Salcedo replied. "When we show them what good these radiophonic schools will do them, and how such education will improve their standard of living, they will willingly support the project."

The priest returned to Sutatenza, and began traveling about his parish telling the people what he intended to do. The peasants were enthusiastic. The first contributions began to flow in. Alverto Lopez, a small valley farmer, stopped Father Salcedo on the roadside and asked if he could make "a little gift for the venture." Slowly the peasant counted out fifty pesos (about $25), a small fortune for him. Another farmer, Sergio Arenas, who heard that Father Salcedo was trying to borrow money from the bank, mortgaged his cattle and brought the priest 500 pesos. A few days later he was back at the rectory with the deeds to his farm which he gave to the priest to use as security for a loan.

WITH THE AID of Enrique Parra, and two new assistants—Juan Salcedo and Andres Sacristan—Father Salcedo built a 300 watt standard broadcast station in the Sutatenza rectory. The transmitter had only a range of 37 miles, but this was enough for a start. Small receivers were purchased from International General Electric Company, assembled at the rectory, and tuned to receive the 1580 kc frequency broadcast by the station. These were battery receivers because no electricity was available. The receivers were installed in public plazas, farm houses, a road junction, or at any spot where a group could be conveniently gathered. An "assistant instructor", an enthusiastic young man with some schooling, was appointed to take charge of each receiver and to lead class instruction.

In July, 1948, the first test began. Slowly, a detailed plan of instruction was formulated. The tests were successful. Priests in neighboring communities asked to be included in the unusual venture. More receivers were added.

A little more than a year after the first tests, on September 6, 1949, Dr. Mariano Ospina Perez, President of Colombia, spoke by radio from the Presidential Palace in Bogota, officially opening the radiophonic schools. Throughout the entire Boyaca region that day, in 90 different locations, an identical procedure

126

took place. The gong reverberated through the hills, and even before it had become silent, people began to assemble from their mountain homes. Men, women and children came, out of the fields, up from the cane plantations, down from their straw huts. Swiftly, they marched along winding paths to their schools. Each group averaged about 80 persons.

FATHER SALCEDO opened the program by stating the aims of the project, and exhorting his people to take advantage of the opportunity that was theirs.

Then from far-off Bogota the President spoke, officially inaugurating the schools. The voice of Enrique Parra was next heard. This young government schoolteacher now spoke to his largest audience. Slowly he began. "This is the alphabet upon which all of our words are built. Your teacher will now write. A...B...C..."

At each receiver, the assistant teacher studiously wrote the letters of the alphabet upon a blackboard. Old men and young men, women with babies, children, all carefully copied on their slates and pads the letters written on the blackboard.

Then the voice of Parra commanded, "Now we will say these letters together. Ready. A...B..."

Throughout the hills, seven thousand voices chanted, "A...B...C..."

With the lessons underway, Father Salcedo set about stabilizing his schools. Reading and writing would be the basic subjects, since these were the greatest needs of the people. Other subjects would be given in limited doses. Once the people could read and write, other things would come easily. Each day Father Salcedo speaks to his people on spiritual topics, mindful of his Bishop's command which sent him to Sutatenza.

But Father Salcedo was not content. He knew that millions of his countrymen were yet to be reached. His work, now well known in Colombia because of favorable press notices, made it easy for him to appeal for and get additional funds. With this money, the energetic priest left Colombia for the United States in late 1949. Here he observed broadcasting techniques, spoke to engineers, and examined equipment. From the International divison of the General Electric Company he purchased $50,000 worth of equipment. When he returned to Colombia he brought with him 700 additional receivers and a powerful one kw. short wave transmitter, capable of reaching to all corners of his nation. When this equipment was installed in May, 1950, the number of schools jumped from 90 to over 700, and the number of pupils grew from 7,000 to 150,000.

With such accomplishments behind him less than three years after ordination, one would think that Father Salcedo would rest. But this dynamic organizer initiated a new project.

Father Salcedo decided to build a large center in Bogota, the nation's capital. Here he installed the most modern equipment, made provisions for the use of TV, began a newspaper aimed at the campesino which taught such basic fundamentals as hygiene, and instituted a whole program of publications, using Colombian talent.

As Monsignor Salcedo himself says, "Christ told us to go to all men. He commanded that we be the light of the world. That is all we are trying to do here in Colombia—to project the social and religious teachings of the Church with the speed of light."

An empty shoe box becomes a magic toy for this young Peruvian of a poor family.

Ecuadorian nurses are taught the fundamentals of what goes into a good nutritious diet.

Ecuador is an Indian world. Most of us think of Ecuador as a little country. Actually it is a region larger than Texas while its four and a half million population equals that of Virginia. The word "Ecuador" comes from a Spanish word meaning "equator." Quito, the capital of Ecuador, sits practically astride the equator.

Nine out of ten Ecuadorians have Indian blood and one out of two is a full-blooded Indian. In eastern Ecuador live the Indians of the Amazon forest. Here are the Jivaros who shrink the heads of enemies and the aboriginal Awishira who fire poisoned darts at white men hunting oil.

Most of the population of Ecuador, however, lives in the Andean highlands. Here the Indians work on the haciendas of the whites or eke out an existence from their small plots of land. Although education is compulsory, few Indian children get much schooling. There is great illiteracy and poverty.

Modern ways are slowly penetrating among the Ecuadorian Indians. The Otavolo tribe, for example, have developed a foreign market for their woolen goods. As a result, they feel the need for education.

The people of Ecuador are nominally Catholics but a shortage of priests has left them without instruction. Spanish missioners work in the highlands but their numbers are too few. Ecuador's future depends on the progress of its poor.

Although the Alliance for Progress was accused of failure, American aid enabled this Peruvian man to build and own his own home. The Alliance had many successes.

There are three Perus. There is chic and sophisticated Peru that is centered in Lima, one of the most interesting and fascinating cities in the world. Then there is highland Peru, where men are made small by mighty mountains. Finally, there is jungle Peru where savage Indian tribes travel silently through the forests, wearing only bows and arrows and perhaps a few beads.

Peruvians live in a land that was the heart of the great Inca empire. After the Spanish conquest, it was the most important colony of Spain. Untold fortunes were spent to beautify Lima, the capital city. Today the people of Lima live surrounded by art treasures of the past. They have not stood still, however. They have built a sprawling city with skyscrapers and one of the most modern airports in the world.

In recent years, however, thousands of mountain Indians attracted by the wealth of Lima have emigrated to the city with the result that slums and unemployment were created on a large scale. The government and Catholic social agencies are hard at work to relieve these conditions.

The main population of Peru lives in the Andean highlands. Here are found the Quechua and Aymara Indians, struggling to exist in a barren world that knows only two seasons—cold and rainy. Although all of the highland Indians are called Christians, for the majority the title is but nominal. Long years without priests, and consequent instruction, have left the Indians with

Old San Marcos University in Peru.

little knowledge of what Christianity is all about. Many have lapsed back into pagan practices, believing in spirits and witch doctors.

It is in this highland area that the majority of American missioners in Peru are to be found. By training hundreds of lay leaders as catechists, the priests have brought many Indians back to an understanding and practice of Catholicism. Old churches are being repaired and reopened, and the praises of God are being sung again from the top of the world.

Peruvians can count four canonized saints from their country alone. These are Saint Rose of Lima, Saint Toribius, Saint Francis Solano and Saint Martin de Porres. No other land in the New World has been so blessed.

The Peruvian lives surrounded by history. His culture and traditions are among the oldest in the Americas. A century before the Pilgrims landed on Plymouth Rock, San Marcos University in Lima was training the youth of the New World. And even before the Spanish arrived, those great pacifiers, the Incas, had built their mountain capital of Cuzco along grandiose artistic lines. All of this is the heritage of the present Peruvian.

Nine out of ten Bolivians have Indian blood. Bolivians live in a land that has tremendous natural resources to support its people but despite this fact most Bolivians live in grinding, degrading poverty. There is a twofold reason for this. First, many of the potentialities of Bolivia are undeveloped. Second, those resources that are developed are controlled by a very few whites.

Three-fourths of Bolivia's three millions lives on the cold, high altiplano—the great plateau that stretches across the Andes between twelve and fourteen thousand feet above sea level. The sparse, rocky soil of the altiplano is unproductive. Here in windowless, unheated, stone or mud huts live the Aymara Indians. To numb themselves against the dull aches of hunger and the cold, they chew coca leaves from which cocaine is extracted.

On the altiplano and the sides of the Andes are the mines where the Indians have wrested a fortune in tin and silver, little of which has gone to the workers. The govern-ment today has a program of giving the Indians a greater share of this wealth but so far it has not been too effective.

Dropping down from the altiplano to the middle lands and valleys, the land becomes more fertile. Here the Indians (mostly of the Quechua tribe) are better off but only relatively so. Most of them are tenant farmers who must struggle to obtain the necessities of life. The government has a program of breaking up the large estates but centuries of serfdom have left the Indians ill-equipped to stand on their own.

At the foot of the Andes the great Amazon jungle begins. This region is sparsely populated and travel is only along rivers. There is great wealth in the jungle but lack of transportation and communications prevents its effective exploitation. For example, Maryknollers working in the northeast corner of Bolivia must either fly in supplies over the Andes or bring them via the Atlantic Ocean up the Amazon River across the great width of Brazil.

Bolivia is also one of the poorest countries in Latin America as regards religious care. Priests are few and far between. As a result, the Indians, most of whom are illiterate, get little instruction in the Faith they claim. Missioners are helping to ease the situation and an attempt is being made to develop a Bolivian clergy. But for many years to come the people of Bolivia will be in serious need of religious instruction.

These Bolivian Indians labor in a tin mine. Their hours are long, their pay low. For many centuries the Bolivian Indians have been extracting tin and silver from the Andes.

The Family That Needs God

JERONIMO AUCA is a square-faced, weather-beaten farmer, who is thirty-four years old. He lives with his wife and four children in a depression in the Bolivian Andes called the Cochabamba Valley. He is typical of the millions of Indian farmers who live on the roof of the Western World and who make up 85 per cent of the populations of Bolivia and Peru.

Jeronimo's village, if a scattering of huts can be called such, is named Canton Chullpas. It is similar to any one of thousands of cantons, or villages, that dot the countryside along the west coast of South America. Thus if we can come to a knowledge of Jeronimo Auca—his life and his problems—we will have an understanding of millions of people who inhabit the highlands of South America.

The canton of Chullpas was part of an original Spanish grant made in the sixteenth century. As late as 1870, the area was owned by a single individual, Colonel Leon Galindo. After his death, it was divided among his ten children, and before long was disposed of in successive sales. Today no Galindo owns property in the region.

The once large estate is today 260 parcels of land assigned to households totaling 1,414 people. Like Jeronimo Auca, most of the people of the region are of Indian blood, although there is a sprinkling of mestizos—people of mixed Spanish and Indian blood.

Jeronimo and his family live on two acres of land on which he grows wheat, potatoes and corn. The family's yearly income is $110, of which it spends $50 for food, $15 for clothing, and $15 for drink. A small portion of the income comes from homespun yarn that Jeronimo's wife, Justa, makes from the fleece of the two sheep owned by the family. More of it comes from soap Jeronimo makes and sells. Another part is from surplus crops. Jeronimo also hires out to several of the more wealthy landowners in the district.

The Aucas live in a little one-room house that has a door and no windows. The walls of the house are made of adobe bricks (mud mixed with straw) and the roof is thatch placed over long poles. The house is lighted by candle. The family possessions are few. The Aucas own one bed, no chairs, ten plates, five forks, five knives, four spoons, and a dog. In addition to the two sheep, there are a wooden plow, two scythes, and a machete.

Two Auca children died shortly after being born. Infant mortality in the region is high. One of Jeronimo's neighbors has lost fifteen children, and it is not uncommon to meet families that have lost four or five. When questioned about the high child death rate, the people of the valley shrug their shoulders and speak of the will of God. The actual cause is malnutrition brought on by a starchy, meager diet.

Jeronimo's oldest son, Antonio, who is sixteen, left home recently to join the Bolivian army. Antonio is the only child who has had any education. He spent two years in the canton's tiny public school, at the end of which he was barely able to read and write, a feat no one else in the family could approach. Maria, the second child, is thirteen. She works for a neighbor who makes chicha, an alcoholic beverage. The next boy, Jorge, nine, spends his days minding the family sheep. Five-year-old Paulina is usually to be found around the house with Mrs. Auca. It is her task to haul water from a neighbor's well as the Aucas have none of their own.

The Aucas, like all the people of Canton Chullpas, claim to be Catholics. Jeronimo and his wife were not married in the Church, simply because the idea never entered their heads. Unknowingly, they were deprived of the beautiful Toledo Rite wedding ceremony that is used throughout the Spanish regions of the New World. In this ceremony, bride and groom are linked together by a silver chain around their necks. The groom drops silver coins in the hands of the bride, signifying that he will support her.

The people of Canton Chullpas know nothing about their religion because they have never been instructed. The nearest priest is in Cliza, many miles away. On rare occasions a priest from Cliza comes to Canton Chullpas and offers Mass in a small run-down chapel. But such a priestly visit is made only on an average of once every two years. As a result the people are unaware of the sacraments, and morality is generally low.

All of the Auca children were baptized because, like his neighbors, Jeronimo has a superstitious respect for this sacrament. To have the children baptized, Jeronimo and Justa had to take them to Cliza. The only exception was Jorge whose birth corresponded with one of the rare visits by a priest.

JERONIMO IS ONE of the elders of the village, serving on the council to Mayor Yaquiri, who is known as the alcalde or leader. There are many communal problems to be settled, and there are communal arrangements to be made for the annual fiestas. It is the duty of Mayor Yaquiri and his council to see that these things are accomplished.

Jeronimo and his neighbors not only respect Mayor Yaquiri but stand in considerable awe of his powers because he is the medicine man or witch doctor of the region. In the absence of religious instruction, superstition reigns unchecked in the area. Jeronimo believes in ghostmen who live deep in the mountains. They are little old men who are forever smiling. But the smiles are only a disguise, for the real purpose of the ghostmen is to lead mortals to destruction.

There is another evil spirit called *mekhala*. This spirit takes the form of a skinny old woman with matted, disheveled hair. Her task in life is to steal a person's brains. She also steals the souls of children, causing their death. The only way to overcome her wiles is a devotion to *Pacha-Mama,* the Earth Mother.

On the roof of Jeronimo's house is a crude wooden cross. It is put there to keep away evil spirits. This also is the purpose of some paper streamers attached to the roof. In Jeronimo's mind, both cross and paper streamers are equally effective. In the corner of Jeronimo's fields there is a big pile of rocks. Jeronimo believes that each of these rocks has a spirit.

Jeronimo's wife, Justa, will usually be found around her little adobe house. Sometimes she goes out over the bleak altiplano looking for manure with which to make fire for cooking, but this task usually falls to Paulina or Jorge. Occasionally, she will be given a gift of cornstalks by some relative. These she will tie in a big bundle and carry home on her back. These too will be used for fuel in an almost treeless region.

Justa actually spends little time in the house. She has a little earthen fireplace outdoors and here she cooks the family's two meals a day. She does not like to sit on the earth floor of the dark house, but prefers to work in the sunlight.

Sometimes she spins woolen yarn on a crudely made foot machine. Sometimes she makes *api*, a mild alcoholic drink brewed from red and white corn. Sometimes a neighbor stops by for a bit of gossip. Sometimes she helps her husband in the fields. When it is plowing time, it is Justa who pulls the crude wooden plow while Jeronimo guides it.

MOUNTAIN LIFE is monotonous. The weather is often cold and damp and an ache gets in the bones. The diet causes teeth to decay rapidly and since no one has even heard of a dentist, there is nothing to do but suffer the pain quietly. Chewing coca leaves helps to lessen the aches but sometimes even this luxury cannot be afforded.

The main diversions of the year come with two fiestas. One is the patronal feast of Canton Chullpas, the other is held in Cliza. Both fiestas are three day affairs. Originally the fiestas had a religious significance but because of the lack of priests to give instruction, the spiritual meaning has been lost.

The principal activity of the fiestas is dancing and drinking. The dances are native and consist mostly of whirling around to the accompaniment of flutes and drums. The drinking is largely done with chicha, a potent alcoholic beverage made from masticated corn. By the end of the second day of a fiesta, Jeronimo has usually passed out from excessive drinking. Justa must sit by his prostrate body until he awakes and she can get him home. While such drinking cannot be condoned, poverty, ignorance and monotony are certainly mitigating factors.

Like most of the people of the region, Jeronimo and his family have little sense of belonging to a country or being Bolivians. To them the government is the soldier who will arrest them if they become a nuisance when drunk, or the administrator who comes around and collects the annual taxes.

Not yet thirty-five, Jeronimo and his wife are already old. Justa is wrinkled and almost completely toothless. The stubble of beard on Jeronimo's wind-etched face is heavily streaked with gray hairs. One does not have to talk to them long to realize that they are tired in body and mind.

The Aucas have no other security than that which their small plot of land offers. One bad year of weather and they will starve. Happiness comes when they can afford a little cheese or spices to put into their ground corn. They have no hope for better conditions. They need many things. They need education. They need medical help and technical assistance. But most of all, they need God.

136

Andean men—anonymity in poverty

Threshing wheat on horseback is fun for these boys of Chile's fertile central valley.

Chileans are a progressive, cosmopolitan people. The nine million people of Chile live in a land of haunting beauty—lovely green valleys, irrigated by swift-flowing rivers; dense, towering forests; and soaring, snow-capped mountain peaks that majestically rise to a greater height than any others of North and South America.

The country of the Chileans is a "string bean" country—long and narrow. If laid across the United States, Chile would stretch from New York to San Francisco. It extends from burning deserts in the north to the damp, cold Antarctic wastelands. In between are the fertile central valleys where the majority of the people live and work.

People of many lands settled in Chile. The Spanish were the first to arrive but after them came English, Scotch, Irish, and Germans. All of them have left their mark on their adopted nation. The leading Chilean patriot in that country's struggle for independence was an Irishman, Bernard O'Higgins. As a result of this mixing of peoples, Chile has been a leader in progressive social legislation and trade unionism.

Chile has a diversified economy. While most Chileans are engaged in agriculture, the country has much natural wealth. In the north, there are borax, nitrates and copper. The Andes hold gold and silver mines. In the central section, there are rich farms and vineyards. Farther south, the people engage in cattle and sheep raising. Below them are the great forests of the lumber industry.

The original inhabitants of Chile were the Araucanian Indians, a liberty-loving people never conquered by the Spanish. Today there are over 300,000 Araucanian Indians in south central Chile.

At the very tip of Chile, a few scattered remnants of Fuegian tribes remain. This formerly was a paradise for anthropologists but today the Yahgan, Ona, and Alakaluf peoples are practically extinct. These Fuegians (inhabitants of Tierra del Fuego) are among the most primitive people in the world. They speak in a language that sounds like a man clearing his throat. Despite the dampness and cold, they wear little clothing.

The people of Chile have two great problems. The first is a more equal distribution of the land. Over 50 per cent of all farmland is in the hands of a few hundred families. The second problem is the disintegration of the faith in Chile because of a lack of priests. Chile also had the dubious distinction of the first freely elected Marxist government, now overthrown.

Argentina grew by immigration. When the Spanish conquest invaded Latin America, Argentina was bypassed. The Spanish attention was focused on the west coast of South America and the towering Andes formed a natural barrier to penetration of the pampas to the east. As a result, Argentine growth

An Araucanian Indian woman of Chile

came from natural immigration from Europe — Spanish, Italian, Irish, German, and Scotch making up the bulk of the population. Today, 78 per cent of the population is Argentine, born of European ancestry, 20 per cent is foreign born from Europe, 2 per cent Indian or mixed descent. There are over 23 million Argentines.

In 1850, Buenos Aires was a sleepy town of about 80,000 people. Today, with close to four million people, it is one of the leading cities of the world, larger than London or Berlin. The people of "B.A." know the last word in progress. Their beautiful city has subways, theaters, skyscrapers.

Half the population of Argentina lives within a hundred mile radius of Buenos Aires. In the outlying provinces are the vineyards, farms and cattle-raising pampas. The bulk of the best land is controlled by only two hundred families. These families are also the main support of the Church. The Catholic religion has relatively great strength in Argentina. Catholic social principles permeate Argentine life. However, the main body of clergy are in the vicinity of Buenos Aires, and the provinces badly need clergy.

Uruguay is a vest-pocket edition of Argentina. Uruguayans are a people of mixed European backgrounds who live in the smallest South American country. They are a cosmopolitan, progressive people with advanced social legislation.

Paraguay is a poor cousin. Although Paraguay is as large as Montana, it has about the same amount of people as Philadelphia, Pa. The country is a dictatorship and is exceedingly backwards. Paraguayans are peons, proud but poor.

Brazilians think big. Brazilians live in a country larger than coterminous U.S. that occupies half the land area of South America, and that has half the continent's population. Although Brazilians compose all races, the culture and language of their country is Portuguese. The population is 61 per cent white, 27 per cent mulatto, and 11 per cent Negro. There is no racial prejudice in Brazil but there are sharp social distinctions.

The great majority of Brazilians live close to the seacoast and vast sections of the interior are uninhabited and some even unexplored. Two cities, Rio de Janeiro and Sao Paulo, have a population of ten million between them. These cities are cosmopolitan and progressive. Sao Paulo is the industrial heart of Brazil, the center of great wealth and expansion. While a middle class exists in these two cities, elsewhere there exists a tremendous gulf between the rich and poor.

The Portuguese were the first to settle in Brazil. They imported large numbers of Negro slaves. After Brazil became a republic, Italians, Germans, and people of the Slavic countries immigrated there. Twenty-five years ago, Japanese began to immigrate to Brazil and today there are close to three hundred thousand of them there. Brazilians enjoy freedom of religion, and it is estimated that 95 per cent of the people claim to be Catholics. However, many people are Catholics in little more than name. In Bahia, large numbers of people belong to pagan sects that are a cross between African voodoo and Christianity. *Macumba,* a spiritist and devil-worshiping cult, has made tremendous inroads among the poor and slum people of the big cities. Protestantism is stronger numerically in Brazil than in any other Latin American country.

The Catholic hierarchy and clergy are untiring in their efforts to revive the Catholic heritage of Brazil but they are undermanned and confined mostly to the large cities. The task of restoring Christ to Brazil must be done by the Brazilian laity.

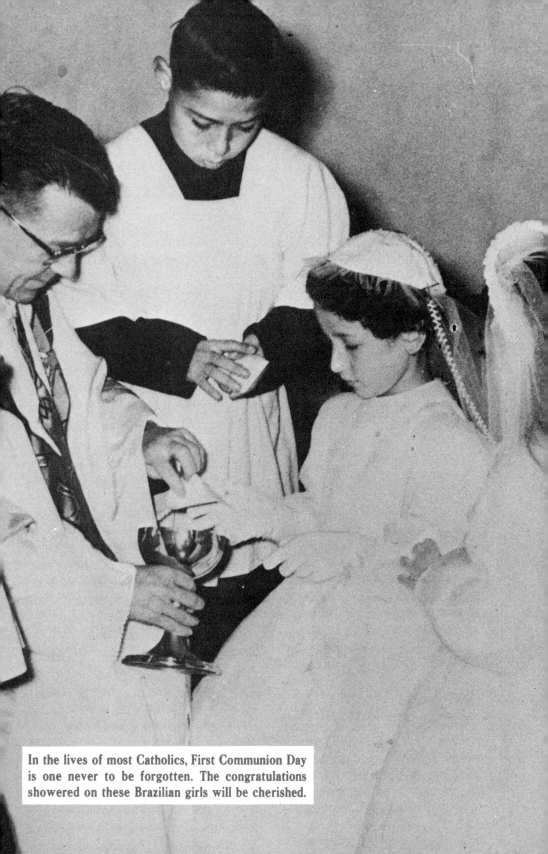

In the lives of most Catholics, First Communion Day is one never to be forgotten. The congratulations showered on these Brazilian girls will be cherished.

A Wedding in Malaya

"I WILL BE GLAD when this day is over," Yusof bin Hussein remarked to his wife, as he breakfasted on rice and curry in the privacy of their bedroom.

"It is what comes from having a daughter," answered his wife, teasingly. "The next one to be married will be our son. Then it will be someone else who will have all this fussing to do and not us."

As his wife withdrew, Yusof thought to himself what complicated business it was to marry off a girl child. It had all begun six months earlier with the engagement of his daughter, Leh, to Othman, a young Malay policeman. The time for the wedding had been set for shortly after the rice harvest. At first preparations had been minor and then the harvesting had so occupied his time, that Yusof hardly realized that the affair was coming to a climax. But once the harvest was in, and with time on his hands, Yusof discovered his house a place of confusion.

Weeks earlier the initial betrothal ceremony had taken place. Yusof and his wife according to the custom of Malaya had carried a box of betel leaves to Othman's parents. Then there was the engagement party and the ceremony of receiving the dowry. In this latter affair, Othman's relatives had brought 300 dollars wrapped in gold cloth and had presented it to Yusof before witnesses. The dowry payment had been a signal for preparations to begin in earnest. From that time on there had been no peace.

For the past week, there had been nothing but hustle and bustle in his house. All peace had gone. Women relatives were forever underfoot. Yusof never realized that so many people were required to prepare a wedding, or that so many things had to be done. Yusof's wife was the overseer, assigning different squads to Leh's bedroom which was being transformed into the bridal chamber. Yusof could hardly recognize the room with its gold embroidered pillows and bed spread, and the fancily decorated sequin net. Others had been at work setting up and decorating the low platform and couch on which the bride and groom were to sit in state. Still others had been busy making paper flowers to which hardboiled eggs were attached. These would be given to the guests, the symbolism being that of fertility. Finally, the kitchen was crowded with people making the cakes and sweet rice that would be used in the celebration and which would be taken home in great quantities by all the relatives and helpers.

Yusof stood up from the floor where he had been seated cross-legged, eating from dishes set on a mat. He stretched himself and walked over to the open window. He saw Leh hurrying in from the bathhouse set near the well under the coconut trees. She was modestly covered by a dry sarong. Yusof noticed that

Leh's fingers and toe nails, ceremoniously stained with henna leaves two days earlier, were still brightly colored. He wondered to himself how long it would take the dye to wash off and why women made such a fuss over such beauty details as painted toenails.

Actually, Leh and Othman were already legally married. That had happened yesterday. But they would not live together until all the ceremonies practiced by good Moslems had been completed. At noon on the previous day, the village elders, Yusof, his sons, and his two brothers gathered in the large front room of the house where the bridal couch had been erected. Othman and a few of his friends had arrived last. When he reached the house, he slipped his shoes off, as no Malay would wear shoes indoors, and hurried into the room.

Othman squatted in the center of the floor in front of the *kathi*, or Moslem marriage official. His friends sat in a row behind him. The *kathi* offered a Moslem prayer and then went alone to Leh's room, where the bride sat waiting. The *kathi* asked Leh if she agreed to the marriage. She replied that she did. The *kathi* then returned and put the same question to Othman. With both parties consenting, the official then delivered a short talk on the duties of the bridegroom. Then the marriage register was signed by the *kathi* and Othman. Finally, the *kathi* had escorted Othman to Leh's room. The youth had touched Leh on the forehead signifying that she was his wife. Then he went out to join his new father-in-law and relatives in their noon meal, after which he went to his own home.

Othman returned to Yusof's house after dusk. Again, relatives and friends assembled in the big room, now lighted with oil lamps. Leh was led in and took a seat on the wedding couch. Her bridesmaid stood at her side, directing her and arranging her dress. Leh sat stiffly, her eyes downcast, her hands extended, palms resting on her knees. A brass tray was carried in with four dishes containing saffron rice, rice paste, bleached rice grains, and pandan leaves.

Each of her relatives approached the platform. Each took grains from the two dishes of rice and threw them over the right and left shoulder of the bride. Lastly, a pandan leaf was dipped in the rice paste and a few drops allowed to fall on the back of each of the bride's hands. The bridesmaid wiped away the paste with a handkerchief and then turned the bride's palms up. Again drops of rice paste fell. When these were removed, Leh folded her hands before her breast and bowed seven times to the relatives. The bows were returned. When all the relatives were finished, the bride was led back to her room. Then the entire ceremony was repeated with Othman in the place of honor.

WHEN THE CEREMONY ended, Othman returned again to his own home, while his friends remained behind. Yusof also retired but was unable to get to sleep because of the singing and beating of drums. The young people of both families continued the party until long after midnight. When they finally did depart, it was with shouts that they would all be back shortly after noon the next day for the final part of the ceremonies. Yusof finally fell asleep thinking how fortunate were Othman's father and mother. Malay tradition decreed that they should not attend any of the ceremonies.

Coming back to the present, Yusof remembered the busy day ahead. He left the bedroom and walked through the large ceremonial room. He spoke softly to several cousins who were busy putting the last minute touches on the wedding couch and platform, and then went outdoors. At one side of the house a long table had been set up. It was piled high with gifts sent in by relatives to help out with the reception. There were coconuts, oil, fruit and baskets of rice. Yusof's brother was listing all the articles and marking each piece of cloth wrapping or basket with the name of the donor. The wrappings would be returned to their owners at the end of the day, filled with small wedding cakes. The names were important because custom decreed that should the daughter of one of the donors get married, Yusof would have to make a gift to her of equal value. Across from the gift table, under some coconut trees, several long thatched-roof sheds, open on four sides, had been set up. Tables and benches borrowed from the town hall were in place under the temporary shelters. A few yards away temporary kitchens had been erected where male relatives were busy with preparations.

About one o'clock, Yusof began receiving guests before the verandah. He was dressed in a white silk shirt, white duck trousers, a brightly striped sarong-like apron, and a black velvet hat, styled somewhat like an Army overseas cap. The guests brought presents which were turned over to Yusof's brother for cataloguing. This time the gifts were mostly household articles—cutlery, cups and saucers, plates, cloth, tablecloths, mats, and so on. Occasionally, an envelope with cash was handed in. All of these gifts would be useful when Othman built his own house.

YUSOF'S SONS ESCORTED the male guests to the covered shed where they were served tea and cakes. They chatted and smoked, content to be in male company. The women made their way into the house to exclaim over the glittering sequins and golden cloth of Leh's bedroom, and the attractiveness of the wedding platform. Then they squatted Malay-style on the floor and were served tea and cakes. By midafternoon there were over 100 people crowded about the house and compound.

It was promptly at four o'clock when a procession of cars came down the road in a cloud of dust and accompanied by the screeching of horns. It was Othman with his friends and relatives. The young policeman was resplendent in a suit of gold cloth and peaked wedding hat. Some of his friends carried suitcases containing all his belongings. He would live in his father-in-law's house until he could build one of his own. Other friends carried Malayan drums on which they began beating by hand as an accompaniment to their singing. The party made its way to the house with Othman in the lead. Just as the groom was about to put his foot on the first step a bevy of women poured out of the house, chattering wildly and blocking the way.

Leh's bridesmaid came to the front of the group, asking what Othman and his friends wanted. They were told to go away. Othman's best man spoke up and demanded admission. The bickering went on for some time. Finally, the best man offered the women a present of money. Immediately, the simulated quarrel came to an end. The women opened a way, and Othman forced his way through the crowd. Leh was already sitting on the couch and Othman made his way to her and took a seat at her side. The guests crowded around to take a look at the newly married couple. Close relatives approached the platform sprinkling ground sandalwood and flower petals on the bridal couple. Close friends of the bride and groom came up and made jests trying to get the happy couple to smile. Most of the time Othman and Leh were able to keep straight faces. Outside the wedding banquet was being served to guests.

About an hour later, the first guests began to leave. They were given flowers containing hardboiled eggs and their gift wrappings filled with wedding cakes. At the entranceway to the compound Yusof and his wife stood saying farewell to the departing guests. "Safe journey," Yusof bid each of his guests in traditional Malay style. "Stay in health," was the answer. When the last of the guests had gone, Yusof and his wife went indoors to take their evening meal with the newlyweds and the few close relatives remaining. Leh served Othman as tradition required, and the young groom was pleased to note that his wife had been well trained by her mother.

AFTER THE MEAL was over, the women took Leh to her room to prepare her for the first private meeting with her husband. The men went out on the verandah.

"Friday we will go to the mosque and thank Allah that all went well these past weeks," Yusof said to Othman. "We will also ask Allah's blessing on your marriage."

One by one the relatives drifted away. At last only Yusof and Othman were left.

"It has been a good day," said Yusof.

"Yes, it has," replied Othman.

There was another silence.

"It is time that we went in," remarked Yusof finally.

"Yes, father. It is time."

Arm in arm, the father and new husband entered the darkened house.

PAGODA CLIMBING

by Margaret Leong

We have watched the turtles swimming
   And have fed the temple's fish
   As they swam among the lotus
   With their silver fins a-swish;

We have climbed the copper stairs
   Of the temple; we have come
   To the foot of the pagoda,
   With its giant, wooden drum;

We have seen the grey gulls fly
   Across the sky in pairs,
   And now we must descend again
   The worn flights of stairs;

To the arch of hanging bridges,
   And the red-vermilion pier;
   O we shall not return again
   For many and many a year;

But we'll remember always
The day when winds were singing
In the sun-drenched gold pagoda,
As the temple bells were ringing.

How People Support Themselves

NOMADIC

Nomads are people with no fixed residence. They are continually on the move. They are usually a pastoral people who follow their flocks of cattle or sheep to new grazing grounds. The Masai, of Tanganyika, are an example of nomads. Nomads are chiefly found in Africa and Asia. Gypsies, a now disappearing tribe, were European nomads.

SEMI-NOMADIC

Semi-nomadic people never settle in one place for long. The Fuegians of southern Chile and some Amazonian tribes live in a semi-nomadic manner. They build a village and reside there until it is full of garbage and refuse. Then they move to another site. Many migrant workers in the United States lead semi-nomadic lives. These people have no real roots.

SEDENTARY

In the beginning, all men were nomads. As the human race developed, men settled down to build permanent homes, to cultivate gardens and tend their flocks. Today, the vast majority of mankind leads a sedentary life. People are content to sink their roots into a community and to spend their lives about one place. Our civilization could not have developed otherwise.

Andean water carrier

Chapter 4

Europe

MOST AMERICANS look to Europe as the homeland of their ancestors. Indeed, for many the ties to Europe are only one or two generations removed. We view Europe with a feeling of warmth, often forgetting the poverty and harsh conditions that caused our ancestors to seek a new life in the New World.

Human habitation of Europe is very ancient. Remains of pre-historic men have been found in many places, the earliest going back a quarter of a million years to the second inter-glacial period. There are many traces of men belonging to the Early Stone Age (about 50,000 years ago), during which period the people were hunters, used stone tools and knew the secret of fire. About 10,000 B.C., following the fourth glacial period, mankind in Europe learned to plant seeds and to harvest. They built primitive wooden homes, discovered the plow, and the first towns began.

With only a few exceptions all the languages of Europe belong to a single family, which philologists call Indo-European. There are people in Asia today who speak related languages and it is believed that they migrated from Europe to Asia. Counter-migrations brought Oriental types (such as the Magyars and Huns) into Europe. Today there are a half billion people living in Europe, practically all of whom belong to the white race.

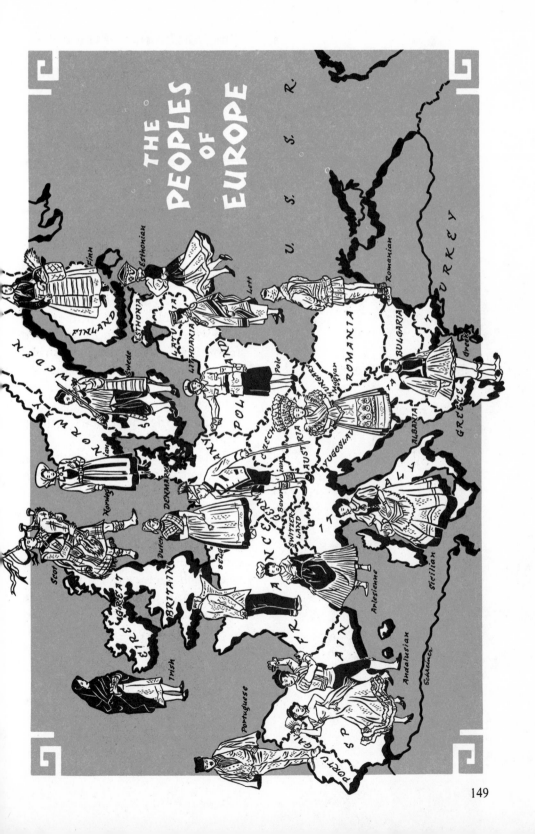

149

Ireland's sons have emigrated far.

The inhabitants of the British Isles are the product of many peoples. Fourteen different tribes have gone into forming the people of Great Britain and Ireland: Angles, Anglo-Saxons, Belgae, Britons, Celts, Cymry, English, Irish, Jutes, Manx, Picts, Saxons, Scotch, Welsh.

It is impossible to break down the physical and mental characteristics of the Englishmen today into their original tribal elements. When Julius Caesar landed in Britain, he found a population of Celtic origin and speech who were supposed to have crossed from Belgic Gaul and absorbed pre-existing tribes. He describes the men of Britain as painting themselves with blue clay, wearing skins, and as having moustaches but no beards.

Following Caesar, Scandinavian and Teutonic elements put fresh blood into the people of Great Britain. The Normans invaded England and Ireland. Later came the Dutch and French. From all of these peoples the English drew various parts to their character and culture. Their tallness and fair complexion were inherited from their Saxon and Scandinavian forebears. Their humor, quick wit and love of sports come from the Celts. Their patience, coldness of manner, and love of adventure is probably Teutonic. From the Teutons the English borrowed their language in great part.

The English character has also been developed by its surroundings.

For many centuries, the English lived cut off from the rest of Europe. As a result, they developed a self-sufficiency and national pride.

Living on a small island with little resources of its own, the Englishman strained for freedom of movement and ambition. To find this liberty, the Englishman turned to the sea. Soon he was carrying his institutions to all parts of the world and building a mighty empire which existed up to our own times.

Today there are over 45 million Englishmen living in an area about the size of the State of New York.

The Welsh are a distinct people with a language and literature of their own. The Welsh belong to the Cymry tribe, a subdivision of the Celts. They are a dark-haired people, short and stocky. They have a strong sense of independence and were not easily conquered. Even today they keep aloof from the rest of Great Britain and encourage the use of their own separate language (Cymric), which about half the three million population speaks.

The Welsh are a musical people and are well known for their outstanding choral groups. They have also produced many excellent harpists. In religion, they are nonconformists, with Methodism and Presbyterianism as the main religious bodies.

The people of Ireland are of almost pure Celtic stock. While the Teutonic element is represented in the five northern counties because of English and Scotch settlers, in the Republic of Ireland proper the inhabitants are almost pure Celts. The Celts did absorb a Neolithic people and there was a small immigration by Normans and Spanish castaways that resulted in black-haired Irishmen and the so called "Dark Irish." But the typical Irishman with light, auburn, or red hair and tall stature exhibits the characteristics of the ancient Celts.

The Irish are noted for their lively imaginations, warm-heartedness, enthusiasm, and quickness of intellect and temper. They lack the patient effort and steady determination of the Teutons. They are individualistic, with a high regard for women and chastity. The Irish have a gift for words, and make good lawyers and writers.

The Erse tongue, which has much in common with the Gaelic of Scotland, is being encouraged by the government. The Irish have an adventurous spirit and have spread to all parts of the world, influencing the people among whom they have settled. The Irish are stanchly Roman Catholics and Irish missioners have spread the Faith to all parts of the earth.

It is possible, however, that the Irish are a vanishing tribe. Outside of Ireland, they tend to intermarry. At home their numbers are diminishing. In 1845, there were eight million of them in Ireland. In 1891, the number was but half and is less today.

Portuguese parents of two of the children to whom the Virgin appeared at Fatima.

These Dutch boys
inhabit Youthland,
near Amsterdam.

Scotland is made up of two peoples—the Highlanders, or Celts; and the Lowlanders, or Saxons. The old name for Scotland was Caledonia and today this ancient land has a population of over five millions.

The Scotch Lowlanders have been strongly influenced by their Teutonic and Scandinavian forebears. The Lowlander is distinguished by his reserve, prudence, thrift, and steadiness. The Highlander, on the other hand, is more romantic, aristocratic, and possesses great family pride. He is clan-conscious. His original language was very similar to that of the Irish. He is superstitious, a believer in folklore and "secondsight." He is also musical.

Three quarters of the people of Scotland live in towns and cities. Glasgow is the largest city (over a million people) with Edinburgh the seat of the courts. Scotch law is based on French courts and law rather than English. Scotland is the original home of Presbyterianism, this religion being the established church of Scotland.

Scandinavia is a term applied to Denmark, Norway and Sweden as the inhabitants of these countries have closely related languages and cultures. The word is derived from a Teutonic word meaning "Land of Darkness." The people of Scandinavia were also known as Northmen in the Middle Ages. The term "Scandinavia" is gradually dying out.

The Danes are an industrious people. The people of Denmark are yellow-haired and fair-skinned, belonging to the Scandinavian branch of the Teutons. Denmark is made up of Danes, Frisians, Jutes, and Scandinavians. They are a courageous and practical people given to deep thought and solid learning. They live by agriculture, dairying, and fishing.

The Danes made education compulsory in 1814 and began consumer and agricultural co-operatives in 1866. This small kingdom of four and a half million people, about the size of New Jersey, exports more butter and produces more bacon than any other country, excepting the United States. Most Danes are Lutherans.

Norwegians live in a land of spectacular scenery. There are almost four million Norwegians living in a land of fjords, islands, and mountains. Since three-fourths of Norway is unproductive, Norwegians are forced to be a maritime people. The average Norwegian is not of exceptional height, but is thickly and strongly built. He is self-possessed, industrious, and resourceful, with a special skill for handicrafts. Norwegians are strong believers in education and social progress. In the north of the country live the strange Lapp people, otherwise all Norwegians are Scandinavian Teutons. Most of the people are members of the Lutheran Church.

Because of comparative isolation, the Swedes have been able to preserve national traits and physical character unchanged through many generations. More than eight million Swedes live tucked away in the upper corner of Europe. Set apart by natural boundaries, the Swedes have been able to stay away from political entanglements and to preserve their neutrality in two world wars.

The Swedes are a tall, fair, handsome people of Teutonic origin. Once largely agricultural, now twice as many people live by industry as farming. The Swedes are great believers in nature and the outdoors; and despite the fact that most of them belong to the state religion of Lutheranism, they have become very materialistic in recent years. Very few are Catholics.

Finns are a hardy, outdoor stock.

The people of Finland have the highest literacy rate in the world. The once common idea that the people of Europe all belonged to the Aryan family (Teutonic, Celtic, Slav, Hellenic, Italic) is disproved by the Finns, a non-Aryan people, whom some people claim to be closely related to the Ainu of Japan.

Finns are a stocky people, blond, with blue eyes. A freedom loving people, they are intelligent with an advanced system of education. The more than four million Finns are industrious and prosperous. Most are Evangelical Lutherans.

Thrift and cleanliness mark Sweden.

The People Who Sold the Wind

LONG, LONG AGO, before history began to be recorded, a great migration of people originated somewhere in Central Asia. What caused these families to pull up roots and take to an almost endless road can only be imagined. Perhaps the reasons are found in some unwritten tale of war or famine or flood. In any event, great masses of mankind became wanderers, seeking a Promised Land of their own.

Some of these people trekked the length of Siberia and made their way across what was then a land bridge to the North American continent. These hardy voyagers became the forebears of the Eskimo and our own American Indians. Among these migrants was one group that settled in northern Scandinavia and who are known to us today as Lapps. For the most part the Mongoloid cast to their features has been lost through their assimilation of Scandinavian blood. But their language even to this day bears witness to their Mongol-Tartar origin.

The Lapps are a hardy and unusual people. In many ways they resemble the Amercan Indians of whom they are cousins. Just as the Plains Indian depended on the buffalo for survival, Lapp life is centered about the reindeer. To the needs and whims of this ungainly animal, the Lapp adjusts his existence. And it is a free and easy existence, like that of the Indian. Clocks have little importance in Lapland. When the mood is upon him, the Lapp can sleep eighteen hours a day. Yet when he is on the trail with his herd of reindeer, he may go for weeks or a month with only two or three hours of sleep a day.

Lapland sprawls across that vast crescent of land of northern Europe that lies between the Arctic Circle and the Arctic Ocean. It traverses four countries—Norway, Sweden, Finland and Russia. In this sparsely populated region of mountains, rivers, forests, lakes, and frozen tundra live some 40,000 Lapps. A few generations ago, anthropologists thought that the Lapp people were dying out. However, in recent years it has been shown through census-taking that the European Lapps are on the increase. Few outside the Iron Curtain know anything of the Russian Lapps.

The Scandinavian Lapps are divided into three groups. There are the poorer Lapps, who lack reindeer, and who live by fishing; these are a small minority. The second group are the Forest Lapps, who have settled down with their reindeer, who cultivate small plots, and who have adopted the ways of modern civilization. The third group, the Mountain Lapps, live the old nomadic life of their ancestors; their Social Security is their reindeer herd; life to them is an exhilarating challenge.

Because of the diverse way of life of these three Lapp groups it is hard to generalize when talking about them. However, since the vast majority (two-thirds) live in Norway, and since most of these are semi-nomadic, they will be the subject of this article.

Not too many years ago, Lapp life was governed by tribal shamans, or witch doctors. There were many taboos. In fact, so great was the Lapp reputation for witchcraft that English seamen used to travel to Lapland to buy "a wind" that would insure good sailing. Some authorities derive the word "Lapp" from a Swedish word meaning "enchanter." Although they retain many of the old superstitions, the Lapps today are Christians, practically all of Lutheran belief.

The dominant reaction of the outsider when meeting Lapps for the first time is one of surprise at their size. The Lapps are the shortest people in Europe. Years ago, a few anthropologists classified them as dwarfs but such a name is not correct. The average male stands about four feet eleven inches, while the Lapp woman is four inches shorter. Lapps also have very short arms and legs, and dainty feet. Because of intermarriage with Scandinavians many Lapps have blond hair and blue eyes. Their faces are open and intelligent.

LAPP DRESS is most colorful. The men wear large, four-cornered caps which they call "hats of the four winds." The women have caps of red, fashioned like a football helmet with ear pieces that tie under the chin; these hats are very similar to the caps worn by Andean Indian men. The Lapps wear no stockings but fill their skin boots with soft, dry grass. A grass, known as sedge, is gathered by the women and pounded with paddles until it is silky soft. Then it is twisted into strands and stuffed into the skin boots. It is surprisingly warm.

Reindeer skins are used to make boots and trousers, coats and dresses. In winter, skin garments are worn with the hair on the inside; in summer, the garments are reversed and the hair is on the outside. In recent years, coarse woolen jackets have been replacing the traditional skin coats. These are Norse adaptions. The jackets are colorful—blue with red and yellow trimming across the shoulders and about the neck, hem and cuffs.

Most Norwegian Lapp families own snug log cabins where they spend the long Arctic night. In Lapland, the sun disappears in October and does not reappear again until March. During this period of twenty-four hour darkness, snow covers Lapland, rivers are frozen, and biting Arctic winds roar over the tundra. The Lapps spend the prolonged night sleeping. They sleep as much as eighteen hours a day, rising only to eat and do necessary household chores.

However, the Lapp winter should not be compared to that found in our own North American Arctic regions. The winter of Lapland is much milder because the Norwegian Current, an offshoot of the Gulf Stream, brings a warmth that makes Lapland more habitable than an equivalent area on our own continent. As a result, barley and potatoes are grown in the thin soil of Lapland and in summer the temperature often gets close to ninety degrees. But even despite the Norwegian Current, winter temperatures often drop as low as fifty degrees.

As soon as the sun returns to the north, the Lapps begin a new life. Now their days are dominated by their reindeer. Animals are usually subject to the whims of man but in Lapland this order is reversed. Here man serves his animals. The reindeer is the heart of Lapp economy. These low-slung beasts, which stand about hip-high to the small Lapps, are almost as domesticated as our cows. These long-antlered deer provide food, clothing, household utensils, and transportation for their human companions. Because of their size, they cannot be mounted, except by small children. But they are amazingly strong when pulling a sled or traverse. They can plod all day at a steady ten mile an hour gait. They are excellent swimmers, especially buoyant because their hair is hollow and air-filled.

When a reindeer is killed, every part of the 300-pound carcass is used. The skin is cleaned and tanned. Highly prized is a white reindeer skin, found only on one in about a thousand animals. A white reindeer skin can bring its owner a small fortune. After the skins are tanned, they are used in many ways. Sometimes they are used for summer tents. The Lapps also sleep on reindeer skins, which are soft and warm, spread over a "mattress" of twigs.

The rest of the reindeer is equally put to use. The hair that is scraped off the skin is made into lifebelts because of its buoyancy. Brains and liver of the beast are boiled and eaten fresh. The meat is smoked and dried for future use. It is kept on a high platform built close to the family tent. Lungs, blood, and other undesired parts are fed to the ever-present shepherd dogs. Sinews are stretched and treated to be used as thread. Horns and bones are fashioned into knives and other household instruments.

Lapps are an open and friendly people who will tell the visitor almost anything he wishes to know. But there is one thing he never reveals and that is the size of his reindeer herd. This is partly due to superstition and partly to suspicion that the information may be some day used against them, perhaps for tax purposes. It takes a minimum of twenty reindeer to make a practical herd but the vast majority of herds are larger than that. Some families are said to have herds as large as 3,000 animals.

WITH THE COMING of the summer sun, the reindeer herd grows restless. The winter fodder of hay grown the previous summer is gone and the animals begin to search out new pasturage. When this happens, the Lapps pack up their necessary belongings and take after their beasts. It is at this time the Lapps most resemble the American Indians. Their summer homes are either sod houses or skin tepees. They live much like the Indians both as regards their tribal structure and habits. Lapp women even carry their babies on their backs in wooden and leather cradles, Indian style.

Once they take to the trail, Lapp life is free and uncomplicated. They pause to eat only when hungry and sleep only when tired. Clocks have little meaning when the sun never sets. Lapps often travel hundreds of miles each summer following their grazing herds. A single animal requires about two acres from which to get its staple food, reindeer moss. (Conversely, each Lapp will eat two reindeer in the course of a year.) The grazing land is not Lapp-owned, but custom reserves certain areas for each family.

Oftentimes, different families join together to make the summer trek. Camp life then is more festive and even easier going. Sometimes when a number of families travel together, arrangements are made for teaching the children. However, most of their education must be confined to the winter months. And while the families enjoy life together, their animals are herded in common and pastured in common. At the end of the trek, each owner will separate his own animals, recognizing each beast by notches cut in its ears when it was a calf.

While on the march, the Lapps live off the land, but this does not mean that they eat poorly. A typical meal may consist of reindeer meat, smoked over fragrant juniper sticks. There will be wild succulent mountain raspberries or large juicy blueberries ripened in a warm, twenty-four hour sun. There will be cakes made of reindeer milk and barley meal, baked in shallow pans over live coals. Often fish—fat, meaty trout or salmon, fierce fighters because of their cold habitat—will substitute for meat. Coffee and salt are practically the only food staples carried on the trail. Lapp coffee, incidentally, is unique. Instead of using milk or cream in their coffee, Lapps drop in a lump of soft, white cheese made from reindeer milk. It gives the coffee a flavor as distinctive as Irish coffee, although not as potent.

HOW LONG the cheerful and contented Lapps can preserve their free and happy ways in the face of the advances of modern civilization is problematical. Already sleek airplanes are landing on their lakes and rivers. Their once free waterways are now being harnessed to provide electric power for far distant cities. The age of Sputnik militates against the friendly life of these hospitable wanderers. But the Lapps possess great courage. They seem to thrive on difficult situations. They have maintained their individuality and integrity over countless centuries. Who is there to say that they will not continue to do so?

Reverence for the Human Person

Coming down to practical and particularly urgent consequences, this Council lays stress on reverence for man; everyone must consider his every neighbor without exception as another self, taking into account first of all his life and the means necessary to living it with dignity, so as not to imitate the rich man who had no concern for the poor man Lazarus.

In our times a special obligation binds us to make ourselves the neighbor of absolutely every person, and of actively helping him when he comes across our path, whether he be an old person abandoned by all, a foreign laborer unjustly looked down upon, a refugee, a child born of an unlawful union and wrongly suffering for a sin he did not commit, or a hungry person who disturbs our conscience by recalling the voice of the Lord: "As long as you did it for one of these, the least of my brethren, you did it for me" (Mt. 25:40).

Furthermore, whatever is opposed to life itself, such as any type of murder, genocide, abortion, euthanasia, or willful self-destruction, whatever violates the integrity of the human person, such as mutilation, torments inflicted on body or mind, attempts to coerce the will itself; whatever insults human dignity, such as subhuman living conditions, arbitrary imprisonment, deportation, slavery, prostitution, the selling of women and children; as well as disgraceful working conditions, where men are treated as mere tools for profit, rather than as free and responsible persons; all these things and others of their like are infamies indeed.

— **Constitution of the Church in the Modern World, Vatican II**

France—land
of traditions

The French are related culturally, linguistically and geographically to the Italians. Fifteen tribes have gone into making the modern Frenchman—Alemanni, Basque, Belgae, Breton, Burgundian, Celt, Frank, French, Gascon, Gauls, Goths, Ligurian, Provençals, Vandals and Walloons. However, the French have undergone so many amalgamations and transformations that it is impossible to analyze them precisely today. Of all the tribes, the Basque and Breton people have best kept their individuality.

Mankind in France goes back beyond prehistoric times. Ancient bones and cave paintings have been discovered in France. It was the Roman legions that stabilized the country, gave it some unity, and developed civilization. From Rome, France received her language and laws. When the Roman influence declined, Teutonic tribes such as the Goths, Burgundians, and Franks overran the country. Later the Normans, a Scandinavian people, invaded. Thus the French are Latin in language but their ethnic basis is Celtic tinged with Teutonic and Scandinavian blood.

The French are vivacious and quick witted. They are frugal and thrifty. Judging by the rapidity with which the French change governments, one might conclude that they are fickle. In reality, the Frenchman is merely disinterested in professional politics and holds himself aloof.

The French have made many contributions to the world, and they built a colonial empire second only to England. We in North America owe much to brave Frenchmen who explored and pioneered in the United States and Canada.

French missioners have been in the forefront of modern day mission advances. In the last century, many of the missioners left their homeland knowing that they might be martyred. The roll of priests and brothers who died to spread Christianity is long.

While the 52 million Frenchmen are today generally considered to be Roman Catholics many of them are indifferent to religion, and tinged with secularism and anticlericalism. The day when France could be called "the elder daughter" of the Church is no more.

A metalworker of the Saar Valley

161

The thrifty French housewife is always ready to bargain with the corner groceryman.

Belgians live in the most densely populated country in Europe, excepting Monaco. The Kingdom of Belgium is approximately the size of Maryland, but has three times as many people (ten million). The Belgian nation is made up from five original tribes—the Belgae, Franks, Flemings, Gauls and Walloons. Like their French neighbors, the Belgians are of Celtic and Teutonic origins. French and Flemish are the official languages of the country but German is also spoken in some areas.

The majority of the people of Belgium are Roman Catholics but there are strong anti-clerical and secularistic elements in official circles. The government is officially neutral, paying part of the salaries of priests, ministers, and rabbis.

The Dutch people are descended from the Germanic family of tribes. At various times different Teutonic peoples overran the area known today as the Netherlands, a country wrested from the sea. To this foundation was added people of other European areas who sought freedom and liberty in Holland. The result has been that the original Dutch type has been considerably changed. The Dutch are a reserved, determined, and honest people. They are blunt and outspoken in manner. They are neat and clean, and Dutch homes are spotless and shining. The Dutch have a reputation for big appetites, esteeming such dishes as salted herring and smoked eel.

The Netherlands is a third larger

Women of
Brittany

than Maryland and has a population of eleven million people. Catholics make up about 40 per cent of the country, the largest single religious group. The Dutch Reformed Church to which the royal family belongs claims 31 per cent of the people. Catholic influence is strongly felt in the social and political life of the nation, and proportionately the Dutch have more foreign missioners than any other country in the world.

Vest-pocket Countries. There are a number of tiny countries in Europe that are interesting historically and because they have been able to maintain their independence in the turbulence of Europe. The smallest is Monaco (one half a square mile); the largest is Luxembourg (a thousand square miles). In between are Andorra, Liechtenstein, and San Marino. The inhabitants of these countries are quite similar to their surrounding neighbors and no individual comment is needed.

The Portuguese are isolated from the rest of Europe. Portugal has been called "the forgotten nation" because of its isolated position. Jutting out into the Atlantic Ocean, it is cut off from all other European countries by Spain. The result has been twofold. First, the Portuguese have remained a unit within themselves. Although closely related to the Spanish, they have

managed to preserve their own language, culture and physical characteristics. Secondly, they were forced to look out beyond Europe and this caused them to become one of the great sea powers and colonizers. With the rise of the English, the Portuguese power declined. The people became insular and agricultural and tended to remain apart from the rest of the world.

The Portuguese descend from two tribes, the Iberian and Ibero-Mediterranean. The Romans conquered Portugal and spread their language and institutions there. The Moors also had a strong influence during their period of occupation. Moorish words entered the Portuguese vocabulary and Moorish blood was added to that of previous tribes. In the days of colonial power, Negro and Asian Indian blood also entered the Portuguese people. Large colonies of Jews were established in Portugal and they contributed to the physical characteristics of the nation.

The Portuguese are a happy people. Although of careless disposition, they are nevertheless frugal about the goods of this world. They are talkative and hospitable, kindly and bright.

The nine million Portuguese are nearly all Roman Catholics. The people of Portugal have a deep and profound faith. It is significant that the Blessed Virgin chose to appear at Fatima to Portuguese peasant children. The message she delivered there has now spanned the world.

Portugal—off to market!

This Portuguese fisherman has blood of Phoenicians, Normans and Spaniards.

Next to the English, America owes its greatest cultural debt to the Spanish. It is not easy to describe the people of Spain, as they are composed of many tribes and stocks. Among those who make up the people of Spain are the Basques, Cantabrians, Castilians, Catalanes, Celtiberians, Iberians, Ibero-Mediterraneans, Moriscoes, Vandals, and Vascones. According to one theory, Spain was originally inhabited by a small, dark-haired Neolithic people known as Iberians. These people originally spread throughout the entire Mediterranean region but were finally forced back into Spain and finally overcome by the Celts, thus producing the Celtiberians. The Basques are said by some ethnologists to be a group of Iberians who were never conquered.

Later came the Romans, Greeks and Teutonic invaders. It was the Moors (Arabs and Berbers), however, who had the greatest influence. Besides their cultural contributions, they intermarried with the Spanish and thus began a new people called Moriscoes. Finally, Gypsies came to Spain to add to the blood lines.

Today it is easier to talk about people by regions rather than tribal backgrounds. The Andalusian is well-built, good natured, clever and gallant. The Castilian is proud, dignified and solemn. The Aragonese is reserved and suspicious of outsiders. The Catalonian is hard working, enlightened, and energetic. The Asturian is independent, honest, and physically strong. The Galician is hard working, thrifty and loyal.

For many years, the Spanish were one of the leading powers of the world. It was not until the United States went to war with Spain in 1898 that imperial power came to a real end. As a result of that war, Cuba, Puerto Rico and the Philippine Islands were lost to Spain. Because the United States was strongly influenced by Anglo-Saxon traditions, the role of Spain is often lost or misinterpreted in our history books. The Anglo-Saxons and Spaniards were bitter enemies, and English rendering of history is not unbiased. The English developed the "Black Legend" which attributed the most evil intentions and crimes to the Spaniards, while Englishmen who practiced the same cruelties were made into knights and heroes.

However, it will be a long time before Spanish influence is lost in the world. The Spanish language is spoken over a large part of the earth. Spanish culture and traditions shaped our own Southwest. Latin America has been formed by Spanish blood and speech.

Spain today boasts a population of 33.9 million people. Catholicism is the state religion. From the confusion following the loss of their empire and from the tragic days of republicanism and civil war, the Spaniards are moving to a new position in the world.

Spain—land of color, gaiety, life.

The Italians were the molders of European civilization. While today the Italian people form one nation and speak the same language, they present an extraordinary variety in character and physical type, as well as in dialect. This is not surprising in view of their complex history, which goes back beyond the Stone Age.

The original inhabitants of Italy were a non-Aryan people called the Etruscans who were related to the Iberic groups of Spain. Also present were the Gauls and Ligurians. The Latin race began in Italy with the great Aryan migrations from Asia. The tribes that made up this invasion included the Oscans, Marrucini, Umbrians, Sabines, and the Samnites. Greek elements settled in Italy, as did Phoenicians from Africa.

After the fall of the Roman Empire, Italy was invaded by barbaric tribes which brought Slav and Teutonic blood to the people. Then the Huns, Bulgars, and other people of Mongol origin added an Oriental touch to the blend. Finally in more modern times, French, Spanish, and Austrian occupation troops completed the amalgam. As a result Italians run the physical gamut from short and dark types to tall and blond.

If it is difficult to analyze the physical characteristics of the Italian people, it is equally difficult to assess properly the tremendous contributions that they have made to the world. It was the Romans who gave civilization to Europe.

The Latin language has influenced other European tongues, including English. The Italians had no peers in the arts—sculpture, painting, architecture, and music bear the impress of these creative people.

It was the Italians who developed and spread Christianity, who gave great religious leaders to the world, who shaped great saints. In the speculative fields of philosophy and theology, the Italian contribution is immeasurable.

Although Italian armed might ended with the fall of the Roman Empire and Italy did not engage in the mad rush for colonial territories, Italians were great explorers. It was an Italian, Christopher Columbus, who discovered the New World.

In modern times, Italians have carried their culture and arts to other parts of the world by emigration. Substantial Italian colonies exist in such countries as the United States, Brazil, Argentina, and the Union of South Africa.

The Italians are a handsome people with charming manners, the gift for expressive speech, and a quickness of wit. They are passionate, generous, volatile, and warm hearted. Every Italian seems to have an innate sense of artistry.

There are fifty million Italians, of whom 99.6 per cent declare themselves to be Catholics, but for a substantial number their religion is only nominal. There are about 100,000 Protestants and half as many Jews. Communism has considerable strength in the political arena.

Boy of Italian Alps

The Germans are part of one of the principal branches of the human family. The word "German" is a political rather than scientific distinction. The Teutonic stock from which the people of Germany descend is one of the principal branches of the Aryan family. Politically, Germany is divided into East and West, Communist and non-Communist sectors.

Seventeen tribes have gone into making the people we know as Germans. These tribes are the Alemanni, Angles, Anglo-Saxons, Bavarians, Cimbri, Franks, Frisians, Gauls, Gepids, Germans, Goths, Huns, Jutes, Ostrogoths, Saxons, Vandals, and Wends.

Today Germans may be divided into two divisions, corresponding to two distinct parts of the country. To the south and west of the Hartz Mountains, we find the so-called High Germans, or Swabians. They are darker than the northern Germans because of fusion with a Celtic people who in turn had absorbed a Neolithic people.

North and east of the Hartz Mountain live the Low Germans, or Saxons. The Saxons have the light hair and blue eyes that are so often taken as the marks of a typical German. However, as with peoples in other parts of Europe, we must be careful not to oversimplify because of the many Celtic, Scandinavian, and Slavic influences that have mixed with the Teuton.

The German temperament is serious and thorough. Excessive militarism in past generations has given him a brusque manner. German education, which is very systematic, tends to make the pupil dependent. The German is noted for his family affection and his intense loyalty. He is fond of music.

Germany has made many contributions to the world. German writers, philosophers, artists, architects, musicians, and scientists are counted among the world's greatest. German products that require precise work, such as cameras and other optical instruments, are among the finest in the world.

The Germans offered more resistance to Christianity than most European peoples. Parts of Bavaria were evangelized in Roman times. At the end of the sixth century, Saint Columban and his Irish missioners made their way into the Germanic wilds. However, it was Saint Boniface and his English co-workers who led all the Germanic peoples into Christianity, except the Saxons and Frisians. These latter were finally conquered and converted by Charlemagne.

It is a great tragedy that so many of the Germanic people were led into Protestantism by Martin Luther and John Calvin. Today a slight majority of Germany's seventy-five million inhabitants belong to the Protestant creed but the areas most deeply furrowed by Saint Boniface's plow remained loyal to the Catholic Church.

The Doberman pinscher will protect this pair of friendly German lassies, off to school.

The Swiss are a unit neither in race, language, nor religion. In an ethnological sense, there is no such thing as the Swiss people. The Swiss are a diverse group of people living in an area half the size of Maine. The original tribes of Switzerland were the Alemanni, Gauls, and Helvetii. Today, the country is made up of three groups, German, French, and Italian. There is a small fourth group that is now almost extinct. This latter group is a Rhaeto-Romance people who speak Rumonsh, a Latin dialect.

The Swiss are a thrifty, vigorous, independent people. They possess fine democratic traditions, tempered by conservative customs. They have a fine school system and practically universal literacy. The Swiss were converted to Catholicism by an Irish monk, Saint Gall. Calvin and Zwingli, leaders in the Protestant movement, led many Swiss from the Catholic Church. Today slightly less than half the six million people of Switzerland are Catholics.

Nine out of ten Austrians are Catholics. The people of Austria are of Teutonic stock—Bavarians, Cimbri, Goths and Germans. They number slightly more than seven million and live in a country about as large as South Carolina.

For centuries, Austria has been one of the great centers in Europe for music, drama, literature, architecture, and painting. Music is in the blood of the people, and Vienna has been called the musical capital of the world.

The Austrian man is industrious and the Austrian woman has all the qualities that are necessary for a devoted and capable wife and mother. Austrian civilization has been deeply influenced by Catholicism and the Protestant Reformation made little inroads on the Austrian people. Today, 89 per cent of the people belong to the Catholic Church.

Hungarians are the descendants of the Magyars, an Oriental people from Central Asia. Many tribes have gone into the making of the Hungarians. The earliest settlers in the region were Slavs and Germanic tribes. Then the Huns and Magyars overran the land. Mongol influences came in and finally Hungary was brought under Turkish domination. Slovaks and Slovenes also settled in Hungary.

Hungarians are among the handsomest people in Europe. They are tall, athletic, and robust. Hungarian women are particularly beautiful. Hungarians are a hospitable people, brave and strong.

Hungary was not Christianized until the end of the tenth century. It was Saint Stephen, the second Christian ruler, who consolidated the Faith in the country. Before the Communists took over about two-thirds of the people were Catholics, the remainder Calvinists and Lutherans.

Swiss mountaineers are world-famous.

Czechoslovakia is the homeland of many peoples. Eleven tribes make up the Czechoslovakian people. They are the Agathyrsi, Avar, Bohemians, Boii, Chechians, Cimbri, Czechs, Goths, Slavs, Slovak, and Slovene. Today three-fourths of the people are either Czechs or Slovaks, with the former in the majority. Both peoples love freedom and independence.

The Czechs belong to the Slav family. They are a handsome people with a keen sense of nationality. They have clung tenaciously to their own language. The Slovaks are a different stock than the Slovenes. They are pastoral, hard working, with strong family ties.

The fourteen million people of Czechoslovakia live in a country about as large as New York State. The land was evangelized in the ninth century by two talented Slavic-speaking brothers from Constantinople, Saints Cyril and Methodius. Despite the fact that the provinces of Bohemia and Moravia were one of the earliest centers of Protestantism, 75 per cent of the people of the country today are Catholics. The balance are Protestants, Jews, and members of the Eastern Orthodox Church. Communists took over the country in 1948 and have been carrying on a subtle war against religion.

The Poles are a religious and patriotic people. The Poles appeared in Europe under the name of Lekhs in the seventh century. Some scientists claim that they were a Norse tribe that overcame and absorbed a Slavonic people. Whatever their origins, they are now recognized as a subdivision of the great Slav family. Today there are thirty-two million Poles in an area almost equal to that of New Mexico.

Poles have always been distinguished for their love of independence, bravery, good manners, and great intellectual gifts.

Because of the country's strategic position in Europe, Poles have had an unhappy history. Their country has been invaded and controlled at various times by Prussia, Russia, Austria, Germany, and the Soviet Union. Once the home of many Jews, more than three million were exterminated by the Nazi occupation forces. Today Poland is Communist dominated. Because of troubled conditions in their homeland, many Poles emigrated to other countries. There are said to be some five million persons of Polish descent in the United States. Poles played important roles in establishing the American nation. Two Polish generals, Pulaski and Kosciuszko, were leaders in the American revolutionary army.

Ever since the tenth century the Poles have been strongly loyal to the Holy See. Today the overwhelming majority of the people are Roman Catholics. In 1683, the last serious Turkish threat to Europe was defeated by King John Sobieski of Poland. It is this religious spirit that still lives in the Poles and fights Russian atheistic materialism.

Poland—dreams of
bread and freedom

Freedom no longer for this Latvian

Lithuanians are a connecting link between Russians and Germans. The people of Lithuania are descendants of three tribes: Jmoud, Letts, and Slavs. The expressive language of the Lithuanians is one of the oldest tongues in Europe.

Lithuanians are handsome, well built, with blue eyes, light hair, and very white skin. Their country is about the size of New York State and is estimated to have a population in excess of three million. Because the people of Lithuania are 90 per cent Catholic, they have suffered greatly under Soviet Russian occupation. Lithuanians have been jailed, tortured, shot, and deported by the thousands. More than two million persons of Lithuanian descent live in the United States, keeping ancient traditions alive.

Estonians have inhabited the shores of the Baltic Sea since history was first recorded. Despite the fact that they have been ruled by Danes, Germans, Poles, Swedes, and Russians, the people of Estonia have been able to preserve their language and customs. The Estonians are descendants of the Tchoud people and their language is closely related to Finnish.

There are about a million and a half Estonians living in a country twice the size of Maryland. They are tall, blond people who love nature and the outdoors. Five out of six Estonians are Lutherans, and like their Lithuanian neighbors they too are suffering under Communist tyranny.

Latvians are an agricultural people. There are more than two million Latvians living in a country slightly larger than West Virginia. They are a progressive people who have suffered greatly under German and Russian rulers. Latvians are descendants of the Letts and Slavs.

Before the Communists occupied the country, attaching it to the Soviet Union, half the people were Protestant, a quarter were Catholics, the rest Greek Orthodox or Jews.

Yugoslavians live in a mixed-up country. Five national groups —the Serbs, Croats, Slovenes, Macedonians, and Montenegrins—make up the twenty million people of Yugoslavia. Four of them speak separate languages, although a mixture of the two main ones, called

Serbo-Croatian, is the official language. To complete the confusion, Yugoslavians use two alphabets, have a number of calendars based on the three main religions—Roman Catholic, Greek Orthodox, and Islam.

The reason for this conglomeration is that the Balkans have served as a bridge between Europe and Asia, and the geography of the area has been the greatest influence on the history of the area. The Vardar and Moravan valleys were natural routes for invading armies.

Yugoslavia was originally inhabited by a people of the New Stone Age who have left many traces of their occupation. A new people, the Illyrians, invaded the area and absorbed the inhabitants. Later Greek colonies were established, then Rome took control. After the Roman empire fell apart, Avars and Huns entered. About 500 A.D., a group of Slav people came in and they are the ancestors of today's Serbs, Croats and Slovenes.

The Serbs are a physically strong people. They are hospitable, proud, brave, and quick-tempered. They are also very pious. Most are Greek Orthodox in religion, although some are Moslems.

The Croats are a branch of the Slav race and are close cousins of the Serbs. They, however, are Roman Catholics, and use the Latin alphabet. They are good humored, loving colorful costumes. As a group they are not as hard working as the Serbs but they exceed their neighbors in hospitality.

The Montenegrins, or people of the Black Mountain, have been called the flower of the Slavic race. They are tall and handsome. In the past they were a warlike people but now they keep neat homes and farms. They are reputed for their honesty and for the lengths they will go to defend the virtue of their women. One Montenegrin tale concerns the days of the Turkish invasion. The men were all absent from a particular village when Turkish soldiers arrived. The women fortified themselves in a tower and fought like Amazons. When resistance was no longer possible, they admitted the Turks to the tower and then exploded barrels of gunpowder, killing the Turks and themselves.

The people of Macedonia are closely allied to the Greeks. The Lake Ohrid region of Macedonia is the cradle of Slav Christianity but it also has large numbers of Moslems because of long Turkish occupation.

Slovenes are found in northern Yugoslavia. They are hard working people who have been strongly influenced by Austrians. In recent years they have become industrialized and today less than half the people of Slovenia live from the soil.

Yugoslavians today live under Communist domination. They are regimented and religion is persecuted. Croatia and Slovenia are the Catholic strongholds. The Orthodox religion claims 46 per cent of the people, Catholicism has 36 per cent, and Islam has 11 per cent.

"It's the Gypsy in My Soul"

WHEN I WAS A BOY, there was one sign of spring more certain than the presence of robins. It was when after the long winter months a gypsy caravan rolled into some wooded and vacant lots on the edge of town and set up camp, the first stop on the annual migration from New York City. The dark-skinned and strange-speaking members of the troupe seldom stayed more than a couple of days because by that time the local gendarmes would have piled up enough reports of petty thefts to force the gypsies to move on.

While the gypsies were around, children remained close to home and housewives kept their doors locked. Everyone stood in awe of these independent spirits who chose to stand apart from civilization—spending their days in travel and their evenings in singing and dancing. The gypsies were surrounded by all sorts of myths, legends and suspicions. They had a reputation for thievery and drunkenness. It was whispered that they were not at all adverse to kidnaping children to increase the population of their caravans. Indeed, there were even rumors that they stole babies to eat them in strange, mystic rites.

There was a very famous kidnaping case in those days. A young boy named Charlie Ross disappeared not long after a band of gypsies had visited his home town. The case was a national sensation and the general opinion was that he had been carried away by the gypsies. Of course, a great deal of the noise was caused by hysteria, and nothing was actually proved against the gypsies. When authorities caught up with the band, Charlie wasn't with it, nor was he ever found. Yet there are people to this day who believe that gypsies made off with Charlie Ross.

The auto eventually put an end to the annual gypsy visitation from New York. When the gypsies became streamlined, they were able to move farther and faster. They still came to my town, however; only now they rented empty stores, covered the windows with heavy drapes, set up some mystic signs, and invited the general public within for palm reading and fortunetelling. I don't ever recall seeing any non-gypsy slipping into this mystic realm, yet somehow the gypsies continued to exist and keep coming back.

World War II sent the gypsies into defense plants when rationing deprived them of gasoline. After the war, some of them took to the road again in sleek chrome trailers but quite a few adopted the sedentary life. I can't remember meeting any gypsies in the last few years but I have been assured by those in the know that they are still around.

Before World War II, it was estimated that there were about two million gypsies in the world, with the largest majority in Europe. The figure is not too reliable since gypsies were never folk who waited around for the census taker. The Nazis singled them out for destruction in Germany and it is estimated that upwards of 18,000 were put to death there. The largest bodies of gypsies existed in Poland, Hungary, and Roumania and since those lands slipped behind the Iron Curtain no one of us can tell how the gypsies fare under the Communists.

According to surveys there are between 60,000 and 200,000 gypsies in the Near East—the spread between the figures gives an idea of the difficulty in accurate estimates. In the United States, the number is put at 100,000 with 12,000 alone in New York City. At one time there was a large number settled around Braddock, Pennsylvania. There are substantial numbers in England and western Europe. There is hardly a part of the world in which gypsies are not to be found.

Although gypsies live in practically all parts of the world, they always remain a people apart. They pretend to conform to the pattern of the country in which they dwell but it is only a surface conformity to spare them trouble. Underneath, they remain contemptuous and independent, proud of their heritage, convinced that they are above all other people, firm in the belief that they have no peers.

Gypsies speak of themselves as *Rom*, their word for "man." It is from this word that the expression Romany comes, a term sometimes used for the gypsies themselves, but more accurately meaning their queer sounding language which today exists in almost as many dialects as there are tribes. It was the English who named these dark, mysterious people "Egyptians"; and it is from a corruption of this word that we get the designation "gypsy."

THE FIRST RECORDED appearance of gypsies in Europe came in 1422 when they turned up in Italy, explaining that they were Christians who had been driven out of Africa by the Moslems. They said that their homeland was in lower Egypt, and they claimed to have a letter from the Pope ordering all Catholic bishops to help them with alms because of what they had suffered for the faith. The letter is the first of their many recorded inventions.

Five years later, gypsies were in Paris. Here, they boasted that they were lords and nobles. They again told the story that they were under the protection of the Holy Father and that they were pilgrims. For this latter reason, they were treated with kindness, showered with gifts of food and money, and forgiven petty crimes. However, the members of this group were finally excommunicated because they insisted on practicing palmistry and fortunetelling.

From this time on, records show that they spread rapidly over Europe. From the evidence at hand, it would appear that these first groups were advance scouts who sent back favorable reports to the home base. In any event, the next few years saw an influx of gypsies into Europe. They turned up in every country and moved into the British Isles. In May of 1596, 196 gypsies were arrested in Yorkshire, England, and charged with idleness and other crimes. They were sentenced to be executed. Some were put to death but the pitiful cries of survivors so moved the judges and people that most of them were spared.

Gypsies arrived in America towards the end of the eighteenth century. France exiled a large group of them to Louisiana. These "Bohemians" thrived so well that they are still there. Most of them profess to be Catholics, many have settled as farmers. But the wild blood in their veins occasionally takes over. Portugal sent a large group of gypsies to Brazil, many of whom later came to the United States. However, Brazilian gypsies are looked down upon by other tribes and are said to have impure blood lines. Gypsies in the United States come from England, Wales, Scotland, Hungary, Roumania, Germany, Russia, Syria, and Persia.

According to Gordon Thayer, of the Cleveland Public Library, gypsies can be traced through records back to ninth-century Persia. Actually they are much older. For a long time their origin was unknown. When the anthropologist, H. M. Grellman, made a study of their language, he discovered that one-third of their words were of Hindu origin. With this lead, other anthropologists took up the trail. Today, it is generally held that their language comes from Sanskrit, that they originated in northern India and are related to the Jats tribe. No one knows what caused them to become nomads, and gypsy legends are far from reliable.

It is significant that gypsies have no Romany words for "possession" or "duty". They are a carefree, independent people who even when they settle down are apt to pull up roots at a moment's notice or on a whim. The gypsy is of slight and agile build, with olive-colored skin, dark flashing eyes, coal black hair, and even white teeth set in a small mouth. They have no national dress but adopt the dress of the country in which they live. The gypsy women love color and the sound of rattling jewelry.

Many Americans think of gypsy women as volatile creatures clad in thick skirted and long dresses, wearing large golden earrings and a kerchief about the head. Indeed, that was the way many of these women traveled about America. Actually, this type of gypsy dress was from Hungary and Roumania and the wearer was merely following European styles. Since the dress was colorful, Hollywood made it the official gypsy movie costume. In reality, a gypsy girl born in the United States appears like any other American girl.

EACH GYPSY TRIBE is ruled by a chief, chosen by election. A tribal mother is also chosen who is custodian of the tribe's moral code. Hollywood and novelists have made these individuals into "kings" and "queens" but such terms are inexact. Gypsies have their own laws and courts and the most severe punishment is banishment from the tribe. The tribal mother performs all weddings, although the presence of the tribal chief is necessary for legality.

Gypsies do not subscribe to our moral code of the ten commandments. They have no ethical principles as we know them. Lying for a reason is considered an art and virtue. Stealing is only wrong when the robber is apprehended or when he steals from one of the tribe. Polygamy is permissible and there is no objection to a man marrying his niece or half sister or even his granddaughter. Gypsies believe in a god whom they respect and fear. They also believe in an evil spirit.

They have a rigid system of superstitions and taboos. Dogs and cats are unclean. It is a serious crime to eat from a dish that has been in contact with a woman's skirt. A woman may not pass in front of a man who is sitting down. When a person dies, all of his or her clothes must be destroyed, and that person's name may never be mentioned again. Their folklore parallels very closely Hindu folk tales with additions picked up in their travels.

180

It was noted earlier that gypsies make a great pretense of adaptation to the customs and people among whom they live. Gypsies from Italy or Hungary say they are Catholics. Gypsies from Scotland call themselves Presbyterians. They preserve this false front to all outsiders. For example, when a gypsy dies, the family will seek to have a funeral service conducted by a priest or minister. After the ceremony is over, the body is taken to the grave and the gypsy ceremony is held amid loud lamentations. The body is put into the grave uncovered. The little finger on the right hand is broken and a coin fastened to it with a piece of red ribbon. The coin is to pay the dead man's fare across the River Styx.

NEXT TO FREEDOM, the gypsy loves dancing and singing. It was the gypsy who gave popularity to the violin and who has had a profound influence on European music. Gypsies inspired and formed the music of Liszt, Brahms and Schubert. The Strausses owe many of their waltzes to gypsy inspirations. George Bizet turned gypsy themes into the powerful music found in the opera *Carmen*. The violin is the favorite gypsy instrument although the accordion has a considerable following.

If the gypsy has agility of body, he also has agility of mind. Education has never meant much to gypsies and the majority of them are illiterate. But they are quick thinkers, able to invent fantastic stories and situations.

Bercovici tells about a gypsy whose child fell sick. The father took the baby to a doctor who performed surgery and cured it. As his fee, the doctor asked the price of a cow that the gypsy owned. The gypsy thought this exorbitant but agreed.

"I shall take the cow to the county fair tomorrow and turn over to you the price she fetches," promised the gypsy.

The next day the gypsy kept his word. He took the cow to the fair and put her up for sale along with a chicken.

"How much do you want for the cow?" asked a farmer.

"Fifty cents," replied the gypsy.

"And the chicken?"

"A hundred and fifty dollars."

"Well, I'll take the cow and you can keep the chicken."

"Oh, no!" exclaimed the gypsy. "I don't want to sell one without the other."

Before the day was over, the gypsy had sold cow and chicken. He solemnly paid the doctor the fifty cents received for the cow and pocketed the $150.

The gypsies in America today are hard to distinguish. They have identified themselves with American life, have adopted American ways. They call themselves Smith, Jones, Stanley and Lee. They work in factories, stores and offices. They are actors and actresses, musicians and salesmen. Yet they never stay put for long. Come spring or a sudden urge, they pack up their belongings, stow them away in an automobile and trailer and take off on the open road.

Next time a trailer family passes through your town, look at it well. The members may be first or second generation Irish, Slovak, or Pole. They may seem like any of your neighbors. But study them carefully, they may also be gypsies. And the next time you yourself get the urge to chuck everything up and go looking for Shangri La, be careful. Somewhere in the dim past a strain of gypsy blood may have entered your family!

Venice, Queen of the
Adriatic, is a city
of churches amidst
canals. Below is
the Grand Canal.

Switzerland is a country where people live between soaring snow-covered mountains.

Albanians are cousins to the Greeks. The Albanians are a remnant of the Illyrian tribe. There are two main divisions of them. The Ghegs live in the north and are Mohammedans or Catholics. The southern Tosks are Greek Orthodox. Both people are handsome and independent. There are more than two million Albanians in a country the size of Maryland. They live under Communist control.

Bulgarians are an agricultural people. Although the eight million Bulgarians who live in a country about the size of New York State speak a Slavic language and are classified among the Slavic people, like the Turks and Magyars, they are of Mongol-Tartar origin. Bulgarians are a dark, stocky people of stolid habits. They are quiet but determined, loving peace.

The main religion of Bulgarians is Greek Orthodox but there are Catholics, Protestants, and Mohammedans in the country. The Bulgarians are suffering under the Communist yoke and looking forward to the day when they can be free again.

The Romanians are an old people. The nineteen million people of Romania trace their origins back to a tribe known as the Dacians. In the centuries before Christ, these primitive people settled on the rich plains where the Danube empties into the Black Sea. From here they spread into the mountains and dense forests which give

Romania its wild beauty. Later other tribes such as the Agathyrsi, Avar, Bastarnae, and Goths settled in the country.

Roman legionaries subdued these tribes and left a heritage in the name of the country and in the peoples' Latin speech. Afterwards, Romania was invaded by Asiatic tribes and the Turks. Another important factor in forming the national character of the people was the Gypsies who settled in great numbers in the country.

Romanians are a dark skinned people, with dark hair and black eyes. They are quite frugal and suspicious of outsiders. They have a developed artistic sense.

The people of Romania are quite poor. Their country has some of the best farmland of Europe and has large oil reserves, but the Communist masters of the country have destroyed the initiative of the people by shipping almost all exports to the Soviet Union and giving little to the people in return.

It is estimated that at least half the people of Romania cannot read or write. Religion undergoes persecution by the government. The Greek Catholic Church has been taken over by the Romanian Orthodox Church and is under complete control of the government. Roman Catholic religious orders have been abolished.

Greeks brought Western civilization to flower. It would be a very difficult task to truly assess the debt that mankind owes the people

Bulgarians who are of Tartar-Mongol origin now speak Slavonic and are classed as Slavs.

of Greece. Today, Greece is a poor country of nine million people who live in an area about the size of Arkansas. It has very little fertile land and many mountains. Yet five hundred years before Christ, the Greeks created out of this wilderness a brilliant civilization, the effects of which remain to this day.

Eight original tribes make up the modern Greek. These are the Achaeans, Dorians, Ionians, Mainote, Molossians, Pelasgi, Thracians, and Tsakonians. On top of this base, many other people were added. Slavic settlers advanced into Greece and were absorbed. Turks also mixed their blood with that of the Greeks. Yet in spite of all this intermingling, the Greeks have kept their blood comparatively pure; and rather than being influenced

by invaders, the actual situation was the other way around—the Greeks Hellenized their would-be corrupters, Turkish and Slav.

The ancient Greeks were skilled seafarers and traders. Greek athletes contended with each other for victors' palms in the first Olympic games. In the arts, they had no peers. Their architects and sculptors raised such magnificent buildings as the Parthenon at Athens. Their playwrights constructed dramas that are still played. Their philosophers—men like Aristotle and Socrates—taught men to love freedom and think deeply about the meaning of life. While the Romans raised a great empire of military might, the Greeks raised an empire of the mind. Greek achievements in politics, science, arts and

185

letters are an essential part of our own traditions today. It is interesting to note that the military forces thrown against the Greeks—first the Macedonians, then the Romans, and finally the Turks—have all vanished while Greek thought remains alive and vibrant.

The average Greek is stocky, well-proportioned, oval faced, dark, with sparkling white teeth and animated eyes. The Greeks are hospitable, thrifty, and temperate. They are clever bargainers, and Greek businessmen are found in all parts of the world. Every Greek is a born politician, and he would sooner argue politics than eat. He is intensely proud of his nationality.

Although Greeks still write in the classical form of their language, their spoken tongue has considerably changed from the time of Socrates. Spoken Greek has been strongly influenced by the Slavonic tongue.

Most Greeks are quite poor and a high percentage of them can neither read nor write. Most of them eke out a bare existence by growing olives, grapes, currants, figs, and grain crops. Others raise sheep and goats. Those who have gone into commerce are better off financially, many of them carrying on their businesses all over the Near East.

Saint Paul introduced the Greeks to Christianity. Today, most Greeks belong to the Greek Orthodox religion which is the country's official faith.

A Greek farmer in his daily garb

Chapter 5

The Soviet Republics

THERE ARE few people in the world about whom there is more interest but about whom there is less known than the people of the Union of Soviet Socialist Republics. The interest we have in Russia and Russians is more than academic because our future depends a great deal on what they do.

It is not easy to become acquainted with the Soviets. The Communist rulers have dropped a curtain around all of the territory they control. The Communist leaders shower the rest of the world with propaganda but all too often it is not based on fact. In recent years television and cultural exchanges have made the Soviets better known, but again in a propaganda sense.

Russians live in the largest country in the world—a great land mass that sprawls over two continents and makes up one sixth of the earth's land surface. There are more than 241 million Soviets, amalgamated out of more than 150 tribes, speaking an equal number of languages. Their religious backgrounds are Christian, Jewish, Moslem, and Buddhist. Yet out of this magnitude and diversity, from fifteen separate republics, the Soviet citizen has been formed.

Russians live in a land of tremendous potential and although they lagged behind the rest of Europe for centuries this past generation has seen electrifying progress. The Soviet Union is a land in ferment. The people of the Soviet Union are restless, anxious to be recognized by the world, but knowing no other life than that imposed by their Communist masters.

THE **PEOPLES** OF THE **SOVIET UNION**

188

A Russian farmer and his three daughters. These are typical faces of White Russia.

Russians are but one nationality in the Soviet Union. Because the largest and most influential of the Soviet Republics is Russia, it is commonly believed that all citizens of the Soviet Union are Russians. The Russians are a European people who make up half the population of the country.

The Russians are a Slavonic branch of the Caucasian family, nomadic descendants of tribes that inhabited the Dnieper, Don, and Vistula valleys. The Northmen, or Vikings, overran them in the ninth century and ruled Russia for the next 800 years.

The thirteenth century saw Russia invaded by Mongols and Tartars under Genghis Khan. This Oriental "Golden Horde" kept control of the region until driven out in 1480 by Ivan III. In the meantime, the Russians had been converted to the Eastern Orthodox religion.

The Russian is a person of great endurance. He lives in a harsh climate with extremes of heat and cold, and this has developed in him a sense of forbearance that is not matched by other people. He alternates between simplicity and prodigality, has a quick and volatile disposition. Having lived under despotic czars and now despotic Communists, he submits willingly

A schoolgirl of the Lesghian people

Georgians are said to be the handsomest people in the Soviet Union. The people of Georgia, who live in the center of Transcaucasia, are not Russians but an independent, freedom loving people. They are a hospitable folk who love nothing better than a song, or a party at which there will be plenty of dancing and wine. They have a flair for politics and polo, for recklessness and arrogance.

There are some four million Georgians living in an area equal to South Carolina.

Armenians have a great sense for business. The Armenians live as neighbors of the Georgians and are just the opposite of these latter people. The Armenian is of Semitic origin, is industrious and serious, intelligent and adaptable. Armenians have undergone many persecutions, and today they are scattered over the face of the earth. Large bodies of them are found in the Near East, England, and the United States. They are solidly Christian, and a large proportion of them belong to the Armenian Church which is in union with the Pope and Holy See.

Circassians are always in a hurry. This Caucasian people are reputedly very handsome. They have great energy and vitality. Like their Georgian neighbors, they would rather play than eat. They are restless and independent, placing great store on athletic prowess. Most Circassians belong to the religion of Mohamet.

to controls that would move other people to rebellion. He is a fatalist, a conservative, and a man of great sociable and hospitable tendencies. He has an ingrained religious sentiment that almost borders on superstition. He is enterprising, with a great love for the land. He is also artistic, as the long list of Russian writers and artists proves.

While Moscow is the heart of the Russian country, the native Muscovite is almost as rare as the native New Yorker. Moscow, today, is a city of peasants who have come there to work, to trade, and visit the Red shrines.

The Swanetians are as wild as their mountains. The Swanetian people are fast disappearing from their mountain fastness in southwestern Caucasus. They are a savage people whom the Russian czars could not tame. They have no organization and are given to feuding among themselves.

The Lesghians are another people who resisted the Russians. Numbering about seven hundred thousand, the Lesghians live on the northeastern side of the Caucasus ridge. They are a hardy and strong people who have a fierce love for independence. They resisted the Russians for many years. They have a reputation for being abstemious. Once converted to Christianity, they are *now* fanatical Moslems.

Ukrainians live in the bread basket of the Soviet Union. Because the people of the Ukraine live in the most fertile part of the Soviet Union, and because this same area is rich in coal and iron, they have suffered a stormy history of wars and invasions. The Ukraine is the most densely populated section of the Soviet Union, and Kiev, its capital, is known as "the mother of Russia." The Ukrainians are a hard working people with a deep religious sense.

Many people of Russian descent in the United States have their roots in the Ukraine because it was from here that much of the Russian emigration took place. There are over forty-seven million people in the Ukraine, practically all of whom dream of the day when they will be free and independent.

Siberian Khakass folk are close relatives of our own Eskimos, as these faces show.

The people of Soviet Siberia are rapidly being Russianized. It can be generalized that the native people of Soviet Siberia are Mongol-Tartars. There are estimated to be about a hundred different tribes who formerly led a nomadic existence much like the American Indian. Russians are moving into the areas formerly occupied by these people and they have been drawn into the Soviet orbit. Materially, this has improved their lives. But it is interesting to note that the Communists who denounce segregation outside their own boundaries, practice it in their homeland. For example, Russians get a third more pay for the same work than do the Asians; schoolbooks are written only in Russian.

Because of space limitations, only a few Asian tribes can be treated here.

Kirghiz. The Kirghiz people live as nomads on the Siberian steppes. They dwell in tents called *yurts* and move from area to area by camelback. The Kirghiz exist by livestock breeding and selling sheep and camel wool. They speak their own language and are Mohammedans.

Buriats. This very numerous people is divided into about a dozen sub-tribes. They are phlegmatic and slow-moving. They are very Mongol looking in appearance and live by tending cattle. In religion, they are divided into Christians and Buddhists although in practice most of them are nature worshipers.

Tunguses. The Tunguses are a number of tribes of Manchu origin. They live from the Pacific to Arctic Oceans and number well over a hundred thousand. They dwell in tents, fishing in summer and hunting in winter. They are said to be very intelligent and to possess high natural virtue. Some of them are Buddhist but the majority are pagans and nature worshipers.

Ostiaks. The Ostiaks are a tribe of Finnish stock inhabiting the most western part of Siberia. They speak a language called Chanti which is very similar to Hungarian. They live in large teepees, tend reindeer herds, and are expert fishermen. They practice a religion called shamanism, which is similar to that practiced by the American Indian. The wolf and the bear are sources of many Ostiak superstitions. There are only about thirty thousand Ostiaks left.

Yakuts. The Yakuts live in a part of Siberia that is said to be the coldest place on earth. During the winter the thermometer goes to sixty below zero and the ground is frozen to a depth of fifty feet. Because of the cold, the Yakuts build log huts with large fireplaces. They are said to belong to the Russian Orthodox church but people who know them well say they are still pagans. They have an inordinate appetite for meat and it is reputed that four Yakuts can eat a horse in one sitting.

Chapter 6

The Islamic Crescent

I SLAM, the religion founded by the Arabian merchant, Mohammed, in the seventh century, today is the second leading religion of the world and claims over 400 million followers. Spread by fanatical devotees, the religion at one time threatened to engulf Europe and the East. After the Moslem invasions were halted by Charles Martel and Leo the Isurian, the religion lost much of its missionary drive and was confined, except for isolated pockets, in a broad sweep of land extending from northwestern Africa across to the borders of India.

For many centuries, the people of Islam lived aloof from and suspicious of the Christian world. As a result, the inhabitants of Moslem lands did not share in the technological and social advances made in European countries. The Moslem peoples lived in underdeveloped countries, experiencing great physical and intellectual poverty.

In recent years, however, great changes have come to the peoples of the Islamic crescent. Discoveries of oil reserves, the failure of colonialism, and the shrinking of the world by advances in communications and transportation have brought the Moslems into contact with their non-Moslem neighbors. In addition, the strategic position of the Islamic countries has made them of great concern to other nations. Today, the religion of Mohammed has become missionary once more and the peoples of Islam are a powerful world force.

The people of Turkey form a bridge between East and West. The Bible tells us that many, many centuries ago, following the great deluge, Noah's ark came to rest on Mount Ararat. This mountain is the highest peak in the modern country of Turkey. Ever since that day, Turkey has played an important role in the history of the world. It was in this country that Saint Paul preached Christianity and from there passed into Europe.

At one time, Turkey was the center of the Roman empire. It was there that Constantine had his seat of government and the city named after him (Constantinople) was one of the grandest in the world. But gradually the forces of Islam closed steadily in on the Roman Empire of the East until in 1453 the city of Constantine fell before the Mohammedan onslaught.

From that time on, Turkish power grew. The Turks became one of the mightiest peoples on earth, threatening to sweep over all Europe. However, at the battle of Lepanto their sea power was

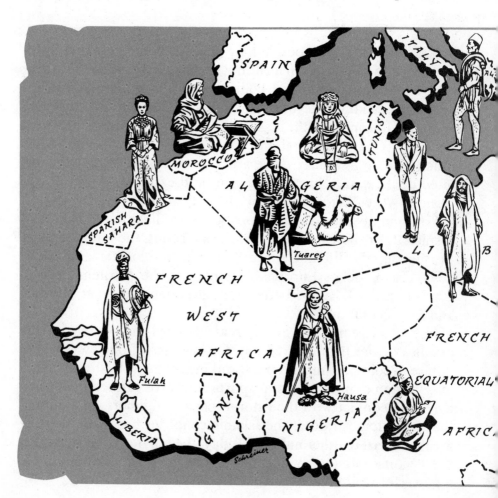

crushed and in 1683, the Polish King John Sobieski halted the Turkish army before Vienna and saved Europe.

Today the more than thirty million Turks are among the most modern and progressive people of any Mohammedan land. They are almost completely Moslem, ninety-eight out of every hundred Turks being followers of Mohamet. It is interesting to note, however, that part of Turkey is in Europe, and 10 per cent of the Turkish population lives in European Turkey.

Three out of four Turks live by agriculture, raising wheat, tobacco, and livestock. The Turks are known for their fine Angora goats which have long, fine hair; these hairs are woven into luxurious mohairs. Turkish sheep give a fine grade of wool which for centuries has given Turkish rugs superlative quality.

The Turks are Western in their ideals and Eastern in their culture. They are a progressive, friendly people, who must be ranked high among the leaders of the Moslem world today.

THE MAJOR **PEOPLES** OF **ISLAM**

People of the Crescent Moon

T HE MOSLEM WORLD extends like its own political symbol—the crescent moon—across northern Africa, up through the Near East, into the heart of Asia. Much of this land is barren and inhospitable yet in this crescent live 250 million Moslems, the world's largest religious body after Roman Catholics.

Today that world is seething with unrest. There is rebellion against the occupying forces of colonial powers. There is resentment against the West, some of it inborn but more created by modern political maneuvers. There is the desire of adaption and readjustment to modern ways of life by a people whose philosophy of life is many centuries old. There is a reawakening of the missionary spirit of Moslemism, long dormant but which has never ceased believing that it is the only perfect religion in a world of unbelievers.

Unfortunately, few of the Western world—and this is particularly true of Americans—know much about the Moslem world and even less about its faith. What knowledge we have is colored by romantic novels and movies—the mystery of the Casbah, the glamour of the Foreign Legion, sheiks astride sleek steeds speeding over the shifting Sahara sands, the treachery of Himalayan mountain princes. But all of these are outside the real meaning of Islam.

No one can understand the people of the crescent without understanding their religion. This is because their religion is so much bound up with their life. The Moslem religion is the real motivating force in the life of the people of the crescent. It gives them a feeling of superiority to the rest of the world, makes them arrogant and contemptuous of the foreigner, and binds them to its practice with sincerity and sacrifice.

Take fasting, for instance. The average Christian wants to temporize with the Lenten Fast. Not so the Moslem in his fast or Ramadan. He accepts its obligation very seriously, not in the spirit of penance but as an opportunity for gaining merit.

One day I was sitting in a car in Nairobi, Kenya, with a young Negro Moslem named Shebangi. I offered him a cigarette, having previously seen him smoke. He declined courteously.

"Have you given up smoking?" I asked.

"It is the time of Ramadan," he replied simply.

Curious, I pressed him for more information. Ramadan, he told me, is the ninth month in the Mohammedan lunar calendar. During these thirty days every good Moslem begins his fast at sunrise and continues it until sunset. During this time not a morsel of food, not a drop of water, not a puff of tobacco will be taken. This is tough going, especially for people who must do a hard day's work.

The Moslem's contempt for Christianity is based on misunderstandings and with some justification.

"Are you a Hindu or Christian?" I asked a young Indian in Uganda.

"Thank God I am neither," he replied.

"What do you object to in Christianity?" I inquired.

"Many things," he answered without hesitation, indicating that he had given thought to the subject. "Christianity is unrealistic. It is too much concerned with the ideal and does not take people as they are. Christians are told to pray for their enemies, to turn the other cheek. This is nonsense. Then too, Christians are idolaters. They believe in three gods."

I tried to explain but he was not interested in explanations. He judged Christianity by Christians he saw around him and whom he met on visits to England and India. It was a judgment based on externals.

"Christians are hypocrites," he interrupted. "They say Jesus was the Prince of Peace but no nations fight as much as Christian nations. Jesus forbade divorce and look how the people of America marry and remarry. Jesus preached brotherhood and see the racial prejudice that exists among Americans and Europeans. And who is there to tell the true Christian faith when there are so many Christian sects quarreling among themselves?

"We Moslems practice our beliefs. We live brotherhood. For us the Koran is the way of life. We even respect Jesus more than the Christians do. To us He is one of the great prophets."

The young Indian went on and on. His accusations were many. About the only charge he left out was the one that makes Christianity the agent of colonialism and imperialism—a charge that has great vogue in the Moslem world.

THE MOHAMMEDAN CREED is summed up in the single word *Kalima*, an abbreviated form meaning "There is no God but Allah and Mohammed is his prophet." The word has been used as a battle cry, a challenge and a reminder for the faithful Moslem to attend to his duties. Five times a day the Moslem muezzin climbs his minaret and gives the cry of Kalima, *"Allah akabar!"* —"God is most great." This is the call summoning the faithful to prayer.

When the call rings out, the Moslem will stop what he is doing, unroll his prayer rug, kneel facing towards Mecca and begin to pray in Arabic—"the language of the angels." There are six distinct postures of the body, ending up with a full prostration to signify complete submission to the will of God. The usual prayer which is said seventy-five times in a single day, goes as follows:

"God is most great. I seek refuge from evil Satan. I praise the perfection of my Lord, the most great. Praise unto thee, O Lord. God is most great. I extol the perfection of my Lord most high. God is most great. Peace be upon you and the mercy of God."

The Moslem will tell you that his is the most perfect religion in the world. If you ask him why he will answer simply that the Koran says so. To the Moslem the Koran is the equivalent of the Catholic Bible. It is the revealed word of God. Since Mohammed was the last of the prophets, the Koran contains the last and most up-to-date revelation.

When Mohammed founded his religion in the seventh century, he borrowed much from Christianity. Indeed, in the beginning, Islamism was nothing more than a Christian heresy. The Moslems have a creed similar to our Apostles' Creed which declares:

"I believe there is no god but Allah. I believe in his angels; in his revelation; in his prophets, and that Mohammed is the last of them; in the Last Judgment; and in the predestination by Allah of good and evil."

Five duties make up what the Mohammedans call "the pillars of religion." These duties are: 1. To bear witness that there is no god but Allah; 2. To continue steadfast in prayer; 3. To fast in the month of Ramadan; 4. To give alms; 5. To make the pilgrimage to Mecca.

MECCA, ON THE ARABIAN peninsula, is the goal of every follower of Mohammed. This is the holy city of the prophet, where he denounced idolatry, and founded his religion, from which he was driven out and to which he finally returned in triumph. The Moslem has a fanaticism about Mecca that far outstrips Christian feelings for Rome and the Holy Land.

Yet despite the hidebound traditionalism of their religion, Western ideas and Western morality are having an effect on Islamism. In the large cities and in the more modern countries, the *purdah* system is fast disappearing. Purdah was the strict seclusion of women. Now the veils are gone, women show themselves freely and girls are allowed to attend schools.

Islamism allows a man to take four wives, but today many Moslems have come out strongly against polygamy. The reason is partly practical—quarrels and jealousy having torn apart many a polygamous family. However, Moslem women are the real leaders in the campaign to destroy the system. Americans got an unusual insight into the problem recently when the wife of an Asiatic ambassador to Washington made the headlines because she took her children and moved from the embassy when her husband took a second wife.

Turkey has legally abolished polygamy and sentiment is rising against the practice throughout the Moslem world. Today it exists largely among the rich who can afford the luxury of a harem, and even here education is making the system unpopular. Moslem women enjoying new freedoms will undoubtedly put an end to the practice within the next couple of generations.

Child marriage is also a Moslem practice that is dying out. Marriages among Moslems are not love matches but are arranged through a third party. Love is no requisite for wedding bells; in fact, in many areas, love matches are not respectable. Moslems are not married in the mosque but in the home. Except in the most progressive families the young man never lays eyes on his bride until the wedding day.

It was the practice for infant girls sometimes to be married to grown men. At a certain age, the girl would be added to her husband's harem. The practice was used to unite families and to get a source of income for a poor family. Education and medical knowledge is putting an end to the practice.

Moslemism has always been a man's religion. Purdah, polygamy, and child marriage all favored the man. Another proof of this orientation is in the ease with which a man can divorce his wife. In some areas all the man has to do is declare "I divorce you" three times in the presence of his wife, and the marriage is ended. He is even favored by the Islamic law that says he has to return to his divorced wife only the equivalent of one-third of her dowry. But often even this third is denied her and she is dismissed penniless.

Under certain circumstances, the wife may divorce her husband. But for the women divorce is difficult and seldom initiated. Turkey is an exception, for that nation has an European divorce code. In the Islamic world at large divorce is accepted as the prerogative of the male, a right that is now being challenged by educated women.

Association between young men and women is rare except in the larger cities where education has broken down barriers. In many areas mixed dancing is thought to be highly immoral, but in Turkey, Egypt, and areas influenced by the American movies, mixed social life is now the accepted practice.

Much of Moslem life is centered around their holy days just as the Christian year is highlighted by Christmas, Easter and other feasts. The Ramadan fast ends in a big feast during which shops close and people go about in their best dress. Greeting cards are sent out at this time and homes are decorated. The birthday of Mohammed is another important feast day, as is the Day of Record when it is believed that Allah records all actions of men for the coming year.

One of the most important feasts of the year is Muharram, the anniversary of the first Moslem martyrs. Among some sects this is a day of public penance. Elsewhere there are processions formed by thousands to honor the memory of the first three Moslems to die for their faith.

While all Moslem children receive religious education, main attention is given to the training of boys. Religious education takes place in the home and the child is exposed to religion, in daily periods of family prayer.

Little children are taught the Moslem prayers at an early age and are read to from the Koran. When a boy is about six he is sent to school in the Mosque to learn Arabic reading. He is trained to memorize extensive parts of the Koran. Often when the boy completes the reading of the Koran for the first time, his family will give a party in his honor similar to a First Communion party.

MISSIONERS WORKING among Moslem people know the difficulty in making conversions. The main barrier is social pressure. A person denying Islam is in effect denying God. He will be lucky if he does not suffer bodily injury.

Yet Christianity has much to offer the Moslem whose religion is naturalistic and deprived of love. The faults that exist in the Western world, exist in spite of Christianity, not because of it. But the faults that exist in the Moslem world are directly rooted in the faith of the people. In the Moslem religion there is no sense of sin or wrongdoing. Polygamy, divorce, child marriage, concubinage, and slavery are all permitted. There is no love of neighbor or respect for his rights.

If Moslem women could be made to see that their homes can never be made stronger than religious sanctions applying to marriage and divorce, that only in Christianity can they find the stability they so earnestly desire, then we would be well on the road to converting them.

A veteran missioner once told me that Islam has no word for "home," only for "house." It is Christianity that can take the Moslem family out of a house and put it into a home.

From behind the veil . . .

The Arab woman is no longer a secluded prisoner. A Lebanese Sister teaches in a Catholic school. The girl (lower right) is as up-to-date as modern Beirut. Arab women are becoming professional career people, as the lawyer (upper right). All are a long way from *purdah*.

The followers of Islam are now engaged in a tremendous effort to shake off ignorance.

Iranians live in one of the oldest countries in the world. Iran, formerly called Persia, is a country that goes back thousands of years before Christ. In the Bible it was called the country of the Persians and Medes.

There are more than 25 million people in Iran, one-third of whom are nomads. They speak the Persian language, and for the most part ar Moslems. There are few Catholics and about ten thousand Parsis.

Except for a small, fabulously rich ruling group, most of the people of Iran live in great poverty. Only recently with some of the money made from Iran's extensive oil fields has the government begun programs of health, education and economics. The largest and most valuable product of native industry are the beautiful, handmade Persian rugs and shawls.

The people of Iraq live in a land that may once have held the Garden of Eden. Some scholars believe that Iraq, which was formerly known as Mesopotamia, was the cradle of mankind and that the human race began there. Certainly it is the most ancient place in recorded history. In this land were the legendary cities of Nineveh and Babylon. Ur, the most ancient city known to man, was built four thousand years before Christ. The people of Ur lived in two-story, fourteen-room villas, set amid plantations of date palms.

Many Afghanistan peasants go to school at night in order to learn to read and write.

The Hanging Gardens of Babylon were one of the Seven Wonders of the ancient world. Then gradually neglect set in. The extraordinarily fertile soil was not irrigated, barrenness spread over the land. Today the more than eight million people of Iraq are so poor that they must use mud to build their houses and have only animal dung for their fires.

The Mesopotamians dress today much as they did in Biblical days, eat the same foods, and travel their great Tigris and Euphrates Rivers in the same-style asphalt-lined boats. The wealth that comes from the oil fields of Iraq does not filter down to the ordinary man. However, plans have been started to control floods and to irrigate the historic Tigris - Euphrates Valley.

The people of Iraq are largely shepherds. Arabic is the general language. Arabs and Kurds form the majority of the population. There are about a hundred thousand Jews and a smaller group of Nestorian Christians in the country.

The Moslem religion is the unifying force in Afghanistan, a country about the size of Texas, with fifteen million people. The country of Afghanistan stands at an Asiatic crossroads, lying between Russia, Iran, and India. It was the route of conquerors and invaders to and from Asia, and as a result traces of many Asiatic tribes and languages are found there today.

The people of Afghanistan are

gathered into tribes, many of which do not recognize the central government. They are a nomadic people, given to raising sheep, and noted for their fine horses and horsemanship.

The principal languages are Pushtu and Persian. The principal peoples found in the country are Pukhtuns (53 per cent), Tajki (36 per cent), and Uzbeks (6 per cent). Multitudinous tribes make up the small balance.

Syrians are an ancient people who have adjusted well in the modern world. The people of Syria live in the heart of the Middle East. There are about a half million Christian Syrians, a half million nomadic Bedouins, and about five million Sunni Moslems. Arabic is the chief language. The people live by agriculture and cattle breeding. The Syrians are a progressive people and are especially good traders. Many Syrians have emigrated to other countries where they usually become merchants. Syrian children have the opportunity to attend school, and the country has a university in Damascus, the world's oldest inhabited city.

Lebanon is a Christian nation surrounded by a Moslem world. Hundreds of years before Abraham left the kingdom of Mari to settle the land of Canaan, the pharaohs of Egypt had discovered the cedars of Lebanon and were using these trees to build their ships and temples. Solomon also imported this wood for his great constructions. Today the people of Lebanon still live among these fragrant, sturdy trees.

The people of Lebanon are the cultural heirs of the Hittites, Phoenicians, Romans, Arabs, Crusaders and Turks, all of whom passed through the country leaving some legacy behind. Marionite Christians established themselves so strongly that in spite of the fact that the country has been surrounded by Moslemism, Lebanon has remained predominantly Christian.

Compared to most people of the Near and Middle East, the Lebanese are quite well off. They are a thrifty, hard-working people. Beirut, the capital, has four universities. Many Lebanese have emigrated to Europe and America. Today there are about three million Lebanese living in a country about the size of Connecticut. The people speak Arabic, the principal language.

The faithful of three religions look upon Israel as a holy land. Israel is an artificial state, created after World War II to give the displaced Jews of the world a homeland. While the name of the area changed from Canaan of biblical days to Palestine and now to State of Israel, the land is held in veneration by religious Jews be-

This Arab man and child are typical of the million refugees wandering the Holy Land.

A scene on the road to Jericho. Much of the Holy Land is as it was in Our Lord's time.

cause it is the place promised them by God, by Christians because of its associations with Jesus Christ, and by Moslems because they consider themselves the heirs of Judaism and Christianity.

There are about two million people living in Israel today of whom about two hundred thousand are Arabs. Almost a million other Arabs, who formerly lived in the area, fled to neighboring states, particularly to the Gaza Strip.

The new Jewish residents of Israel have taken as their text, those words of the prophet Ezekiel: "And the desolate land shall be tilled." By irrigation and farming, they have caused once barren land to blossom with every possible type of crop. They have developed indus-

tries, opened mines, begun pumping oil, founded an international airline and shipping company. Schools have been founded.

The settlers of Israel are prepared to fight to keep what they have wrested from the desert. The combined might of the Arab world does not daunt these spirited people.

Jordanians live in an Arab country. There are estimated to be over a million and a half people in Jordan, a country about the size of Indiana. These are Arab Moslems except for 180,000 Arab Christians and 11,000 Moslem Circassians. The people are poor, depending on farming and some mining for employment.

This aged settler is helping to build the new country of Israel. He came from Europe.

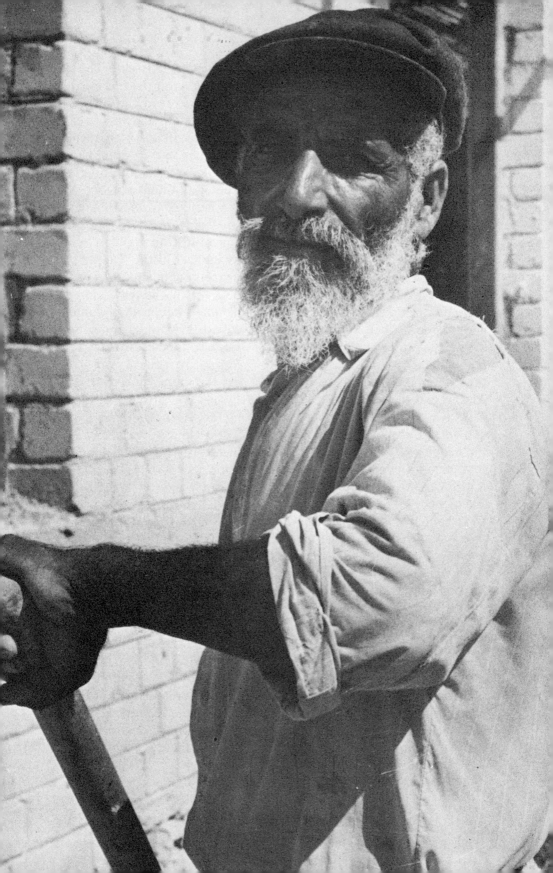

The people of the Arabian peninsula are one of the most homogeneous in the world. The Arabian peninsula embraces an area of a million square miles, equal to four times the size of Texas. But in this vast region there is estimated to be not more than seven million people because the country is mostly barren desert—although underneath the burning sands flows liquid gold in the form of huge oil reserves.

Saudi Arabia is the most important country on the peninsula with about six and a half million people. Smaller countries are Yemen, Aden, Kuwait, and Oman. The people of the region are all Arabs, speaking Arabic, and the religion is Moslem. The town Arabs are merchants and craftsmen but the great majority of the people are desert Arabs, called Bedouins—a people, tall, graceful, tanned by the ever-present sun. These people live in tribes, each tribe being ruled by a sheik. They move from place to place seeking grass and water for their herds of sheep, goats, camels, and world-famous horses. Their food consists mainly of milk and meat, with rice and dates to round out their diets.

The people of the Arabian peninsula are the very foundation of the Islamic religion. The holy city of Mecca, to which every good Moslem must make a pilgrimage, is in their land. They are a devout people, giving daily worship to Allah, attributing everything that happens to His will. The name of their religion, Islam, means "submission to God."

In principle, Islam treats Jews and Christians with respect and tolerance, but in practice the Mohammedan has an underlying hatred of all things non-Moslem. This is a heritage from Mohammed who so deeply resented the refusal of Jews and Christians to accept him as the last of the prophets that he heaped condemnations on all "unbelievers." The revelations of Mohammed were collected into a book called the Koran and other traditions connected with him into the Sunna. It is these two books that are the foundation of Islam.

The Western world has a long history of indifference to Moslem culture and social needs. It is only in recent years that leaders from both camps have been trying to find a common ground that will permit co-operation to achieve various social and economic goals. Actually, there are many points of similarity in these two great monotheistic faiths. Both believe in one God, creator of all things. Both believe in the remission of sin, resurrection, and a life in the world to come. Both share the Jewish traditions. Moslems respect the Blessed Virgin and look upon Jesus as a great prophet (but not the Son of God). Each religion asserts the dignity and freedom of the human will. Indeed, there is plenty of room for agreement.

In an Arabian school room burnoose-covered students learn of the world without.

The Moslem Crescent extends into Africa. Directly across the Red Sea and Gulf of Aden from Saudi Arabia are some narrow strips of land known as Somalia. Although the people of this land are black skinned, they are Moslems and can be considered part of the Moslem Crescent. There are almost three million people in Somalia, representing twenty-one different tribes, of which the Somali and Danakil are the most important.

The Somali are a dark brown people who lead a nomadic desert life. They are cheerful and light-hearted with a tendency to fanaticism in religious matters. They are a hardy people, and the men make excellent soldiers. They belong to Hamitic stock.

The Danakil, or Afar, speak a

The Sudanese were mighty warriors.

210

language akin to the Somali. They are darker than the Somali, and it is difficult to distinguish them from Negroes, the main distinction being that their hair while coarse and curly is not spiraled. The Danakil are lukewarm Moslems.

Sudan is a country of many peoples. More than 120 distinct tribes have been identified in Sudan. The Arabs and Nubians (people of mixed Arab and Negro blood) control the country and are nearly all Mohammedans. The Negroes are mostly pagans, and it is from this group that converts to Christianity are made. The Arabs and Nubians are found mostly in the north.

While it is impossible to discuss all of the tribes of the Sudan, mention of a few will illustrate the variety of the region. The Baggara is an Arabic tribe known for its fine cattle-breeding. The Baggara people are nomadic and they wander over southern Sudan. They carry as much if not more Negro blood than Arab, producing handsome individuals. dark skinned with clear-cut features. They are the most warlike of all tribes in the Sudan.

The Copts are a Christian tribe found not only in the Sudan but also in Egypt. They are usually town dwellers. The Dinka are a tall, black Nilotic people related to Zaire tribes. They are completely pastoral, often not growing enough grain to keep themselves in food. They are pagans. The Negrillos are a pygmy people whose racial history is shrouded in mystery.

When the Mauri travel, a shelter is
built to keep off the equatorial sun.

The Egyptians are heirs to one of the cradles of civilization. The history of the people of Egypt goes back to 4000 BC and the blood of the people of Egypt has been mixed with the many other peoples who came to conquer or rule this strategic land—Persians, Greeks, Macedonians, Romans, Saracens, Turks, French, and British. In return, the Egyptians have placed their mark on many other African Negro tribes.

There are thirty-four million Egyptians today, living in a country somewhat larger than Texas. However, great areas of Egypt are uninhabitable desert and the country's population is confined to a narrow strip on either side of the Nile River and to the Nile delta.

Egypt, particularly Cairo, is the intellectual capital of Islam. The University of Al-Azhar, founded in 968, is the most famous Moslem school in the world. The population of Egypt is 91 per cent Moslem, 8 per cent Christian, and less than 0.30 per cent Jewish. There are 28 different peoples represented in Egypt, from white to black.

The basic racial stock of Egypt is Hamitic. No one is sure where the Hamites originally came from; some anthropologists believe that they originated in Arabia, others say they came from farther east. They were closely related to Semitic stock. They were the great civilizing agent of black Africa from the earliest times. The proof of this is seen in the fact that approximately one-fifth of the people of Africa today speak languages of Hamitic origin. In relatively recent years (after the time of Christ), Semite peoples entered Egypt and mixed with the Hamites. Thus the modern Egyptian is a mixture of Hamite, Semite and Negro, and possibly other races.

The people of Egypt are peasants, called fellahs. They are hard working, highly religious, and peaceable. They are extremely poor, depending on an unstable agricultural economy for their living.

The people of North Africa are of Hamitic and Semitic origins. While the people of North Africa are often referred to by political divisions—Libyans, Algerians, Tunisians, and Moroccans—these terms are misleading. Actually the peoples of all these lands are related, belonging mainly to the Hamitic and Semitic families.

The Northern Hamites include the Berbers of Tunisia, Algeria, Libya, and Morocco, as well as the Tuareg and Tibbu of the Sahara. The Semites include most of the other peoples of Northern Africa usually referred to as Arabs, with the Hamitic exceptions already noted. In addition, there are many Jews and Europeans in the various lands of North Africa. Finally, Negro blood has been added, producing such mixed people as the Moors.

The Tuareg people of the Sahara are of Berber stock, and closely resemble the people of Southern Europe. The men are tall and slim; the women are of delicate features but usually fat because of their diet

An Egyptian scholar

and lack of exercise. The Tuaregs are a fierce and proud people, quick to take insult. They have great courage, and their hospitality is proverbial.

The Hausa are a mixed Hamitic, Semitic, and Negro people who are the traders of North and Central Africa. Their language is often used as the language of commerce. They carry on numerous industries and handicrafts. They are very Negroid in appearance, being dark, short, with broad noses and woolly hair. They are Moslems, but easy going in their religion.

The Berbers, who are often called Arabs, are actually Hamites. They are a Caucasian people with strongly-built bodies, and sometimes blue eyes and fair hair. They are an industrious and practical people. Berber tribes are numerous. As a rule these tribes are peaceful but some tribes, such as the Riffs, are notorious brigands. It is said that the greatest insult that can be given to a Riff is to say, "Your father died in bed."

The Arabs of North Africa are intruders who conquered Algeria and Morocco as part of the Moslem advance in the eighth century. They have many clans, often feuding among themselves. Their way of life is very similar to that of the Arabs of Arabia. Their women are veiled and heavily ornamented; they dye their hands and nails yellow, and blacken their eyebrows with antimony. The Arabs along with the Jews and Negroes are a minority in North Africa.

The Moors are closely allied to the Arabs. However, because of Spanish blood introduced into the tribe during the days of Spanish rule, the Moors are often of lighter complexion than their Arab cousins. The Moors are a brave and courageous people. They are more vivacious than the Arabs, and have a keen sense of humor. Moorish women go in for elaborate costumes with as much jewelry as can be afforded. Moorish architecture is the finest in Africa, and Moorish remains in Spain attract tourists from all parts of the world. Moorish men like their women to be stout and girls are often fattened before marriage on a diet of bread. Islam is the creed of the Moors but they have also picked up many Negro superstitions through inter-marriage with slaves. For example, many Moors will not say the number five but use the expression "four plus one."

The Tibbu tribes inhabit the region of the Tibesti Mountains, along the southern border of Libya and Algeria. Some members of the tribe travel about the desert on camels. They are a mixed people. In the beginning, they were probably of Hamitic origin but they have adopted much from the Negro cultures. The Tibbu men wear veils while the women go half naked. The Tibbu people are extremely poor, living in caves and crude branch huts. They exist on dates and goats' milk, and a flour made from a palm tree. They are only nominal Mohammedans.

By day a scorching, searing sun beats on this Moroccan camel driver but at night the desert becomes freezing. Sharp winds have etched his face and a scarf keeps out the biting sand. Desert life is hard and the desert people know poverty and danger.

The World's Leading Religions

The following figures are based on informed estimates. Few religious bodies keep accurate census figures. Totals are given to the nearest thousands.

Christianity		1,051,591,000
Catholicism	633,000,000	
Protestantism*	294,714,000	
Orthodox	123,877,000	
Islam		471,338,000
Hinduism		472,358,000
Confucianism		304,595,000
Buddhism		301,436,000
Taoism		55,000,000
Shinto		60,130,000
Judaism		14,491,000

Protestantism is divided into many sects with varying beliefs. For example, in the United States alone there are 250 Protestant sects or divisions.

Chapter 7

Sub-Sahara Africa

THE PEOPLE of northern Africa received attention in the previous chapter. This section will be concerned with the people who live south of the great Sahara Desert.

For many years, the rest of the world paid little attention to the peoples of Africa. It is only in recent years with the breakdown of colonialism and with the shrinking of the world through advances in communications and transportation that Africa has taken on great importance.

Usually when the outsider speaks of Africa, he considers the people of the continent as a homogeneous group. Nothing could be further from the truth. For one thing, ethnologists and anthropologists point out that Africa is the home of five principal races: 1. Hamites, 2. Semites, 3. Negroes, 4. Bushmen and Hottentots, and 5. Negrillos. The Semites, except for some mixture in Ethiopia, have been in Africa for only a thousand years. It is even suspected by some scientists that even the Negro is a comparative newcomer since no Negro skulls of any considerable age have ever been discovered.

Racially, Africa can be divided into two parts by drawing a line from St. Louis at the mouth of the Senegal River on the west coast to Khartoum in the Sudan, and then down around the western border of Ethiopia to the Indian Ocean. North of this line is Semitic and Hamitic Africa; south of the line, Negro Africa.

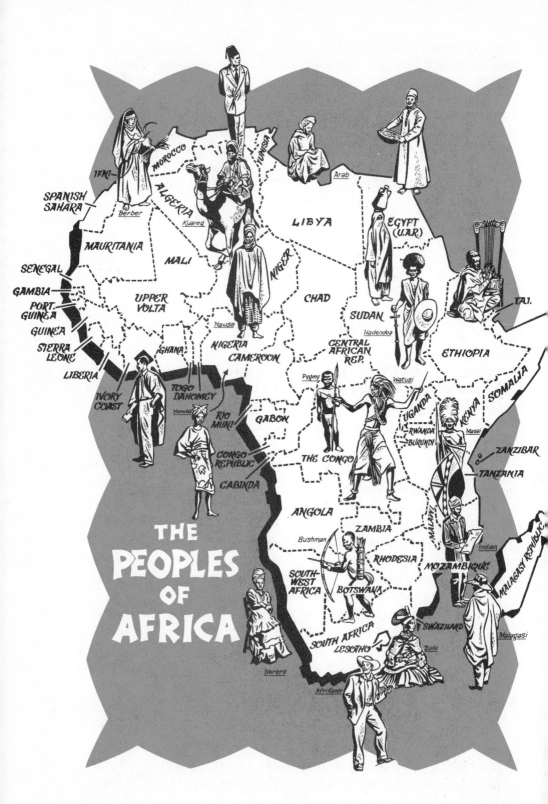

THE PEOPLES OF AFRICA

IFNI

SPANISH SAHARA

MOROCCO

ALGERIA

Berber

Kuareg

TUNISIA

LIBYA

EGYPT (U.A.R.)

Arab

MAURITANIA

MALI

NIGER

CHAD

SUDAN

Hadendoa

T.I.

ETHIOPIA

SENEGAL

GAMBIA

PORT. GUINEA

GUINEA

SIERRA LEONE

LIBERIA

UPPER VOLTA

GHANA

Hausa

NIGERIA

CAMEROON

CENTRAL AFRICAN REP.

IVORY COAST

TOGO

DAHOMEY

Yoruba

RIO MUNI

GABON

CONGO REPUBLIC

CABINDA

THE CONGO

Pygmy

Watusi

UGANDA

RWANDA

BURUNDI

KENYA

Masai

SOMALIA

ZANZIBAR

TANZANIA

ANGOLA

ZAMBIA

Bushman

SOUTH-WEST AFRICA

BOTSWANA

RHODESIA

MALAWI

MOZAMBIQUE

Indien

MALAGASY REPUBLIC

SWAZILAND

Malagasi

SOUTH AFRICA

LESOTHO

Zulu

Herero

Afrikaner

West Africa is the homeland of the true Negro, and here he reached his highest cultural achievements. Crossing the Senegal River from the north, the traveler steps into a maze of states that were once French Africa — Mali, Volta, Niger, Chad, Cameroon and the Central African Republic are the main ones. The first people that the visitor will meet are the Wolofs. They are moderately tall and are said to be the blackest and most talkative people in Africa. Most Wolofs are Mohammedan, a few Christian, and some still pagans who worship lizards. The Wolofs have three castes — nobles, craftsmen, and musicians and slaves.

The Mandingo, or Mande, are a tall, slender people with lighter skin than the Wolofs. They are the merchants of Senegal.

The Mossi are another important tribe of West Africa. They developed a complex native government. The Mossi are mostly farmers, and millet is the staple crop. They possess few cattle but own many horses. The Mossi are pagans who worship the sun, moon, new fire, and their ancestors.

The Songhay are a tall, well-featured people who have intermarried with the Tuaregs and Fulas. Their skin color is copper-brown, rather than the black of their neighbors. They have a single speech, number two million, and practice Islam.

The Bambara are another important tribe among the seventy tribes that once composed French West Africa. For the most part the Bambara have resisted Mohammedan missioners and still practice their ancient worship of spirits. Each Bambara village has its own god, who is said to live in a particular sacred tree.

Although Sierra Leone has two million inhabitants and fifteen tribes, the Temne are the most important people. The Temne today are a very mixed people because of intermarriage. Their skin color varies from light brown to dark black. They have complex and highly organized secret societies which play an important part in their social and ritual life.

Liberia was founded as a home for freed American slaves. Liberia has long been an independent country with its own government. The country is about the size of Tennessee and has over a million people. Liberians live under a constitution modeled after that of the United States. While the control of the government rests in the hands of descendants of ex-slaves, Liberia has almost twenty different tribes within its borders. The most important tribe is the Kru who number about a quarter of a million. They are brave and skillfull seamen, and are important to west coast commerce. They have a reputation for high intelligence and fine physiques. The Kru have a very complex social structure and like so many other tribes of this part of Africa they have religious and judicial secret societies.

Catholic Action workers of the Wolof tribe are married in Western-style in Dakar.

After a megalomaniac beginning Ghana has settled down to a strong political unity. Ghana is a country the size of Oregon with eight million people. Formerly known as the Gold Coast because of the wealth taken from it in both gold and slaves, Ghana today is a progressive state.

The Ashanti are one of the best known and most important tribes in Ghana. There are over a million people living in the Ashanti territory and from the area's rich forests and mines have come great wealth in cocoa, gold, and diamonds. The Ashanti have a long history as a highly organized nation-state and have always been leaders in education, commerce, and government. Among the Ashanti, in-

heritance of property and succession to kingship are governed by matrilineal descent. The Ashanti believe that a child gets his body and blood from its mother and its personality from its father. The most important Ashanti possession is the Golden Stool which the Ashanti believe was given to the tribe by the Sky God. As long as the Ashanti people have this stool in their possession, they will have wealth and health. If it should be destroyed or lost, the Ashanti believe that their nation will come to an end. The American Divine Word Fathers have been doing excellent work among the Ashanti and have built up an exemplary system of schools.

The Ewe speaking people, which include tribes not only in Ghana

This contrast between old and new in Upper Volta dispels many stereotyped ideas.

but also in Dahomey and Nigeria, are of interest because from them came many of the slaves brought to the New World. The Ewe religion was carried across the Atlantic Ocean and is to be found today in Haiti and other West Indian islands. Voodoo is a Ewe word, meaning superhuman spirit.

Fifty-six million Nigerians live in a country larger than France and Great Britain together. One-half of them are Moslems and a fourth Christian. In 1966 the Christian section of Biafra attempted to break away from Moslem domination and a bloody civil war followed. The Ibos, a progressive and commercially minded people, lost the war and suffered about a million dead. An uneasy peace reigns.

There are three million Yoruba-speaking people. Despite the fact that they are gathered into different tribes, they are remarkably similar in culture and way of life. Yoruba religion is a mixture of ancestor worship and animism. They have a whole series of gods, beginning with the Sky God, Olorun, and going down to local village gods. Yorubas have a patrilineal society and their chiefs, or kings, have great authority.

The Mohammedan Hausa tribes, which number eight million people, are centered in Kano and Northern Nigeria. In the Middle Ages they had great political power. They are still politically strong in Nigeria because of their numbers and organization.

The Fulah tribes who conquered the Hausa are not classified as Negroes despite their dark skins. They are probably a Hamitic race with many Berber characteristics. Their facial features are sharp, and their lips are thin. Their hair is slightly curled. They are an intelligent people, ready to give up pastoral ways for industry.

Former Equatorial Africa is the beginning of the Bantu world. Equatorial Africa, formerly French, which includes Cameroon and Chad, extends from the Atlantic seacoast to the border of Mediterranean Libya. Except for the northern regions, it is a land of dense tropical forests. Over eight million people live in this area.

There are over 115 tribes in these new countries, most of them of Bantu stock. The Bantu are a group of people of Central and Southern Africa who take their name from the peculiar language they speak. Their word for people is *abantu,* hence their name.

The Bantu are divided into three groups. The Eastern Bantu live in Kenya, Tanzania and Uganda. The Southern Bantu are found in Zambia, Rhodesia, Mozambique, South and Southwest Africa. The Western Bantu dwell in Equatorial Africa, Zaire and Angola. The distinction between these groups is more than geographical. There are cultural and historical differences as well.

The main Bantu tribes of old Equatorial Africa are the Apingi, Apono, Ashango, Ashira, Ishogo, and Okanda. They are fetish worshiping tribes who believe in immortality.

The Ashira live near the coast, and subsist on a staple diet of bananas. Marriage between blood relatives is prohibited by the Ashira, although a man may marry all the wives of a deceased uncle. He may also marry his stepmother.

The Ishogo are a progressive people who live in large villages, arranged with well-planned streets. Their houses consist of several rooms. Formerly, they filed their teeth to points. The men shave the crown of their heads, and both sexes remove eyebrows and eyelashes. Fetishism is very strong among them.

The Ashango, who live close to the Ishogo, have many of the same customs as their neighbors. They cultivate peanuts and raise bees. They also keep flocks of chickens and herds of goats, but the flesh of these is forbidden to women.

An unimportant tribe in the torrid equatorial region, but one well known to many Americans, is the Ubangi. At one time it was popular to have Ubangi women as part of circuses and carnivals. Ubangi women had the custom of stretching their lips into grotesque sizes by using wooden discs, continually replacing them with larger ones. The custom is seldom practiced any longer. The reason for this strange practice was to make the subject unsuitable to be sold as a slave. The wearer would not be taken into captivity because of the strange and frightening disfigurement.

A Baoulé man of the Ivory Coast

An unmarried Arab girl of Algeria

A Tuareg trader living in Libya

A Christian Azanda in the Sudan

223

The people of Zaire, formerly the Belgian Congo, are making rapid industrial and social advances. Zaire is a big sprawling country, as large as Texas, New Mexico, Arizona, Utah, Colorado, and California combined. In it live over eighteen million people who are divided into 174 different tribes. They occupy the very heart of the African continent, an area once known as "darkest Africa." Today, the nation's youth can attend a university in Kinshasa, live in small modern cottages, swim in Olympic swimming pools, and find plenty of job opportunities in Zaire's copper-rich economy. For example, Zaire is the world's larg-

A woman from the Ashanti tribe.

He is a Cotocoli charmer from Togo.

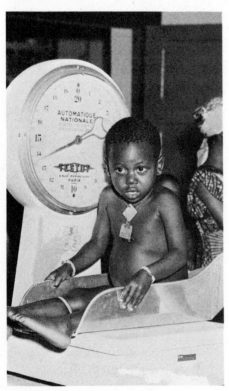

est producer of industrial diamonds, has 60 per cent of the world's known uranium ore, and 90 per cent of the world's supply of radium.

Despite industry, 70 per cent of the people are farmers. The Congo Bantu excel in the arts. It is one of the few areas in Africa where sculpture and music have developed on the native level.

Some of the important tribes are the Bakongo, the Balolo, the Bakete (one of the oldest settlers), the tattooed Bangala, and the Baluba. There are four million Catholics, 800,000 Protestants and a half million Moslems. French is the national language.

Whites and blacks are taught to play together in new Zaire.

Blanket Boy's Paradise

LESOTHO is an oasis of freedom, surrounded, by a vast racial desert called South Africa. Driving down to the country from Johannesburg, one passes through a land that could easily be transplanted to the American midwest. There is mile after mile of flat or very gently rolling countryside with well kept farms, rich in their acres of wheat and corn. But as soon as one rumbles across the little narrow-gauge railroad bridge that separates the new nation from the Orange Free State, he passes both literally and figuratively into another world.

For the first time in many miles you see dark-skinned men conscious of their dignity. The Basuto, wrapped in his bright blanket, astride his sturdy pony, is a far different man than the one you saw crowded into the South African locations along the Rand. Here you can almost smell the clean air of freedom. Not that Lesotho is wholly a paradise—once in the country you come face to face with ritual murder and the ever-present African poverty—but at least here a man has choice and freedom of movement.

Even the very face of the land is different. Lesotho is a tortuous region of mountains and canyons. There are great outcroppings of yellow and red rock. A citizen of Arizona or New Mexico could be set down here and never know that he had left home. On every side is the evidence of erosion. Except for the willows bending low over dried-up gullies, trees are mostly lacking. Up in the hills wild flowers break the blinding monotony. In the distance over the Drakenborg Mountains, huge thunderheads gather with their teasing promise of rain.

Once across the bridge, the traveler enters the little city of Maseru, now the capital for one million people of this former British protectorate. British policy had been the exclusion of foreigners from the protectorate, and the only whites to be found are a few officials, missionaries, and the few traders who have been able to get permits. Mineral exploitation and farming are prohibited to whites. The result has been the creation of a true African nation, long familiar with ruling itself in a monarchial manner.

The people are represented by chiefs, under a single paramount chief, who are formed into the Legislative Council, which meets regularly at Maseru. At the present time, the King is mainly a figurehead and control rests with the Prime Minister.

Lesotho is entirely surrounded by South Africa, and there was considerable pressure by the South African government for annexation of the territory. The Basutos themselves wanted no part of the Union. They knew that they would lose their national identity and individual freedom if the Afrikaaner took them over. For many years the British resisted transferring administration to the Union, and in 1966 settled the question once and hopefully for all time by granting the protectorate full independence. Now that Lesotho is a member of the United Nations, its future independence seems secure from further South African threats.

There is no question but that South Africa could strangle Lesotho anytime it desires. Every import of the country must cross South African soil. The products of Lesotho—wool, mohair, and hides—must go out through South Africa. Lesotho is also a large reservoir for cheap South African labor. One out of every six citizens goes to the Union to find work. If South Africa should close off imports and exports, and seal the border against labor migration, the tiny nation would be in serious trouble. The country is promoting tourism and has legalized gambling. These are efforts to gain outside recognition. South Africa's own repressive racial policies leave little sympathy for its ambitions.

The highlight of any visit to Lesotho is to see the excellent works of the Oblates of Mary Immaculate. These missioners—mostly from Canada, but also from France, Ireland, Holland and South Africa—have established the Church on firm footing. Forty per cent of the population is now Catholic. The country even boasts of a native archbishop, Alphonsus Ligouri Morapeli, O.M.I., a scholarly man who is respected for his preaching and writings.

THE OBLATES HAVE inaugurated two projects in Lesotho which have no equal in Africa. One is Mazenod Institute, not far from Maseru. Here they have set up a Catholic Action center whose effects actually radiate to all parts of the continent. Heart of this activity is the excellent printing establishment founded by Father M. Ferragne and now directed by Father Matthias Garreau. This printing plant of composing room, presses, and bindery has up to date equipment and is housed in a large modern fireproof building. Native workers operate the linotype machines and the huge presses.

The output of Mazenod in a single year gives an idea of the amount of work being done. The figures for the most recent year available gave the following totals: 39,725 copies of magazines in four languages; 129,967 school books in three languages; 345,444 circulars and tracts in nine languages; 24,000 calendars in three languages; 306,000 copies of the weekly Sesotho journal, "Moeletsi."

The publications of Mazenod go out to Lesotho, South Africa, Rhodesia, Uganda, Kenya, Tanzania, Malawi, Nigeria and Ghana—in fact all English-speaking Africa. Walking through the bright modern plant we saw posters in various languages that had been produced publicizing Marian devotion, other posters promoting the Bible. We saw Catholic catechisms, a cleverly designed pamphlet condemning ritual murder, magazines, and books on the Bible and the history of the Basuto people.

"The percentage of Basutos who attend school is larger than anywhere else in Africa," Father Ferragne told us. "Right now we are aiding in a literacy campaign. We want everyone in Basutoland to be able to read."

The director showed us a clever book that had been worked out by Father Hamel, an Oblate, for the purpose of teaching people to read and write. The only classroom needed was the outdoors, the blackboard being the earth itself. The book shows the teacher how to trace lines on the ground, how to evolve these lines gradually into letters, and then the letters into words. The idea is to get literacy classes started in every village, and all the pupils need are sticks with which they can trace lines along with the teacher. School texts now account for eighty per cent of output.

The weekly newspaper "Moeletsi oa Basotho" (Counselor of the Basutos) has a picture-studded, lively typographical format that is superior to the average Catholic newspaper in the United States. Published in the native Sesotho language, 15,000 copies of the paper go to Basutos at home and in the Union. The paper is full of religious exhortation, Catholic and general world news. Through "Moeletsi" education is being given and literacy advocated.

YOU HAVEN'T SEEN anything until you've been to Roma." I had heard this many times from Catholics in South Africa, and it was to see Roma that I had made the long journey to Lesotho. Roma lies about thirteen miles inland beyond Mazenod. It is set in a deep canyon at the foot of sheer cliffs and must be seen to be believed. Here is an educational setup that cannot be surpassed in any other mission country.

At the top of the list is Roma's University, once called Pius XII University, now simply referred to as UBLS. Then there are Roma College, Roma Teachers' College, St. Mary's Institute, St. Theresa's Junior Seminary, St. Augustine Seminary, St. Mary's Juniorate (for training Brothers), a novitiate for training Sisters, primary schools, a large hospital, a cathedral, and scores of other buildings.

In this remote canyon cut off from the rest of the world, the Oblates have erected a huge university city. Out of the rock walls surrounding them they have quarried the stones for their many buildings, purposefully constructing them to last through the ages.

Yet even with the tremendous building program that has been going on at Roma, space is at a premium. We visited a primary school taught by Canadian and native nuns. Every classroom was jammed to capacity and classes were being held on the open porch of the school. Under the trees behind the school a half-dozen more classes were going on. Barefooted Basuto youngsters sat on benches and shouted back their lessons in English and Sesotho. You could actually feel their desire for knowledge.

LATER WE WALKED up through a long row of trees (planted by the missioners) to St. Mary's Institute. Here girls were receiving high school training, and here the future women teachers of Basutoland are prepared. Dressed in neat uniforms these girls were practicing games they would later use in their teaching. They followed the crisp orders of their leader, moving with precision and grace.

In one of the classrooms we found a session in domestic science in progress. A native Sister was demonstrating how to put up preserves.

We went to Roma College, taught by the Brothers of the Sacred Heart, some of whom are Americans. Once again we were caught up in the apparent zeal for learning. Here we met young Constantine Bereng—tall, handsome and soft-spoken, who since has become the paramount chief of Lesotho. He is the son of the famous chief, Nathaniel Griffith, who died in 1939. Griffith was a wise and able leader who did much to advance his people. He was converted to Christianity towards the end of his life, got rid of his many wives, and led an exemplary life following his baptism. After graduation from Roma, Constantine studied in Europe. His ascent to the throne was permitted but his uncle, Jonathan, seized actual power and ended free elections in 1970.

Roma's glory, however, is its University. Father Romeo Guilbeault, formerly educational secretary for Lesotho, was the rector when I visited. He is now back in Canada and the University has undergone transition.

The University began with six students, three teachers, and an abandoned elementary school in 1945. Today it is called the University of Botswana, Lesotho and Swaziland—all countries too small to found a good university by themselves. Actually its students represent South and East Africa. The Oblates have made a tremendous contribution in starting a Catholic university and then broadening its scope internationally. Four Oblate missioners are on the University staff.

ONE CANNOT VISIT the University and go away unaffected. Academic standards are high, and mediocrity on part of teacher or student is not permitted. The main task of the University is to create a Catholic intelligentsia—an intelligentsia devoid of Marxism, and one that believes in a supernatural basis for life. Africa is in turmoil, and out of this cauldron are arising new leaders. Up to now the Church in Africa has not been able to equip these leaders to meet the challenge offered by Marxist and materialistic theorists.

If priests and lay faculty are working under handicaps and at disadvantages, the same applies to the students. We remember stopping to talk with a group of students engaged in an impromptu jam session. The young saxophonist introduced himself as Tarcisius Silundika, working towards a Bachelor of Arts degree, majoring in psychology and politics. He hoped later to go into medicine or law. Tarcisius comes from Rhodesia. He is one of ten children. His father earns ten pounds a month (not quite thirty dollars). On this meager salary Tarcisius had been put through primary and secondary schools. Now the college fees of two hundred dollars a year were proving more than the young man's family could manage. Yet the family was willing to make any possible sacrifice to see Tarcisius educated.

Before leaving Lesotho we drove up to the rim of the canyon. As we stopped the car and looked down on Roma bathed in the golden glow of late afternoon sunlight, we noticed a young, blanket-clad boy off at the side, guarding a flock of sheep and goats. Here was the contrast of today's Africa. Here, too, was the promise of the future. Just a few years earlier the vital young men and women we had met at Roma had been like this young shepherd. What changes had come into their lives in so few short years! What changes might there not still come before the almost present tomorrow.

Pygmies, properly called Negrillos, once roamed much more widely over the African continent than they do today. In modern times, Pygmies are confined to the dense tropical forests found five degrees on either side of the Equator. The average height of the male Pygmy is four feet eight inches. The Pygmies live in small communities, building their houses from branches and large leaves. They are excellent hunters, using bows and poisoned arrows. They are friendly but easily excitable, given to sudden bursts of rage. When they do become enemies, they are cunning and revengeful. Their religion is animistic and few have been converted to Christianity. They have borrowed freely from the Bantu culture, particularly as regards language.

The Watusi are the deposed aristocrats of Rwanda. The Watusi are a very advanced people who live in exceptionally clean villages, in well constructed reed houses, and who have long-horned cattle that might be the envy of any livestock breeder. The Watusi are believed to have emigrated to Central Africa from Ethiopia. Their area of Africa is the fastest growing as far as the Church is concerned. Two out of every five inhabitants of Rwanda, and neighboring Burundi, are Catholics.

The tribes of Portuguese Angola are similar to the Congo peoples. Portuguese West Africa has a coast line extending a thousand miles south from the Congo River. In this country, twice as large as the state of Texas, live about five million people. The region is divided between three groups. In the north live the Bakongo, already spoken of as the principal inhabitants of Zaire. The southern coast is inhabited by the Abunda, while inland live the Ganguella, or the "stammerers." These tribes are broken up into some sixty-five sub tribes. The Portuguese have controlled the area since 1575, and for many years outsiders were not welcomed.

Some of the most primitive people in the world live in Southwest Africa, a territory controlled by the Union of South Africa. Despite its immense size (twice as large as California), this largely desert-like region has less than a half million inhabitants.

Among the native peoples are the Herero, who although of Bantu stock, show the results of Bushman and Hamitic intermarriage. The Herero raise livestock and work in the diamond and lead mines. They are pagans, worshiping a sacred fire.

The Bushmen, who extend into South Africa, are of very ancient origin. They are the most backwards of all Africans, and are just emerging from the Stone Age. They are short people, and to Europeans have ugly, blunt features. Each

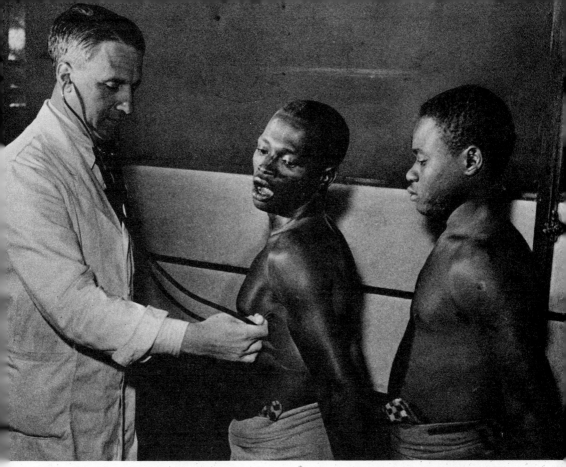

These Basuto youths are being examined for employment in a South African diamond mine.

Bushman tribe speaks its own language. The Bushmen do not practice agriculture but live by hunting and gathering edible roots and weeds. They wear little clothing, often going naked. They worship the moon and stars, have many taboos, and are governed in religious matters by medicine men who are also rainmakers. They are excellent mimics and love to dance.

The Hottentots who also spread into the Union of South Africa are very similar to the Bushmen. They are believed to be the result of a mixture between Bushmen and invading Hamites. The Hottentots are a disappearing people, and few old customs and beliefs survive among the remnants.

Integration is treason in South Africa. The Union of South Africa is a country equal to the size of Texas, Arizona and New Mexico. It has a population of twenty-one million people, of whom over three million are whites of European origin, a half million are Asian Indians, and the balance of Bantu stock. Because the Negro population is multiplying faster than any other and because the whites do not wish to jeopardize their standard of living, the government has strict segregation laws.

231

The artistic sense of the Ndeble is shown by geometric designs they paint and use.

The Afrikaners got their name from the language they speak, Africaans. They are descendants of the Dutch Boers who were the white pioneers in South Africa. Like the American pioneers, they crossed prairies in covered wagons, fought hostile tribes, and built homesteads in the wilderness. Fashioned by their strict Calvinistic religion, they are unbending in their treatment of the native population. They control the government and enact laws against the Negro population aimed at protecting their way of life. Other European nationalities in South Africa are only minority voices opposed to Afrikaner policy.

While the Indians are a very small percentage of the South African population, both in South and East Africa, they are very important to the commercial life of their regions. Many of these Indians come from families several generations in Africa, others belong to newer arrivals. They are merchants and tradesmen. Most of them are Hindu, although a surprisingly large number are Catholic Indians from the Goa region.

A century ago the name of the Zulu people was a symbol of terror, much as was the word Apache in our own Southwest. A Zulu warrior, Shaka, organized his people and through warfare and natural increase formed a great nation. Tribe after tribe fell beneath Zulu spears. Zulu karaals grew crowded with fat cattle, and every man was wealthy. The Zulus resisted the white invaders, and conducted terrifying and murderous raids on Boer settlements and wagon trains. The British guns finally halted the aggressive Zulus.

Today, the largest majority of Zulus live outside Zululand. It is estimated that there are over two million of them. They are a robust people of great athletic prowess. In Zululand, they are pastoral and agricultural. The Marianhill mission has had marvelous success with this once-warlike tribe. Today, one-third of all the Catholics in the four provinces of the Union are in the Marianhill area.

The Sotho, sometimes called the Basuto, are a happy, progressive people living in their own nation, Lesotho. The Basuto nation was welded from many tribes and is estimated to count over a half million members today. Large numbers of the Sotho are Catholics and a strong native clergy is being developed among them.

Closely allied to the Basutos are the Bechuanas, again a name under which many tribes have been collected. The Bechuanas are not as progressive as the Zulus or Basutos. They support themselves by livestock and limited agriculture. There are thirty-three tribes in Botswana, all of them Bantu save for some Bushmen, with a total of approximately five hundred thousand people.

The Swazi of Swaziland are another important Bantu tribe found in South Africa. They raise livestock and grow corn and tobacco. Some minerals are found in their region. There are close to two hundred thousand Swazi.

There is a special class in South Africa called the Colored, or Cape Colored. They are people of mixed blood and as such are looked down upon by the race-conscious Afrikaner. Most of them live in the Cape Province. They speak both Africaans and English. Once skilled artisans, they are now reduced to the most menial tasks because of restrictive laws.

Mozambique, or Portuguese East Africa, is roughly the size of Texas. There are estimated to be more than eight million natives in the area. Two tribes are predominant. The Gaza are related to the Zulus. They get their name from a Swazi chief, Gaza, who was sent as head of a Zulu army to drive the Portuguese from the area. Failing, he dared not return to Zululand, so he and his men absorbed the tribes living there and began the Gaza people.

The Tsonga people, closely allied to the Basuto, include those tribes of the south not of Zulu origin. In the north are Balempa tribes who show traces of Semitic blood. Many of these tribes do not follow national borders but spill over into the Union and Rhodesia.

The Bushmen of Southwest Africa are a disappearing and almost-extinct primitive race.

The people of Malagasy are of Malay origin. Malagasy, an island off the coast of Africa, is about the size of Texas and has six million people who were French colonials. Although for many years the people of Malagasy were considered Negroes, it has now been established that they have a Malay origin. The general term for the people of the island is Malagasi, the name of their language, which is derived from an ancient Malay dialect. The Malagasi have also borrowed from the African and Arab so that their culture is quite complex. They are divided into a recognized ninety-four tribes.

The leading tribe of the island is the Hova, a well formed and intel-ligent people. For the most part, they live by agriculture, raising rice, maize, sweet potatoes, and coffee. The Hova have features very similar to those of Europeans, and their hair is straight. The Betsileo, who live near the Hova, are much darker and have woolly hair. Other tribes that should be mentioned are the Ikongo, Anti-Mana, and Bara.

The people of Malagasy are very similar in cultural patterns. They are all agriculturists, and own cattle, sheep, pigs, and poultry. They are skilled at weaving grass mats and baskets, and in working metals. The original religion of the island was idolatry and ancestor worship; however Christianity is now widespread.

The people of Rhodesia, Zambia and Malawi live in what was called the Central African Federation. Rhodesia declared its independence in 1965. It is a rich country of five and a half million people of whom a quarter million are white and who rule the country with an iron hand. The country has been embargoed by the UN for its racial policies but the boycott has been ineffective.

The Matabele, formerly fierce warriors, are the oppressed aristocracy of Rhodesia. They are related to the Zulus, are powerfully built, standing about six feet high. They live in round huts that have doorways only two feet high—a means of protection against enemies. The Matabele are an agricultural people, fond of cattle. Many of them now work in mines.

Unlike the Banyai and Makalaka, who were swallowed up by the Matabele, the Mashona people were able to preserve their independence and identity by retreating among their granite hills to safety. The Mashonas are peaceful and hard working. They raise grain crops and keep livestock and poultry. They are also skilled blacksmiths who formerly made some of the finest spears and battle-axes in South Africa. They could not stand up against the Matabele because they were unorganized. They do not lack bravery, however, as is shown by the way they formerly hunted elephants. They would slip up on the big beasts while the latter were asleep and hamstring them with an axe.

Most Pygmies inhabit the dense forests.

The Babemba and Ila are the main tribes of poorer Zambia. The Babemba are hoe-farmers, raising mostly millet. They live in small villages and are governed by a native king. They are a totemistic people, each clan adopting an animal and giving it protection. The Ila raise cattle and hunt and fish. One of their favorite foods is sorghum porridge made with sour milk. The people of Zambia like those of Rhodesia are of Bantu origin.

The natives of Malawi are among the best farmers in Africa. They are intelligent and cultured, having their own written language (Nyanja). They are also unusually well educated for Africans, the result of excellent Catholic mission schools. The main tribes of Mala-

235

wi are the Wangindo, which includes many subdivisions; the Angoni; Makololo; and the Shangana. The ownership of cattle is a sign of wealth. Gardens yield millet and maize, and cassava root is a staple food. Bananas, beans and tobacco are also grown.

More than 10 per cent of the people of this area of Central Africa are Catholic. A strong nucleus of native clergy is being developed. The first martyr of southern Africa, Father Gonzalo da Silveira, a Jesuit, was murdered in Rhodesia.

The people of Tanzania have little national identity. Tanzania is a large country, about one and a half times the size of Texas. It has over twelve million people, divided between almost a hundred tribes. Some of these tribes, like the Watusi and Jaluo, have spread into Tanzania from other regions where they more properly belong, and will be treated under those sections.

Along the jungle-like coastal regions of Tanzania live the Swahili people, also referred to as Suahili. It is their language that has become the trade language of East Africa. The Swahili are a hybrid people formed by intermarriage between the coastal Negroes plus Negroes brought from the interior as slaves and Arab settlers. The name of this people comes from the Arabic *sahel,* meaning coast. Their language is studded with Arabic terms. The language is unusual in that the beginning of the word is altered instead of the end. Thus the verb "to get" becomes *mapata, napata* and *tapata* in its present, past and future tenses. In addition, the Swahili tongue has been influenced by Portuguese, Galla, and Somali. The Swahili mixture has been going on since the seventh century with the result that it is impossible to define the physical characteristics of these people. The Swahili are a merchant race, and in the past were the slave raiders. They are mostly Mohammedans, although more tolerant than most followers of Islam.

The Chagga are a prosperous people who live on the slopes of Mount Kilimanjaro, Africa's highest peak. The Chagga are Bantus who are descended from Kamba or Taita stock. They are comparatively new to Tanzania. They do not live in villages but each family has its own homestead centered in a banana grove. The Chagga also grow coffee, and this crop is the source of their wealth. Although the country is thickly inhabited, the Chagga keep cattle, many of which must be fed on cut grass. The Chagga practice circumcision of both boys and girls. They believe in a Supreme Being called Ruwa, and worship their ancestral spirits. They have faith in modern education, and boast progressive social ideas which have given rise to strong co-operatives. The Holy Ghost Fathers work among them and have made many converts.

The Basukuma, who live in central Tanzania near Lake Victoria, raise cotton as a cash crop. They are a Bantu people who were once part of Kituara Empire. As such they are related to the Baganda, the Rundi, the Nyamwezi, and other tribes around Lake Victoria. However for many hundreds of years, they have existed as an independent kingdom. They have a Hamitic strain of blood, probably brought in by the Huma. The Basukuma are an agricultural and pastoral people who are among the progressive tribes of the country. They number about a million, boast of many Christians, and have seen their sons become priests. Maryknoll Missioners are at work among them.

In northern Tanzania, there are many small tribes, some of which are offshoots from the Masai. One of the most interesting is the Bakuria tribe. These people have settled in one area, raise cattle, and grow maize and other foods. They formerly had the reputation of being cattle thieves. They also punched holes in the lobes of the ears, attached weights, and thus spread their lobes to fantastic lengths—some of the holes being large enough to pass a baby through. The young people, spurred by mission education, are departing from this custom. Likewise disappearing is the skin dress worn by the women. However, the women still bedeck themselves with many strings of beads, and bind their arms with copper wire.

The Masai are a nomadic people who roam over a large area of Tan-

Muganda miss of the Baganda of Uganda.

zania and part of Kenya. The Hamitic strain is very noticeable in their physical characteristics. They are tall and slender, with fine featured, long faces. Their language originated in the Nile Valley. It is impossible to tell of the importance of cattle to the Masai. They wander with their herds from pasture to pasture, subsisting largely on the diet of milk, meat, and blood. The blood is drawn from the necks of their cattle.

The men wear very little clothing, while the women wear leather petticoats and masses of beads about the neck and copper wire about the arms. In the olden days the men were fierce warriors and raiders. They proved manhood by engaging in combat with a lion. Few Masai are Christians because of their nomadic life.

237

Life Among the Baganda

JOSEPH NYMBOZE and his wife, Florentia, live in Uganda, a rolling, hilly country in central Africa about the size of Minnesota or Utah. Uganda is bisected by the equator, and the climate varies from tropical along the shore of Lake Victoria to frigid in the heights of the Ruwenzori Mountains.

Uganda is composed of several tribes. Joseph and Florentia belong to the Baganda people, the dominant force in Uganda. (A single tribesman is known as a Muganda; their territory is Buganda; their language, Luganda.) The history of the Baganda people is quite modern. The first known visitor from the outside world (an Arab) arrived in 1850 and the first European in 1862. The early explorers found the country well organized, under a native king, and progressive. The people wore beautiful clothing and lived in well constructed houses.

In 1877, Anglican missionaries arrived and two years later the first Catholic priests entered the country. Religion took a firm hold. Today Catholicism is the leading faith. Joseph and his wife come from old Catholic families. In fact, Joseph counts a canonized martyr among his ancestors. He also spent three years in a Catholic mission school.

Joseph is a member of the lion clan while his wife belongs to the goat clan. Clan relationship plays an important role in the lives of the people of Uganda. It is forbidden to marry within a clan. Joseph would never think of killing a lion and Florentia will eat no goat meat.

The marriage of Joseph and Florentia was a union of two clans. Unlike the custom of many other African tribes where marriage is completely arranged between parents, Joseph chose his own wife. When Joseph felt that it was time for him to marry (and after he had saved up money from his cotton patch), he set about looking for a suitable wife. There was no idea of romantic love in his approach, because like all Baganda men he believes that physical attraction is no reason for marriage.

Joseph finally settled on several possible partners. The merits and demerits of each girl were carefully weighed and discussed with one or two close friends. Finally, he decided on Florentia, a girl who attended the same mission church as he did. Florentia struck Joseph as being an obedient girl. A friend told him she had a reputation of being a good cook.

One Sunday after Mass, Joseph approached Florentia and made his proposal. It was the first time he had ever spoken to her. Florentia told him that she would give him her reply the next week. On the following Sunday after Mass, Joseph received his answer. Florentia had spent the week investigating him and was satisfied with what she had learned. She told Joseph that he might make a formal request for her.

Joseph then began his courtship, a courtship not only of Florentia but also of her immediate family. In a series of letters to her, her parents, her two brothers and her aunt, Joseph announced his desire to marry Florentia. In each letter he enclosed a gift of money. He also sent presents to Florentia's parents—cloth, meat, and sugar.

At last a letter came to Joseph. Florentia's parents had taken note of him. He was invited to appear on a Thursday evening for formal introduction. Joseph hurried out and bought a dress for Florentia.

ON THURSDAY EVENING, Joseph, accompanied by his own brother and sister, went to Florentia's home. Her whole family was assembled to meet him. Florentia wore the new dress Joseph had sent and she sat modestly silent in the shade of the house.

"This is the man who has made me rebel against my parents," said Florentia's aunt, who spoke in the first person in Florentia's place.

"My sister will make a fine wife," spoke up John, Florentia's brother.

"That is probably so," replied Joseph's brother, not wishing to seem too anxious lest the bride-price be set too high.

"The bride-price will be two hundred shillings," declared John. The current price was between 100 and 300 shillings. This set the cost about $28, just about what Joseph was able to pay.

"It is agreed," said Joseph's brother.

"There are other presents," continued Florentia's spokesman. "There must be beer and a small calf for the feast. And a bark-cloth garment for my mother. A tin of paraffin for my father. A cotton dress for my aunt."

"I will also give a *kanzu* for yourself," promised Joseph, speaking for the first time. A kanzu is an Arab-style gown worn by Baganda men.

A date three months away was chosen for the wedding. In the weeks that followed, Joseph sent the promised money and gifts to Florentia's family. The next meeting of the engaged couple was in the mission church at the wedding ceremony. Florentia was dressed in European style with a white veil, while Joseph wore a European-style suit. The ceremony followed the usual Catholic Ritual.

JOSEPH HAD BUILT a new house for himself and his bride in the middle of a small banana plantation that had come to him from his father who had died two years previously. Because Joseph was a second son, his mother lived with his elder brother. The new house was circular with a high pointed roof. The house was carefully and neatly constructed, with fine cane-work and a wide porch. The homes of the Baganda are far superior to those of most other African tribes. Behind the house is a small shelter built for cooking, and a privy.

Joseph owns about fifteen acres of land. On this parcel he has a grove of bananas, a small grove of coffee trees, a cotton patch, and a vegetable garden which produces sweet potatoes mostly, but also other vegetables such as cassava, beans, chili, ginger, and so on.

Joseph and Florentia arise each day as soon as it is light and go into their fields at once. About ten o'clock, Florentia returns home to prepare the noon meal. Joseph continues working for another hour or so. At that time, because it is usually very hot, he throws his hoe over his shoulder and goes home.

About twelve, the noon meal is served. The household revolves around Joseph because in Uganda the husband is the boss supreme. Everything is organized for his convenience. Florentia would never think of eating in his absence or not having a meal ready when he expects it. After dinner Florentia will sometimes ask her husband's permission to go to the village market or to visit friends. Sometimes Joseph will join her in one of these excursions. Other times, he will nap.

At three o'clock, when the afternoon has begun to cool, husband and wife will be back in their fields. Florentia will leave again at five to get water and prepare supper. Joseph continues working until dusk. After supper, they may visit or entertain visitors, or just sit in the coolness of the porch. Sometimes there is a business or political meeting for Joseph to attend or services at the mission.

Joseph sells his coffee and cotton through excellently operated native co-operatives. He has not too great a need for much ready money. His wants are simple —a little tobacco, an occasional new shirt for himself or dress for his wife, a little bit of cash to put by in case of need, and the money to pay his taxes. Even in remote Africa taxes have become a necessary part of life.

Although Uganda was once under British control, the country always had its own king and native government. After independence the king was deposed and he died in London in alcoholic poverty. Although a republic it is presently a dictatorship.

Many of Joseph's friends have left the land and gone to the cities to work. Uganda is undergoing an industrial invasion and there is a big demand for labor. Joseph has no desire for city life, however. He is content to remain on the land of his ancestors.

Joseph's main concern is with coffee and cotton prices. He approved of the exile of the Indian merchants who had a strong grasp on his economic life. He does not completely approve of the new type government since the Baganda do not have the dominant role in national life that they formerly exercised.

THE WORLD about Joseph is changing rapidly. Old tribal ways are disappearing. The mechanization of the West has caused many upheavals in African cultures. If Joseph could have his way, he would shut out the present and retreat into the past. He wants to be left alone with his wife to build their own future.

Life for Joseph and Florentia is a co-operative affair. The family unit is the basis for Baganda social structure and economy. Although the husband is the head of the household, he holds his wife in great respect and talks over his problems and plans with her, and she does the same. Recently, Florentia told Joseph she is to have a baby. When the child comes (to be followed by many others, he hopes), Joseph's life and happiness will be reasonably complete.

Impoverished Zulu Father

The Masai are a nomadic tribe of Kenya.

Closely related to the Masai are the Turkana who are also nomadic herdsmen. The Turkana are found in northern Uganda and in the southern Sudan. The Turkana are as tall as the Masai and have similar features except that their noses are broader. The Turkana were not as warlike as the Masai, and they have not been as much affected by civilization. They live in a remote area, seldom visited by white men.

Although Uganda takes its name from the Ganda people, it is the homeland of seventy-six tribes. The Ganda, a Bantu tribe, is one of the most progressive in all Africa with a high regard for the white man's civilization, education, and religion. While the Buganda people play the most important role in the life of Uganda because of their organization and central location, there are other important tribes in the country.

The Acholi are a Nilotic people whose original physical characteristics have been changed by marriage with Bantu stock. They are a pastoral and agricultural people who lack the drive of their Ganda neighbors. They raise some of the finest cattle in Africa—beautiful, long-horned beasts which receive as much care and attention as would children. The Acholi are close relatives to the Luo who are also found in Uganda in large numbers but who will be considered under Kenya.

The Basoga resemble the Baganda. They live in large villages of circular huts, dress in the style of the Baganda. They are blacker than the Baganda, thus showing a greater proportion of Negro blood. They are good farmers. Bananas are their staple food.

The Banyoro make up the second most important region in Uganda. They are a Bantu people, who have adopted some of the customs of the Nilotic tribes. They are shorter than the Baganda and lighter complexioned. They had a high tribal organization when discovered by the first white explorers. Like the Baganda and Basoga, they wore bark-cloth garments and the royal court was very complex. They did not build as good houses as the Baganda, and in other respects did not have as high a culture. The Banyoro are polygamous. Their religion was fetishism in which human sacrifice played a part. Islam has made considerable progress among this tribe.

There are some Pygmies and Negrillos in Uganda, however the largest bodies of these people are across the Zaire border. It is also possible to find many fragments of Congo tribes in Uganda. Many of these people are attracted to Uganda because of greater opportunities for employment and thousands fled to escape the civil war that racked the former Belgian Congo.

The Yao are a numerous Bantu people found in Uganda. They are related to the Nyanja of Nyasaland from where they seem to have originally come. They scar their temples and file their upper teeth into points. They are tall and strong, and in the days of exploration were sought as carriers. When a Yao boy marries, he builds his home on the bride's property. His first duty is to hoe a garden for his mother-in-law. The Yao believe in a Supreme Being, and every village has a prayer tree under which sacrifices are offered.

Uganda is one of the most

Twins are usually considered bad luck in Africa. This pair brings good luck.

Christian countries in Africa. The penetration of Central Africa in 1878 by the White Fathers was the beginning of the modern mission era. Uganda was the heart of the effort by both Catholics and Protestants. Today half of the ten million population is Christian, with Catholics outnumbering Protestants about three to one. Almost a fourth of the people is Moslem, while the remainder are animists. The first African bishop of modern times came from the Ganda people, and today Kampala has its own African archbishop.

Religious success did not come easily, however. The first days were turbulent and marked by a savage persecution of Christians. One outburst saw fifteen page boys of the king perish by being burned alive because they would not apostatize. Twenty-two of the Catholic Uganda martyrs were canonized by Pope Paul VI in May, 1964.

243

Kenya is a country of blacks and whites that avoided the mistakes of Rhodesia. In the pioneer days of the British in Africa, it was intended to make Uganda the center for colonial activity. To establish communications, the British decided to build a railroad from the coast, across Kenya to Uganda. Railroad yards were set up about halfway, at a place called Nairobi. From this humble beginning, one of Africa's most modern cities arose. The railroad attracted white settlers, and before long the Kenya highlands were covered with neat farms and homesteads that might have been in England. Today the children of those early settlers do not call themselves English but Kenyans.

The area where the whites settled was the ancestral home of the Kikuyu tribe. The whites thought that they were buying their land from the Kikuyu but in the Kikuyu mind, instead of an outright purchase, the white settlers were given temporary leases. The Kikuyu land was held tribally and not individually. This misunderstanding was to have serious consequences years later when it became one of the causes for the Mau Mau rebellion.

The Kikuyu inhabit the slopes of Mount Kenya and the volcanic highlands. They attribute their origins to the Wakamba with whom they are similar in language and customs. They are a well-built, muscular people of average height. They live in sturdy circular houses with high walls and a conical roof.

They are the best farmers in East Africa, growing beans, millet, sweet potatoes, sugar-cane, tobacco, and bananas. They keep sheep and goats and also raise bees.

In many ways, they resemble the Upper Congo tribes. They are intensely superstitious and attach great importance to fetishes. They are great believers in blood-brotherhood and are hostile to strangers. They live in clans that are connected by blood ties. They have many rites, one of the most secret being "second birth" which is undergone by both sexes about the age of ten. Until the "new birth" is celebrated, no person can be circumcised, inherit property, or take part in religious rites. The fanatical Mau Mau leaders capitalized on these Kikuyu beliefs to terrorize and control the tribe.

However, the Kikuyu are not a backward race. They attach great importance to education. Many of them are Christians—Catholics and Church of England. There are Kikuyu priests and Sisters. It was these Christian Kikuyu who provided resistance to Mau Mau. Many of them were killed, including several Kikuyu nuns. Numerous problems remain to be settled for the Kikuyu but now that they have members in the Kenyan government there is hope that some solutions will be found to provide more living space for this growing tribe.

The Wakamba, or Kamba, one of the largest tribes in East Africa, are neighbors to the Kikuyu. It is believed that their original home

These Bakuria women live in rapidly modernizing Tanzania.

was in Tanzania from which they were driven by their enemies, the Masai. They are well-built, brave but not aggressive, born traders, and good farmers. They build rectangular houses with thatched roofs. The houses are collected into family villages. Agricultural work is still done by many Wakamba with wooden tools because they believe that iron tools will drive away rain.

The Wakamba grow beans, bananas, pumpkins, maize, and the staple, millet. These foods are planted in common plantations, being the property of all the family. When the surplus crops are sold, the money received belongs to all the family. Cattle, sheep, and goats are kept, and the milking is done by women. The Wakamba occasionally bleed their cattle in Masai-fashion, to get blood for food. This blood is often used to thicken millet-flour soup, a Wakamba favorite.

He calls himself a Kenyan, not English.

Her Kikuyu tribe produced the Mau Mau.

The Wakamba are divided into totemistic clans and the members of each clan are said to possess the characteristics of their totem. Thus the members of the Lion Clan are supposed to be brave and fearless while those of the Hyena Clan are sly and greedy. The Wakamba believe in a Supreme Being but pay little attention to him. Most worship is ancestral. The medicine men of the tribe are supposed to be able to prophesy and cure sickness. Charms also play an important role in Wakamba life.

Many Wakamba are now Christians, and mission education has broken down some of the old superstitions. During the Mau Mau rebellion in Kenya, the white settlers, unable to trust the Kikuyu, hired the Wakamba people in their place. This has improved their economic status, and they are not easily

ousted from all their new positions.

Another of the fifty-five tribes of Kenya is the Jaluo, or more simply, the Luo. The British settlers refer to the Luo as the "Americans of East Africa." The name is given to them because of their drive and tribal pride. The Luo are great wanderers and pioneers. They are spreading all over East Africa, occupying new territory and oftentimes crowding out the original settlers. Large groups of them are in Tanzania as well as in Kenya.

The Luo are a Nilotic people and possess the characteristics of that group. They are tall, very black, and speak a Sudanic language. They have the custom of knocking out the six lower front teeth, and hence are easily identified. They are quick to adopt Western ways and are great believers in modern education. They consider no one their equal. This feeling of superiority is carried over into their language. The original Bantus are *mwa,* foreigners; the Luos are *ji,* people.

In the old days of warfare, the Luos were a feared people. They were forever on the attack. They absorbed their enemies into the Luo tribe. Today, they are no longer able to expand by show of violence. But this doesn't stop the Luo. They simply move into unoccupied country and make it their own. They arrange marriages with members of Bantu tribes but the offspring of such unions always end up speaking only Luo. Where there is some resistance, they are not averse to casting a spell on a Bantu's water hole or making off with his cattle so that sooner or later he decides to move and leave the field uncontested.

Young Luo males leave the tribe to go off and work to earn money to buy a bride. As a result, the Luos are found all over East Africa as policemen, railroad workers, busboys, waiters, or what have you. They were quick to take advantage of the eight year Mau Mau trouble (begun in 1953), moving into jobs formerly held by the Kikuyu, jobs that the Kikuyu never got back because there was always a Luo brother or cousin to take over.

The Luos are particularly receptive to Catholicism, and large numbers both in Kenya and Tanzania have entered the Church. There are Luo priests and Luo Sisters. Some missioners believe that Luos will

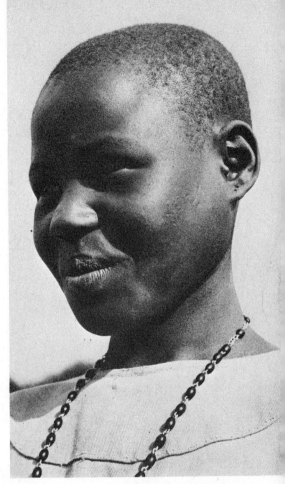

Florentia is a Bakwaya Christian girl.

play an important role in spreading the Faith in East Africa.

Another Nilotic tribe of Kenya is the Nandi. The word "Nandi" refers to a single tribe of that name, and also to a group of tribes such as the Kipsikis, Keyo, Suk, Dorobo, and others. In appearance and culture the Nandi are very similar to their cousins, the Masai. Like the Masai, they have the greatest respect and love for cattle. Milk is so sacred among the Nandi that they will not mix meat and milk in the stomach. If meat is eaten, no milk

247

Feeding a Wachaga baby requires no bottles or dishes when African ingenuity is used.

may be drunk for twelve hours, and then only after the meat-eater has purified his stomach with salt and water. Unlike the Masai, most Nandi are agriculturists and not nomads. They live in small settlements where each family has its house in the center of its farm.

The Nandi have a curious burial custom. Only the very old or very young are interred in the earth. Otherwise, the deceased is taken out at night and left on the ground several hundred yards north of his hut. Men are laid on their right sides, women on their left. Before leaving the body, the relatives cry out, "Hyenas, come and eat!" If after four days the body is not de-voured by wild beasts, a goat is killed and its blood sprinkled over the corpse. If the animals still do not eat the body, it is believed that the deceased perished through some witchcraft.

There are many other tribes in Kenya, a country slightly smaller than Texas and with a population of eleven million. Space does not permit a discussion of all of them. The Swahili have already been treated. The Galla, another important people, will be covered under Ethiopia, their proper homeland. Worthy of mention are such people as the Embu, Meru, Kipsiki, Suku, Watwa, Kavirondo, Elgeyo, Waboni, and Banyara.

This is an African beer pot. The warm, malty brew is drunk through long reed straws.

Ethiopians live in one of the world's oldest kingdoms. The people of Ethiopia believe that they are descended from Ethiops, one of the twelve children of Cush, a grandson of Ham and great-grandson of Noah. Ethiops is supposed to have migrated from Arabia to Abyssinia (another name for the country) after the flood. The children of Ethiops brought all the tribes of the area under their influence.

In any event, the people of Ethiopia are a very mixed stock today. They are the result of a Hamitic, Semitic, and Negro blending. Also within this country are found many of the races existing in a relatively

This Talib girl is Arab and Negro.

249

pure state. There are close to twenty-five million people in Ethiopia and the country is as large as France and Germany combined. Ethnologists count forty-three different tribes in the country.

The typical people of Ethiopia are represented in the Cushite and Amhara tribes. Racially, they are said to be 80 per cent Hamite, about 15 per cent Negro, and the remainder Semite—these figures refer to the blood lines of the average person and not to a population breakdown. Their language, Ethiopic, is believed to be the oldest Semitic language in Africa.

If Ethiopia is racially confused, it is also a land of many religions. The prevailing religion is Christianity. Ethiopia became Christian about 350 A.D., and by the seventh century the Bible had been translated into Ethiopic. The Christianity is Coptic, not in union with Rome. There are over eleven million Coptic Christians. Mohammedans number about three and a half million. There are Jews and also pagans.

The Falasha, or "black" Jews, are of interest. They claim to have descended from a son born to the Queen of Sheba and King Solomon. They live aloof from the rest of the Ethiopians and never marry outside their own group. They are forbidden to enter a Christian house under penalty of ritual purification. They have high moral standards and many ancient Jewish practices. They are a hard-working people who are good farmers. They also manufacture pottery, ironware, and cloth. They are relatively prosperous.

The Galla, another important tribe in Ethiopia, invaded the country in the sixteenth century. They are mostly pagans, although small Mohammedan and Christian groups exist. Excellent horseman, they provide the bulk of the cavalry for the Ethiopian army. They are farmers but also raise large herds of cattle, horses, sheep, and goats. They plow their fields with oxen-drawn plows in contrast to the Bantus who use hoes. While they are black in color, they are Caucasian people with European features. Their staple foods are meat and bread.

The Amharas, the dominant people of the country, are very intelligent. They too use a plow in preparing their fields. They grow cereals as their staple food, but raw meat is their favorite meal. Amhara architecture varies widely. In the city one can find stone houses, two stories high. In the country, the Amhara build crude huts of twigs and mud. The Amhara are quite tall, have oval faces, high foreheads, and frizzly hair. Their color varies from yellow to dark brown.

The Shangallas, who live in the northwestern plains, are Negroes. They are a very primitive people, living in caves during the rainy season, otherwise living without shelter other than the shade of trees. They are fierce and warlike, living on meat and wild honey. They practice a religion of fetishism, and govern their lives through omens.

When this Kenya Luo blows,
his toot can be heard for miles.

Never in history have any people made as rapid an advance in civilization as have the people of central Africa. In hardly a decade they evolved from a complicated tribalism into complex nationhoods. They have taken their place in such world bodies as the United Nations and have given Cardinals to the Church. Many problems remain to be solved, particularly poverty and industrialization, but advances come.

The ancestors of this Panamanian senorita reached the New World in a slave ship.

Chapter 8

Asia

A SIANS live in the world's largest continent, a vast sprawling region that covers one-third of the earth's surface and is homeland for almost two-thirds of mankind—one and a half billion people who despite wars, floods, famines, droughts, liquidation, and the new Western import of birth control, are increasing at the rate of fifteen million a year. The Asiatics are not evenly spread over their continent, for vast areas are inhospitable to human life and people must gather where they can grow food and exist. The people of Asia are also the most complex racially of any continent, for several hundred ethnic groups live here. India alone has more than 200 languages. Even with the most simple of groupings, sixty-eight different peoples must be recognized.

Nevertheless, the peoples of Asia do have many things in common. Most of them go to bed hungry every night, for Asia is a region of vast undernourishment and starvation. It is an area of high infant mortality. Most of the people of Asia live in under-developed countries despite the fact that many of them have been colonial subjects of Western powers. Asians have one other thing in common—very few of them are Catholics, although Christianity began on their continent.

Human life originated somewhere in Asia, therefore the Asian peoples are the oldest inhabitants of the earth. By migrations, invasions, and commerce, they have also contributed much in culture and history to the rest of the world.

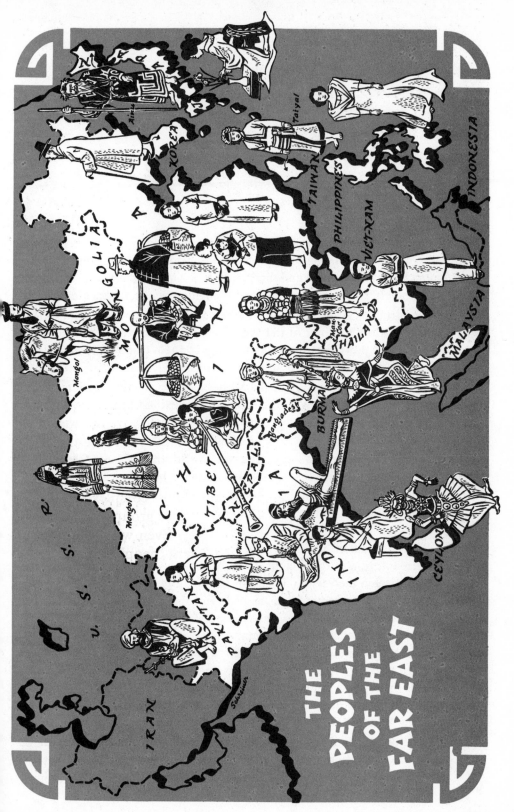

THE
PEOPLES
OF THE
FAR EAST

The Rise of the East

THERE IS a principle that the affairs of history move in cycles. Anne Morrow Lindbergh, in one of her books, interpreted this principle by means of a wave that first begins as a trough and then swells to gigantic force. Others have pictured the principle as a pendulum of time, swinging relentlessly back and forth.

Before the birth of Christ, Persia and Egypt dominated the world. Afterwards, the pendulum swung in favor of the West. The nations of the Western world became strong and powerful, and a small group of them came to dominate the rest of mankind.

Because of the Christian nature of the Western world, this domination helped in the spread of Christianity. With the explorers, went the Christian missioners. Whole peoples were enrolled under the banner of Christianity. This was all to the good. But unfortunately, there were some effects far from desirable.

In the minds of many people in the Eastern world, the Catholic Church became identified as a Western institution, and not as a boundary-less Church of all peoples as Christ meant it to be. This false idea was further strengthened by the slow growth of local clergy—a clergy that would identify the Church with local people.

Today the pendulum of historical power is swinging back to the East. Bishop Fulton J. Sheen attributes the decline of the West to the fact that many Western nations have rejected the very principles of Christianity that brought greatness.

China and India, representing half the people of the world, are giants aroused from the slumber of centuries. In a single decade they have adopted the skills of the West to advance themselves by a century. They and other nations of the East are using modern technology to build a new way of life. No serious student of history can fail to realize that the tremendous resources and populations of these countries will make them dominant in the world within a few generations. The unbalanced power of the West is ended. The pendulum is moving rapidly Eastward.

In view of this historical fact, the development of the Catholic Church in the East during recent generation, and particularly since the end of World War II, is of prime significance. For during this period, the inspired direction of the modern Popes has sought to remove the stigma of Western culture from Ca-

256

tholicism and to identify the Church with local cultures. Christ meant His Church for all men, and the Holy See is proving that very point by its insistence on the development of local clergies and hierarchies.

Vatican Council II was a dramatic demonstration of the change that has come to the Church. Hundreds of African and Asian prelates filled the Council halls, representing tens of thousands of native-born priests, Brothers and Sisters. Pope Paul VI also dramatized the Church's concern in the Third World by his journeys to such places as Hong Kong, the Philippines, India and Uganda.

It is shortsighted to accept the thesis that Christianity is suffering a mortal blow in the Far East because of various restrictive acts of some governments. It is true that in some areas prohibitions have been placed upon the importation of foreign missioners, and that missioners are being forced to work under handicaps. But a long-range analysis can only lead to the conclusion that the Church is being helped immensely by the trend of events.

Until recent years, the Church in the Far East had been largely a colonial Church with great masses of the Catholic population conditioned in their thinking by a feeling of dependence on the West. The Christians adopted Western clothes, sought jobs from the colonial ruler, and looked forward to a peaceful security as protegés of such powers as the British.

Now that foreign support has gone, the Christian must stand on his own two feet. He must prove that his religion is not a foreign intrusion but indigenous to his own customs and culture. This is all to the good. Strength, initiative, and local identification can only result.

The Church made the greatest forward strides in those free areas where religion was not tied up with an occupying Western power. In pre-Communist China, for example, Christianity had great prestige and was accepted as one of the religions of the country.

Thus it seems that the present turn of events towards independence and freedom will immeasurably aid the Church. Once the transitional difficulties and inconveniences are passed, the Church will assume a role of creativeness and vigor that it has never before experienced. With a completely national hierarchy and with the main body of clergy native, the Church will become an important factor in the national life of the new countries.

Western missioners will go to these new nations at the request of local bishops, and as a result their whole thinking and approach will be changed. They will go as assistants and helpers. They will be only temporary assistants to be replaced as more and more local clergy are ordained. The national clergy, in turn, will accept the responsibilities that will rightly be theirs.

The turn of events in the Far East is but one more evidence of the providence of God. Asia is becoming the focal center of the world, and will in the foreseeable future be the controlling power of the world. When that day comes, the Church will be strongly entrenched and ready to play its role in world conversion.

INDIA--the great

WE are the people of India. There are over 500 million of us living in a country half the size of the United States. We are Hindus, Christians, Moslems, Buddhists, Sikhs, Parsis. We represent peasants, Untouchables, factory workers, artisans, domestic servants, princes. We live in a land of great contrasts, of famine and food, of flood and drought, of great wealth and deep poverty, of giant steel mills and crude wooden plows. We are overcrowded, yet vast areas of our country are empty. We

sub-continent

number more than 300 tribes, speaking a babel of 179
languages and 544 dialects. We live in hovels and pal-
aces. Most of us are unimaginably poor yet in our land
lies untold buried treasures—coal, iron, mica, manga-
nese, and many others. While millions of us starve,
unowned cows wander our streets and are fed and cared
for. We believe in social predestination and talk of
democracy. Our very essence is religious, yet we scorn
pity and misery. We are the people of India.

Indians live in a land of great antiquity, beauty, disease, dirt, and division. The people of India are a complex and polyglot group. They are the result of many races and peoples intermingling. Most scientists believe that the population resulted by mixing the dark-skinned Dravidians who lived there long, long ago, light-skinned Caucasians and other invaders who came from the northwest, and the Mongolians who entered from Tibet and China. The result has been many types of people with cultural and racial differences.

Every sixth person in the world today is an Indian. The typical Indian is a Hindu and peasant. He is patient, a hard worker, gentle, kind, courteous, with a sense of humor. His annual income is hardly fifty dollars a year, so he is pitifully poor. He wears a loose shirt and a loose cotton piece called a "dhoti" —a long piece of cloth wrapped around the waist and between the legs. His wife wears a sari, a colorful piece of cotton wrapped to form both a skirt and upper part of the dress, with the end thrown over the shoulder or head. He owns a small piece of land but cannot grow enough to feed himself and his family. He believes that his life has been predetermined and that therefore there is no use fighting against conditions. If he tries to lead a good life he will be born to a higher position in his next reincarnation.

Despite India's awakening to the modern world, the caste system still prevails. Every Indian is inferior to another Indian because of a complex system called caste. Each caste is a world of its own from which there is no escape. No one knows how many castes there really are in India; more than 4,800 have been counted. The word "caste" is of Portuguese origin. The Indians use the word "varna" to mean the four main families of castes. This latter word is of Aryan origin and means "color." The system was probably set up by Aryan invaders and conquerors to preserve blood lines.

The Brahmins, or priestly caste, are the top of Hindu society. They are the rulers, and most politicians are Brahmins. The Brahmin's person is sacred. There are 1,800 Brahmin caste divisions. The Kshatriyas, or Warriors, are the second caste. They are supposed to protect the Brahmins and sacred cows with their lives if necessary. Unlike the Brahmins, they are permitted meat and fermented drinks. This caste is dying out.

The third caste, Vaisyas, or merchants, have the duty of increasing the prosperity of the country. In doing so, they usually benefit themselves. This caste is also dying out and many of its duties are being taken over by the fourth caste, the Sudras, whose duty is to serve the others. Most Indian peasants belong to this caste.

Some of the Tribes of India

Figures in parenthesis show number of millions of speakers. Tribes lacking a figure number less than a million are not included in census totals.

1. HINDUS *(by language)*
Kashmiri (1½)
Punjabi (16)
  Sikhs
  Jats
Sindi (4)
Gujarati (11)
Kachi
Marathi (21)
Konkani
Hindi (79)
Urdu
Bengali (54)
Uriya (11)
Assamese (2)
Nepali (2)

2. DRAVIDIANS *(by language)*
Telugu (26)
Tamil (20)
Kanarese (12)
Malayim (10)
Tula (10)
Kodagu
Oraon
Rajmahal
Khondi (2)
Toda
Khota
Singhalese (2)
Vedda

3. KOLARIANS *(by tribes)*
Santhal (2)
Munda (1)
Kharia
Mal-Paharia
Juang
Gadaba

Korwa
Kurku
Mehto
Savara
Bhil

4. TIBETO-BURMANS
(by tribes) (3)
Garo
Ladakhi
Champa
Garhwali
Magar
Lepcha
Manipuri
Meithei
Miri
Kachari
Kuki
Mikir
Khasia
Naga
Sherpa

5. UNCLASSIFIED
Malayan
Negrito
Indo-Arab
Baluchi
Afghan
Swati
Wazir
Yusufazi
Persian
Parsi
Eurasian

Mother's Day

THE MEHTA FAMILY lives in a small, modern two-story house on the outskirts of Delhi, India. Mr. Mehta is a minor government official. His family life is typical of his class but far superior to that of nine-tenths of India's people, most of whom are poor farmers.

The Mehtas are Hindus, the religion of eight out of ten Indians. Mr. Mehta, who was educated in Madras and London, is something of a religious skeptic while his Indian-educated wife is very orthodox. She believes fully in the Hindu doctrine that creation is a process of life, death, rebirth, and finally Nirvana, the eternal resting place of the spirit. She does not hold to all the taboos and is not overly caste conscious, but she does read every day from the Veda, or Hindu bible.

The Mehta day begins about five o'clock when Mrs. Mehta arises quietly so as not to awaken her husband. She dresses quickly, wrapping her graceful *sari* about her and over one shoulder. The sari is a cloth about nine yards long. One end is tucked in at the hips while the other is gracefully wound about the body. For outdoor wear, the sari is draped over the head. In olden days it was also used to cover the face. Mrs. Mehta has some saris made from beautiful fabrics for formal wear and one woven with silk thread particularly delights her. About the house, however, she wears saris made from colorful cottons.

After washing, she gets a fire going on which to prepare breakfast, sets the dining room table and wakens her three children—two boys and a girl. By seven o'clock, breakfast is ready. Outside the house, the street has become noisy with horns honking and various vendors shouting their bargains. While the children eat, Mrs. Mehta takes the morning newspaper and coffee upstairs to her husband, who by this time is sitting up in bed and rubbing his eyes. He is always served breakfast in bed.

Mrs. Mehta returns to the lower floor to find the children quarreling over breakfast. As she quiets them, the maid arrives for work. The maid immediately draws water and sets off to wash down the entranceway and the porch. Mrs. Mehta hurries about getting the children ready for school—no easy task. One of the boys is up in the mango tree behind the house. The other does not wish to take a bath. The girl resists having her hair combed. From upstairs, Mr. Mehta is calling for clean clothes, shouting that he will be late for the office.

In the Mehta household, all conversation is carried on in English. Mr. and Mrs. Mehta each speak Hindi, while Mr. Mehta also knows several other of the

179 Indian languages. Hindi, along with English, is the official language and is the native tongue of more than a quarter of India's 400 million people.

By nine o'clock, the children are off to school and Mr. Mehta, dressed in Western-type clothing, has gone to work. The house is strangely silent after all the rush and confusion. While the maid begins sweeping out the rooms, Mrs. Mehta goes into her small *puja,* or prayer room. Here she lights the oil lamp, reads from the Veda, and spends a short time in prayer and meditation. Then she returns to the kitchen for her own morning meal.

It is after ten o'clock before the morning dishes are cleaned and put away. Mrs. Mehta then opens the laundry hamper and begins sorting clothes with the maid. The boys wear white clothes most of the time, and these quickly become dirty. The children's clothes and her own *saris* are given to the maid for washing, while her husband's shirts are put aside for the washerman who will call the next day.

Mrs. Mehta then turns to the kitchen. It is a daily ritual that pots and pans must be scrubbed and made to shine. When everything is spick-and-span, she picks up a basket and rushes off to market to buy food. Time is at a premium since she must be back in the house before twelve to have the children's lunches ready for the woman with the basket who will deliver them to the school. Then she has a quick lunch for herself. The maid, who only works a half day, goes home.

At one o'clock, Mrs. Mehta picks up her favorite magazine and takes it up to her room. After reading for a while, she naps. This siesta is the only break she gets in her long day. After resting for about an hour and a half, she arises and begins her mending and sewing. Sometimes a friend will drop in during this period and gossip over a cup of tea. The talk is usually centered about home life and is typical of the talk of women everywhere.

Shortly after three, Mrs. Mehta is back in her kitchen getting ready for the evening meal. She is cleaning vegetables when the children come rushing in from school, calling for their tea and afternoon snack. She takes care of them with tea, jam and chappatties (wheat cakes), before sending them out to play. Her husband arrives home from work in the government's Community Welfare Department—the heart of India's program to rejuvenate 600,000 country villages. He tells his wife of some of the day's doings, then hurries upstairs to change his clothes so that he can be off to play cards with some of his cronies.

OCCASIONALLY, he reminds himself that he should spend more time with his wife of whom he continually boasts to his friends. His marriage had been arranged by his parents—in fact the arrangements were made while he was in England. The choice was a good one for Mrs. Mehta was truly a *sati* —an ideal wife.

"It is all right for Americans to talk about marrying for love," he is wont to say to his friends, "but look at all the divorces they have. It is better our way. Marry first, then love. After all, the parents are wiser in their selection than would be a lovesick youth. Here in India the love of a husband for his wife grows stronger year by year. In free-loving America the love is all used up by the time marriage takes place."

At seven o'clock, Mrs. Mehta summons the children indoors, an act that usually involves considerable struggle. She tells them to wash for dinner, but must supervise the operation. When this is done, she sets them to doing their homework. From the kitchen she must continually remind them to be quiet and study.

About eight, the children are summoned to dinner. The youngsters chatter away while they are fed, recounting the day's happenings in school. Sometimes they play guessing games in which mother joins. After dinner, they are hurried up to bed. This is the story-telling period, and Mrs. Mehta recounts tales from ancient Indian legends that she herself heard when she was a girl. In this way she teaches the elements of the Hindu religion. One by one, the three youngsters drop off to sleep.

WHEN MRS. MEHTA returns downstairs, her husband is back from his club, waiting for his dinner. About nine-fifteen, the two of them sit down at the dining table. Mr. Mehta does not talk much while he eats, and her remarks about the day's activities get monosyllabic answers. When the meal is over, Mr. Mehta goes upstairs to prepare for bed.

Mrs. Mehta clears the dining room and washes the dishes. After everything is put away, she takes the coals from the stove so that there will be no danger of fire. After a last glance around, she puts out the light and wearily climbs the stairs to her bedroom. She glances in at the children and notes with satisfaction that they are all sleeping soundly. Mr. Mehta is propped up in bed, reading a detective story. He puts the book down and talks to his wife as she prepares for bed. He has big plans for their annual vacation. He continues chatting away about the ideas that have come to him.

Suddenly, Mr. Mehta notices that his conversation is very one-sided. He glances over at his wife. She is already asleep. With a shrug of his shoulders, he looks at his watch. It is ten-thirty. He wonders why his wife is so tired when she has had nothing to do but stay at home all day. Pondering this new problem, he puts aside his book and pulls out the electric light.

Another day has ended for the Mehta family.

The Love of Man for All Men

"There are some unfortunately, today especially, who proudly boast of enmity, of hate and spite... Let us, however, follow on after our King of peace... He has taught us not only to have love for those of a different nation and a different race, but to love even our enemies. While our heart overflows with the sweetness of the Apostle's teachings, we chant with him the length, the breadth, the height, the depth of the charity of Christ, which neither diversity of race or culture, neither the wasteless tracts of ocean, nor wars, be their cause just or unjust, can ever weaken or destroy."

—Pope Pius XII, *Mystici Corporis*

An Indian bishop united with the Pope

The Untouchables are a people without caste. The Panchamas, or Untouchables, are at the bottom of India's social scale. In the Hindu world, these unapproachables are rated higher than beasts but less than men. The government would like to ignore them, calling them "depressed classes" or "scheduled classes." They perform the lowest and most menial tasks, have no rights, and are forced to live in the most squalid slums.

The lot of the Untouchables has improved somewhat in recent years. The late Mahatma Gandhi took in an Untouchable family and adopted the daughter of the family as his own. When the constitution for new India was written, the document declared that untouchability could not exist in any form. As a result, when a government official is asked about Untouchables, the standard reply is that they no longer exist. But it will take much more than words written on a piece of paper to convince the sixty million Indian Untouchables that the autocracy of Hinduism has ended.

No one will go so far today as to forbid the Untouchables to wear clean clothes but in the villages they are still forbidden to walk on certain streets lest a Brahmin might look upon them and be defiled. They are still not allowed to draw water from wells used by people of caste. They are banned from schools, temples, and cemeteries. When they enter their homes, they must do so bowing down. If an Untouchable dared to build a house of stone or mud brick, the Sudras would tear it down in holy rage.

Caste is the big stumbling block for India, and caste is the result of the Hindu religion. The only way one can enter a caste is to be born in it; the only escape is by death. Caste keeps India from being truly democratic. Caste hinders progress. Caste is country, family, faith, all in one. Despite the fact that the government has tried to end the caste system, it is too strongly engrained in the people. Hinduism may be a religion without theology, of pre-determinism, of frightening and vengeful gods. But it holds the minds of the people. It must be replaced by another idea, another philosophy.

265

Human labor is cheap in India. Women serve as beasts of burden while men supervise.

Prehistoric tribes live in the dense jungles of India's Andaman and Nicobar Islands. In 1949, a team of anthropologists stumbled through the Andamanese jungle to discover the Onges people who wore no clothes and who had not even achieved the progress of Stone Age men. The Onges did not know how to use or make stone implements for hunting or fishing.

The Onges are almost Pygmies, are distinctly Negroid in appearance, live on a diet of wild pork and fruits, and dwell in communal huts. They are hostile to all outsiders, killing strangers.

Two other primitive Andamanese tribes are the Jarawas and Sentinels. Little is known about them because of their hostility.

The people of Ceylon live on an island of tropical splendor, rich in history and legend. Ceylon is a country about the size of West Virginia with a total population of about twelve million. At one time Ceylon was connected to India by a strip of sand called "Adam's Bridge" which according to legend Adam and Eve crossed after being expelled from the Garden of Eden. It was by this land bridge that the Singhalese entered the island long before the time of Christ. Today, they make up two-thirds of Ceylon's population. The sandbar has disappeared and Ceylon is now an island.

The original inhabitants of Ceylon were the Veddas, a people similar to the native Australians. By

266

India has made great technological progress; but even in Bombay old ways survive.

retreating into the jungles the Veddas were able to survive from the invaders. Veddas still exist today, many of them in the most primitive states.

Ceylon owes much to many peoples and many cultures. Moors, Greeks, Tamils, Dutch, and Portuguese all left their mark. Ceylon was among the first Asian countries to make Buddhism a national religion. In Kandy, the island's cultural capital, each August a wild celebration takes place when what is supposed to be Buddha's tooth is carried in procession. On one of the peaks of the island is the famed "Footprint of Buddha." It was from here the great religious leader is said to have stepped into heaven.

The people of Ceylon support themselves by growing rubber, tea, and coconuts. The mountains of the island have brought a fortune by yielding rubies, sapphires, emeralds, and amethysts. But because there is no coal or iron, the island is without heavy industry. Ceylonese craftsmen turn out fine ceramics and lacquerware. In making the latter, many of the hand-carved wooden dishes, trays, and vases receive as many as thirty-five coats of lacquer.

Although Buddhism is supposed to be a religion of tolerance, Buddhist monks on Ceylon have been violent in their opposition to Christianity. Communism is strong on the island, using friction between the Singhalese and Tamil peoples to its advantage.

267

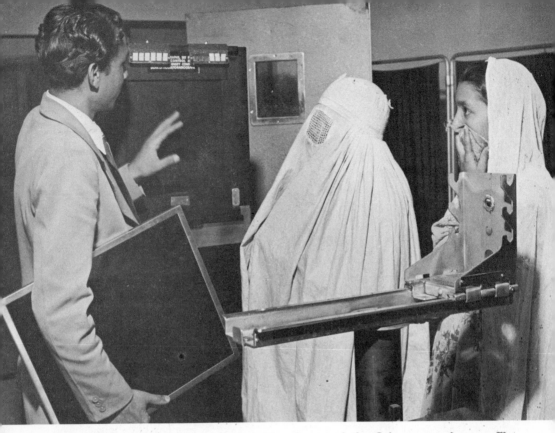

At an X-ray center in Pakistan, the old and new of the Orient come into conflict.

The Pakistanis are a Moslem people who were once part of India. In the days when the British were preparing to withdraw from India, the people of Pakistan let it be known that they wanted no part of Hindu India. Hence, the country of Pakistan was set up, divided into two parts and separated by a thousand miles of India. Today 86 per cent of the population of almost 80 million are Moslems. In 1971 India invaded East Pakistan, created 9.5 million refugees and set up the separate state of Bangladesh.

There are many languages spoken in Pakistan. The most common is Bengali. Urdu has been promoted as the official language because it is used by influential people. Other tongues used are Punjabi, Sindhi, and Pashtu. Only 13 per cent of the people of Pakistan are able to read or write.

Most of the population is engaged in agriculture, growing wheat, rice, millet, cotton and jute. The country has little industry. The people of the country are poor. The government is trying to improve conditions by offering free education to youth and adults and by developing industry. However, age old traditions and customs make change difficult.

Pakistan is the fifth largest country in the world, and the largest Moslem country. It is a traditional Moslemism that keeps its women veiled and in seclusion. It is a Moslemism that carries out strict Moslem practices. It is a Moslemism that is hostile to Christianity. Few converts are made; and if a Moslem does become a Christian, he is cut off from family and friends and can hardly find a livelihood. Yet the Pakistani is a religious man who puts his trust in God. The Pakistan constitution declares: "The entire universe belongs to God Almighty, and the authority which He has delegated to the State of Pakistan is a sacred trust." Here is a solid basis on which to build any new country.

The Burmese are called the happiest people in Asia. Burma is almost the same size as Texas and has twelve million people. Although it stands between the Indian peninsula and China, it is to the latter country that the Burmese look. In place of Aryans, its people are Mongols; instead of Hinduism, the prevailing religion is Buddhism.

The Burmese make up half the population of the country, and these literate, cultured people have a strong disdain for the hill tribes. In all, there are some eighty tribes in Burma, with the Karens and Shans the largest (each 10 per cent of the population). There are over a million Indians in Burma, and a quarter million Chinese.

The Burmese are an attractive and friendly people who receive strangers with great hospitality.

A social worker in Karachi, Pakistan.

In the Terai area of India, a hundred thousand acres of land have been made free of malaria and cleared for settlement by refugees from Pakistan. Here the homeless are building a new life.

They live a free and independent life. Eight out of ten Burmese live from farming, and there is always enough to eat and usually a surplus of rice to be exported. Burmese children attend school and literacy is thus higher than anywhere else in Southeast Asia.

Burmese women are attractive and well dressed. Nowhere else in Asia do women have the freedom and independence that they do in Burma. They keep their maiden names after marriage, and share equal property rights with men.

Burma is probably the most intense Buddhist country in the world. All Burmans enter monasteries in their youth as novices. The stay may be short or long, but it does give every Burman a good knowledge of his religion. Buddhist temples dot the Burmese skyline and Buddhist monks in their saffron colored robes are seen everywhere.

Living in eastern Burma on a great plateau are the Shan people —the Chins, Shans, Kachins, and many more. Many of these people still tattoo themselves from waist to thigh. Some of these mountain tribes are warlike and hostile. Most of the hill tribes are pagans, believing in omens and witchcraft. The Karens are unfriendly to outsiders, liking seclusion, but they are not warlike. They dress in colorful costumes, wearing pounds of beads and other jewelry. The Chins have a proverb: "A man should drink, fight and hunt, for only women and slaves should work." Visitors report they live up to this philosophy.

Among Padaungs of Burma, beauty is a matter of long necks stretched from childhood.

The Pacific and Indian worlds meet in Malaysia. The Federation of Malaysia (exclusive of Singapore, which is almost completely a Chinese city) is about the size of California in land area and half the size in population. Of the nine million people in the country, 40 per cent are Malay, 40 per cent Chinese, 15 per cent Indian, and the remainder divided into some twenty primitive tribes. Malaysia has the world's richest source of tin, the finest rubber plantations, and is one of the most advanced agricultural lands in the Orient.

While the Malays call themselves "Men of the Country," they are wrong on several counts. They are not the original inhabitants, having come there from Pacific Islands, and they have practically ceded their country to the more aggressive Chinese. Singapore was once a Malay city from which the Malays withdrew as the Chinese arrived. Today the Malays are small farmers while the Chinese and Indians work for wages and control the business life of the country.

Two other racial groups in the peninsula are the Negritos and the Sakais. The latter are the original inhabitants. They are a small, light-colored, wavy-haired people who keep to the densest part of the jungle. The Sakais paint their faces, live in communal longhouses, and hunt with blowguns. They plant tapioca and rice. The women wear only skirts, and the men loincloths. They are pagans.

Thailand is a country of prosperous and freedom loving people. Once called Siam, the country was renamed in 1939 as Thailand, which means Land of the Free People. Thailand is somewhat smaller than Texas and has close to 35 million people. The majority of the inhabitants belong to the Thai tribe, but there are large numbers of Chinese and Indians, and a dozen other tribes of whom many are primitive hill people.

The earth has made the Siamese people prosperous. They grow rice for export, and there has been no famine for a long time. About 85 per cent of the people live by agriculture, most of them owning their own land. There is very little manufacturing or mining in the country.

The Thais are friendly and hospitable people. They were always able to keep their independence in a world of colonies. They are quick to laugh and make jokes, enjoy plays and dances, and easily adapt themselves to the conveniences of the Western world. They love to talk and gossip, eat hot and spicy foods. They move between the Eastern and Western worlds easily and with sure confidence.

Buddhism is the official religion, and plays an important role in the life of the people. As in Burma, young men enter a monastery for at least a few months. Every family makes a daily gift to the monks who come around each day to beg. Buddhist temples are unbelievably beautiful and artistic. The Temple of the Emerald Buddha is one of the most extraordinary buildings in the world. Surrounded by hundreds of other buildings, enclosed by galleries painted with artistic murals, it represents the high point of Thai art and devotion. One curious Thai trait is shown in this group of buildings. As the visitor walks through immense thresholds and massive carved doors from one area to the next, he is followed by the unexpected tinkling of thousands of wind bells hung in the eaves. This is an imaginative touch that is distinctly Thai.

In the hills of northern Thailand live tribes that are not of Thai stock. Many of them are the same tribesmen who live in eastern Burma and southwestern China. Some of them like the Khas and Laos are wild and free. The Karens are also an interesting people who prefer their own way of life to that of their more numerous Thai neighbors; they are excellent jungle hunters. The Lisa, Meo, and Yao are isolated Tibeto-Burman groups. One other interesting group are the Kui, Indonesiod aborigines who live on the Korat plateau near the Cambodian border. Despite their remoteness and many primitive ways, they hand-weave silk garments that are attractive and artistic. Finally, there are the Phi Thong Luang (Yellow Leaf People) who elusively hide away in the jungle, and who are nearly extinct.

Siamese dancers in the ruins of Angkor Wat mark a once-great Oriental civilization.

Laotians live in a "never, never" land that is off the Asian main line. The three million people of Laos live in an Indo-China country about the size of Missouri. They are a charming, easy going folk whose favorite expression *"bo pen yan,"* meaning "It really doesn't matter," best illustrates their philosophy of life. They are of Thai origin and therefore have all the admirable qualities of the Siamese.

Laotians live in a rich but Red exploited land. There is enough food for everybody. Most of the people are engaged in agriculture, but they only cultivate enough land for their own needs. Fish and fruit round out their diet. They practice a casual sort of Buddhism with many festivals which give the opportunity for spectacles and enjoyment. Because their country borders two Communist nations (China and North Vietnam), Laotians try to get along with the Reds. An old proverb gives a clue to the Laotian reasoning: "The water drops, the ants eat the fish. The water rises, the fish eat the ants. It is better to love than hate."

There are a number of hill tribes in Laos, of which the Meo is the most interesting. These people build their villages on the crest of hills, grow opium for barter. They wear dark blue trousers and blouses held together with wide sashes. The Meos are pagans, superstitious, and quite averse to change.

Cambodians at one time ruled all of Southeast Asia. The visitor to the great crumbling ruins at Angkor Wat can see in the sculptures and magnificent bas-reliefs the history of Cambodia when it was a great power under the Khmer tribe. Today the Cambodians lead a leisurely life, content to work their small farms and live in small villages. Their pleasures are simple —chewing betel nut, talking, and taking part in Buddhist festivals. They are little concerned with the happenings in the outside world, worrying only about North Vietnamese military incursions. Their country is about the size of Utah, and there are about seven million of them.

The Vietnamese live in a country divided. Vietnam is a country approximately the size of New Mexico, containing thirty-five million inhabitants, equally divided between North and South governments. As a result of the war following the French withdrawal, the Communists seized the northern half. The northern section, known as Tonkin, was heavily Catholic. Many of these people fled as refugees to the south. The main people of Vietnam are the Annamese, but in the hills are Thai, Man, Meo, Montagnards, and Lolo tribesmen.

Vietnam was the meeting point for Asia's two leading cultures— Chinese and Indian. In the end, it was the Chinese culture that prevailed, although the Indian left traces in ruined monuments and forts. Yet, today, in many parts of

Rice is the staple of the Orient. This Vietnamese farms in a fertile rice area.

Vietnam, one can almost believe that he is in China.

The richest part of the country is the Red River delta in the north. This was the rice bowl area not only for Vietnam but for other Asiatic countries that needed surplus rice. Hanoi, the former capital, also in the north, produced the country's intellectuals and one of the great schools of Chinese landscape painting began there. But now that section is firmly closed off from South Vietnamese life.

The Vietnamese, or perhaps better, the Anamese, do not have the friendliness of the Laotian or Cambodian. They are more remote and withdrawn. The reason is probably that they have been under the control of one domineering outside group after another. First by the Chinese, then the Cambodians, then the French, and finally Americans and Chinese. They have suffered much. They are a freedom loving people, and as proof of this, one need but recall the long line of refugees who fled the northern tyranny, many at the risk of their lives. Now busy trying to reconstruct their country after many years of war, they have little time for outsiders or the luxuries of life.

The people of Vietnam are a family people. They live in family units and farm in family groups. They are a loyal and faithful people, many of them becoming martyrs rather than deny their faith. South Vietnam is the most Catholic country on the Asian mainland. The first two presidents of the country were Catholic. There are Buddhists in Vietnam and also some strange hybrid sects.

The NEW COLOSSUS

One fourth of mankind lives in China. Most people think of China as a country of one people, yet anthropologists list more than 275 tribes within the borders of the colossus we know as China. The Chinese proper are the Han people but in addition to them there are twenty million aborigines in the southwest — Meos, Thai, Lolos, Hakka, Mon-khmer, and many others. Mongol, Turkish, and Tungan people number two million. There are more than a million Manchus. Yet despite these differences, there is a remarkable similarity among all Chinese. Dialects may differ but the written language is the same, and excluding small pockets of Chinese Jews, Chinese Moslems, and the larger body of Chinese Christians, the people of China are remarkably alike in their religious ideas which are formed from Confucianism, Buddhism, and Taoism.

The history of China begins in the early Pleistocene era. This is proved by the discovery of skulls and other bones (called the Peking Man), representing some forty-five people. The earliest written records date back to 1200 B.C. Where the Chinese came from before the Peking Man era, no one knows. We do know that over the years many other tribes and nations invaded China, only to be absorbed within the Chinese. Even today the exact population is not known but it is believed to be in excess of 780 million people.

Protectors of the Legacy of Chinese Culture
THE OVERSEAS CHINESE

Asia 12,500,000		Africa 50,000	
Malaysia	3,500,000		
Thailand	3,000,000	Oceania 41,000	
Indonesia	2,000,000	Hawaii	32,700
Hong Kong	3,800,000	Australia	17,390
Americas 500,000			
United States	300,000	Europe 15,000	
Brazil	65,000	Great Britain	13,000
Canada	47,000		

With the culture of the China mainland being systematically destroyed by the iconoclastic Chinese Communists, it will be the task of the Overseas Chinese to preserve ancient traditions until their homeland is once again free.

—CHINA

The roots of China are in the good earth. The Chinese belong to a nation of farmers. Everywhere one goes in China, the landscape shows the results of man's preoccupation with the soil. Generation after generation has toiled on the land, changing and forming it. Although China has some large cities, 80 per cent of its people live by farming. Thus the country can truly be called a nation of farmers. Centuries of famine, invasion, and growth have pushed the Chinese into every area of their country that can possibly support life. It is not an exaggeration to say that no good land remains uncultivated.

Because of the high population density on what is good land, the Chinese live on the edge of want. The balance is precarious. Disease, flood, or drought can mean disaster for there is no surplus to fall back on. Some geographers estimate that within the last century a hundred million people of China have died from famine alone. The problem is a complex one because all the available soil and natural resources are being utilized. Modern techniques are lowering the death rate, and China's population is increasing at the rate of three million a year. The Communist government has liquidated millions of peasants in an attempt to find a solution, and now is promoting birth control.

Mehong tribesmen are a Chinese-Tibetan mixture.

These Chinese lumbermen are mountaineers. They represent typical faces of their land.

The average Chinese is poor. His home is small, and he and his family must labor incessantly on his couple of acres to grow enough food to keep all alive. His diet is monotonous, seldom varied by meat. Even rice to many families is a luxury.

Despite his lot, the Chinese is a man of ready humor. It is a humor born of realism, common sense, lack of hurry, and tolerance. His is a wisdom of the centuries, for the Chinese are the most mature race on earth. The Chinese have a high code of honor. They are shrewd businessmen. Their friendship is generous. They have all the necessary qualities to live at peace with themselves and their fellowmen. Chinese conservatism is rooted in pride and satisfaction in their ancient culture. This is a source of national strength and a guarantee, that despite surface changes enforced by Red masters, the fundamental pattern of Chinese life will endure.

The Chinese have long had a respect for learning and the arts. From the most ancient times, scholars have been held in esteem, and a man can do nothing more noble than to cultivate his mind. Poetry has also been a favorite form of literature, but it is a gentle poetry painting magical pictures with but few words. Chinese art follows the same technique, eliminating nonessentials, and leaving the imagination to supply many details. Chinese architecture is distinctive, yet it harmonizes with nature and blends into the landscape. Chinese artisans have created works of beauty in metal, bone, wood, jade, ivory, and porcelain.

279

Two views of Communist China. This butcher shop is well stocked with pork sides. China places great stress on universal education and for this the Reds must receive credit; unfortunately, all education is propagandized and distorts outside reality.

Rice is the back-breaking staple of the Orient. This Japanese mother is weeding.

A Lolo tribesman from the remote hills.

Family life is the secret of understanding Chinese society. The Chinese way of living derives its strength from the teachings of the sage, Confucius. Filial piety, respect for one's ancestors, is the basis for his ethical code. As a result, the family, with the father as center of authority, has been the foundation of Chinese society. A married son does not set up a separate household, but merely adds rooms to his father's house. The family system breeds a sense of family honor; any disgraceful act on the part of any member of the family reflects on the whole family. The family gives the Chinese a sense of social survival, and so satisfies his craving for immortality. Only a son can perform ancestral rites, hence it is the greatest of disappointments for a Chinese not to beget sons.

The Church had built a strong nucleus in China before the Communists arrived. In 1294, Father John of Montecorvino, a Franciscan, began preaching the Catholic religion in Peking and was later appointed the first archbishop. However, the overthrow of the Mongol empire and the conquests of Tamerlane undid his work. Saint Francis Xavier died trying to get to China. Other Jesuits, such as Father Mateo Ricci, did get in and reestablished the Church.

In 1949, when the Communists took control of China, there were a Chinese cardinal, 30 Chinese bishops and prefects, 2,700 Chinese priests, 5,200 Chinese Sisters, and 650 Chinese Brothers laboring with 5,380 foreign missioners. The Church conducted universities in Peking, Shanghai, and Tientsin. There were three and a half million Catholics. Today, the foreign missioners are expelled, churches closed, and Chinese clergy killed or in jails. The number of Chinese martyrs will probably never be known.

The Chinese have known invaders and persecutors many times in their long history. From the viewpoint of time, Communism is but a passing nightmare. China will be free again, for the Chinese people are too sane to perpetuate the disease that is Communism. When that day comes, the Church may have to begin anew; but Christ assuredly will return to China.

The racial types of Southeast Asia are predominantly of Chinese and Malay origins.

A Buriat of Outer Mongolia

Nothing in Asia is quite like the home of the Tibetans. Although Tibet is twice the size of Texas, there are hardly a million people in this vast territory because most of the country is desolate plateau that will support neither man nor beast. The strong, hardy people who do live there are a branch of the Mongolian race. Most of them are nomads wandering over the bleak plateau, hemmed in by the Himalayan and Karakorum ranges where there are fifty peaks over 25,000 feet high. The nomadic Tibetans live in black tents woven from the hair of their yaks, a beast whose milk forms an important part of Tibetan diet. In the few valleys, some Tibetans have small farms, raising barley and other grain crops. The farming Tibetans live in small stone houses.

Although Tibet is now a part of Communist China, it was for many years a religious kingdom ruled by Buddhist monks called lamas. The many monasteries of the region serve as centers of learning and government. Practically every aspect of Tibetan life is governed by lamaism, and the Dalai Lama, or head abbot, wields great power.

The city of Lhasa is the Mecca of Tibet. It is here that all lamaistic Buddhists wish to make pilgrimage. Lhasa itself is set in a sheltered valley and the people are able to grow vegetables and fruit trees. The palace of the Dalai Lama, one of the most imposing buildings in the world, rises over the city, an ever-present reminder of lama power.

"The primeval home of the Mongols is the region known as Mongolia, where every mountain is a king and every lake or stream a national divinity." Thus does one writer describe the bleak country known as Mongolia, a vast and desolate land half the size of the United States and numbering no more than one million people. Yet it was from this unprepossessing region that Ghengis Khan launched an empire that extended all the way to Europe.

The Mongols, sometimes called Tartars, are a robust and hardy people, capable of enduring great hardships. They prefer to live as nomads wandering over their sparse country, seeking grasslands for their sheep, goats, cattle, horses, and camels. They are expert horsemen, often spending fifteen hours a day in the saddle. They are a hospitable people who easily become suspicious of outsiders. They live almost entirely on meat and milk. Mare's milk is a particular delicacy. Mongols eat meat from horses, camels, or dogs and find each perfectly satisfactory.

Their religion is the superstitious type of lamaism practiced in Tibet. They go on frequent pilgrimages to the various monasteries and shrines. It is the custom for one son from every family to enter a monastery and become a monk. As in Tibet, the lamas wield great power.

In recent years, large numbers of Chinese emigrated to Inner Mongolia, taking over whatever fertile areas they could find for farms.

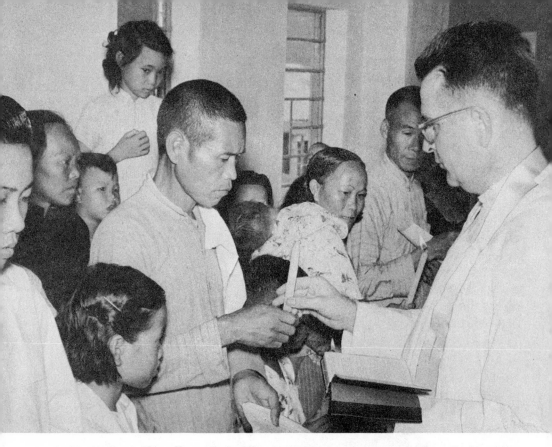

At his mission in Hong Kong, Father Howard Trube baptizes refugees from Red tyranny.

Emigrants have been put as high as two million but population estimates are uncertain. The Belgian Scheut Fathers developed flourishing missions in Inner Mongolia, ministering to almost 160,000 Catholics. However, all conversion work has been halted. The Soviet Union controls Outer Mongolia and has halted the nomadic life of the people by collectivizing herding. Outer Mongolia is a completely closed land with the power of the lamas broken. Inner Mongolia has been taken over by the Chinese Communists, the people have been regimented, lamaism has been subverted, and Catholicism persecuted by closing the churches and driving out or arresting the priests.

Hong Kong is like a New York City subway train at rush hour. It has been established that people were living on the British island we know as Hong Kong as many as three thousand years ago. Later the Mao and Yao tribes settled there. Today, this small island set off the coast of China is crowded with over four million people of whom well over half are refugees from Chinese Communism.

These refugees arrived in Hong Kong with nothing but a love for freedom. They wandered through the valleys and bleak hills of this British Colony seeking any spot of land where they might set up a shack built from scraps. Until they found such a spot they slept in alleys and doorways or any hole that might provide shelter. Their only bed was a straw mat over the ground. They ate what scraps they could beg or scavenge.

The refugees are a cross section of China, and the refugee settlements a babel of dialects. There are mountaineers from Szechwan, farmers from Honan, shopkeepers from Kwangtung. There are lawyers, engineers, dock workers, people of every imaginable trade. And most of them had fled with their wives and children.

The task of handling this influx of humanity was too much for the Hong Kong officials. They needed help and the charitable organizations provided it. Schools and clinics were set up in the refugee areas. Housing projects were begun. Work projects were initiated and later replaced by home industries and co-operatives. The results were twofold: the immediate problems of the refugees were taken care of and the Church won tremendous good will that is now resulting in thousands of conversions each year. Hong Kong's problems are far from completely solved but the refugees are being integrated into the busy life of this island of freedom. Also the presence of so many people who gave up everything for freedom is a reminder to the free world to value its own freedom.

There are a half million people in Hong Kong who make their living by fishing. Many of these people spend their whole lives aboard tiny fishing craft. There they are born and there they grow up and there they eventually die. Often four generations live on one tiny craft. Boat people do not even go ashore to do their marketing. Sampan vendors, selling groceries, dry goods, vegetables, or anything desired, pole their way daily around the boat anchorages. Some of the boats, usually the larger ones, fish by day. The smaller boats fish by night, using bright kerosene lamps to attract the fish into the nets. At dawn the boats return to the harbor and the weary fishing family finally lies down to sleep.

It is estimated that two hundred thousand people live on these fishing boats. Many of these boat people are Catholics and on their sampans one can find small shrines to the Sacred Heart or the Blessed Virgin. The Church has long been interested in the boat people. Each year the Bishop of Hong Kong blesses the Catholic fleet. Missioners have also been active in trying to improve the lot of these hard-working fishermen, who provide the colony with food, often at the cost of their own lives; no season passes without the loss of ships and men in the changeable South China Sea.

Several priests assisted the Government to organize a co-operative Fish Market, eliminating the middlemen. The fisherman now gets 94 per cent of the wholesale price of his fish whereas formerly he received but thirty. Loan societies were set up and schools opened for the children of fishermen.

Taiwan (Formosa) is the homeland for three peoples. Formosa is a Portuguese word meaning beautiful and the people of Formosa believe that their island is one of the most beautiful places on earth. They, however, call it by its old Chinese name, Taiwan, which means Great Bay. Formosa itself is about twice the size of New Jersey and today has a population of fifteen million people.

There are three different types of people on Formosa. First, there are the native Taiwanese. They are of Chinese origin, many of whom are descendants of ancestors who emigrated there in the seventeenth century. There are about ten million Taiwanese on the island. Most of them are farmers, using the methods of China. They have terraced farms, water buffaloes, two-wheeled carts, and ducks. Rice is the main crop and two harvests a year are not uncommon. They also grow sweet potatoes, sugar cane, bananas, and oolong tea.

The second class of people on the island are recent arrivals. They are refugees from Red China. Formosa is the seat of the Free China Government and many of these people are employed in administrative posts. Others are professional people — teachers, doctors, lawyers, engineers, and so on. They number over three million. Under their impetus, the island is being rapidly developed. New roads are being built, new schools erected,

A Free Chinese sentry stands guard.

and new industries established.

The third people are the aborigines, the original inhabitants of the island. There are nine original tribes on the island. These people mostly live in the thickly forested mountains; and up until a few years ago, many of them were head-hunters. Even today they live apart from the rest of the people, carrying on old traditions and customs, protected by the government. They are of Malay origin, speaking a number of dialects. Some of the aborigines are tattooed on their faces. Several of the tribes have attractive and colorful costumes, but often now these are only worn for the benefit of tourists.

Up until the end of World War II, the Japanese controlled the island. Some few Japanese remain. During the Japanese period, mission work on the island was in the hands of Spanish missioners, few in number. With the expulsion of missioners from China, large numbers of priests, Sisters, and Brothers were transferred to Taiwan, including over a hundred Chinese priests. The result has been a concentrated mission effort in all parts of the island with phenomenal success. New parishes are springing up everywhere, and large numbers are studying for baptism. In the beginning, conversions were mainly among the mainland refugees. Now progress is being made among the Taiwanese and aborigines.

Catholic aboriginals of the Sun Moon tribe pose with their Maryknoll pastor.

The Spot Below the Candle

PAK YANG WUN lives with his wife and four children in a broad and fertile valley southeast of Seoul. Conservative and industrious, he has cultivated his little farm so that every inch of ground helps support the family. By American standards he would be called poor, but by Korean standards he makes a fair living.

It was not always thus. Pak and his family suffered under the rigors of war. Security is only several years old. Before that the Pak family was a refugee family, and before that Pak and his wife lived under the Communists in North Korea.

Pak originally lived near Pyongyang, the North Korean capital. Both he and his wife belonged to farming stock. It was in Pyongyang that the Paks were married and it was there that the first two children were born.

"It was not good living under Communism," Pak reminisces. "But that was our ancestral home. My parents were there and my grandparents."

Pak never saw his wife but for one brief glimpse before he married her. The marriage was arranged by a *chungma,* or "go-between." The chungma had been called in by the elder Pak and hired to find a bride for his son. The old lady had a ready list, and it was not long before she suggested the name of Okpoonie, White Crockery. She was a girl of marriageable age who lived with her parents on a farm in a near-by village.

The wedding was arranged. One day Pak Yang Wun went to the village to get a look at the future bride.

"My friends had been telling me that she was cross-eyed and full of marks of chickenpox," Pak recalls. "I didn't dare go close, but I saw her from a distance. She was not bad to look at, and the chungma said she was used to hard work. I figured I was lucky."

"I did not see my husband until our wedding day," Mrs. Pak remembers. "I will never forget that day. I was so frightened! I remember sitting in our house waiting for the women to dress me. I dared not speak for that would have been bad manners and bad luck. Mine was a very traditional family.

"Finally, the women came and oiled and coiled my hair. My eyes were sealed shut, and my face was painted a dead white except for four red spots, one each on my cheeks, forehead and chin. My dress was red satin. I wore a fan-shaped crown that my parents had rented from the chungma. My friends came to see me and tried to make me laugh. But I never smiled. Then the room began to fill up with guests. Suddenly, I heard a cry that the bridegroom was coming. I thought I would die! Of course, I couldn't see my husband with my sealed-up eyes. But I remember hearing his voice. I thought it was very manly."

At the time of their wedding, neither the bride nor the bridegroom was Christian. Pak entered his bride's home accompanied by his best man who carried a goose, symbolizing faithfulness in marriage. After bows were made to the ancestral tablets of the bride's family, Pak and his companion took places at the end of a mat spread on the floor of the *kahn*, or main room of the house.

The bride was led in by the chungma and her mother and stood at the opposite end of the mat. Her bound hands were lifted level with her eyes and she made three solemn bows, sinking each time almost to the floor. Pak made two bows from the waist and a sort of half bow. The ceremony, following Confucian principles, indicates that the wife must humble herself before her husband and can never be his social equal. The husband, though courteous, is always to show his dignity and authority.

After the bowing a wine drinking ceremony took place, followed by more bowing. Then the bride was led away while the husband and guests took part in a banquet. When the banquet was over, White Crockery was led to the house of her father-in-law where she and her husband were to live. The wedding was over.

"My mother-in-law was a very wise and kind woman," Mrs. Pak said. "She did not make me do all the work as so many mothers-in-law do. The life of a daughter-in-law can be very hard."

In 1948, the young couple had their first child, a son. He was simply called Pak One. The following year a girl was born and named Kneedengah, Precious One.

"Life was becoming more and more difficult under the Communists," Pak recalls. "Taxes were high, many men were being taken into the army, and there was a great deal of uncertainty. Then the war began. That was in June, 1950. We thought the war would soon be over because the North Koreans quickly pushed the ROK and United Nations troops back to a little area around Pusan.

"Then in September the whole picture changed. The South Korean troops counterattacked. Seoul was recaptured and within a month the Communists were driven across the Yalu River. We were very happy to be free once again."

BUT FREEDOM was not of long duration. Within a few days, the situation was reversed. At the end of November, 200,000 Chinese Communist troops crossed the Yalu into Korea. The United Nations force had to retreat. Many North Koreans decided to flee south while there was still time.

"I decided to take advantage of the opportunity," declared Pak. "My wife and I packed what few belongings we could carry—food and winter clothing. My parents and grandparents were too old to travel, so they stayed behind. My wife and I each took one of the babies and set out. We did not know what was ahead of us but anything seemed better than life under the Reds."

Thus the Pak family became two statistics among the nine million Koreans made homeless or refugees by the war. The journey south was a nightmare. The roads were clogged with refugees and retreating troops. There was bombing and shooting all around. They had to crawl across wrecked bridges and sleep among the ruins of burned out towns.

When they finally reached the south, behind UN lines, they found great con-

Korean gentleman: grace and dignity.

fusion. They were just four among suffering millions. Over a half million homes had been destroyed by the war. Another half million had been damaged. Two million Koreans were dead or to die from bombs, bullets, and exposure. Over a hundred thousand children were orphaned and wandering the streets.

The Paks reached a refugee area near Pusan. It was winter and some shelter was imperative. Out of scraps of tin and wooden boxes, Pak built a crude shack. Then he went looking for work. He finally found a job as porter for American troops. The work was hard and the pay little but it at least kept them alive while so many were dying.

It was in Pusan that the Paks had their first contact with Christianity. Both their babies became ill and it was feared that the boy would die. On the advice of friends, Mrs. Pak took the children to a clinic operated by American Sisters. Here she received help in the form of medical attention and food. The Sisters sent her to Father Joseph Connors, an American priest from Massachusetts, who gave her more food and used clothing. With care, the babies became well.

The war meanwhile settled down to a stalemate and long truce negotiations. Mr. Pak found a better job and things improved slightly. He was able to save a little money by drastic economies. With this he bought a small patch of ground from a desperate refugee family whose father had been killed along with several sons. Pak went up to this property and built a small house.

When he returned to Pusan, he discovered that his wife had given birth to a girl. Because of the kindness of the Sisters and the priest, Mr. and Mrs. Pak had started to study Catholic doctrine. They were baptized just before they left Pusan, two among a quarter-million Catholics. Father Connors also helped Pak with seed and farm implements, through Catholic War Relief Services.

THE FIRST TWO YEARS on their farm were a desperate struggle. There were times when they had nothing to eat. But gradually things improved. The Catholic mission helped with food and clothing. Their crops brought them a little cash. Pak took odd jobs to fill out his income. He built a better and more permanent house. A fourth child, a son baptized Paul, was born in 1955.

Today the family is self-supporting and, by Korean standards, comfortable. The hard days are behind. Pak considers himself a lucky man. No one in his immediate family died as the result of suffering, he has a home and land of his own, and he is grateful to God for his new religion. Pak One is now in college.

"You cannot catch even one rabbit if you chase two at a time," Pak says. "We succeeded in getting started again by concentrating on one thing at a time. Also we didn't look back and mourn what we once had. It is foolish to worry about a broken vase. We did what we could and God did the rest."

The Paks are typical of the Korean spirit. The nation has been invaded periodically. The people were enslaved by the Chinese, Japanese and Communists. But they refused to be subjected or assimilated. Their headstrong patriotism gave them the title, "the Irish of the Orient." Hospitable, friendly, humorous, quick tempered, graceful, and proud, they refuse to be daunted by adversity.

"The darkest spot is just below the candle," says Mr. Pak. This is the eternal optimism of one of the Orient's most charming people.

These Buddhist monks of Korea represent the major religion of the Orient. Buddhism is many centuries older than Christianity and plays a major role in the Oriental thinking.

Koreans are a people who have known much suffering. The people of Korea live in a country about the size of Kansas, of which only one-fifth can be farmed. There are forty-six million Koreans which means that the average man, woman, and child must secure his or her livelihood from less than a half acre of cultivated land.

The Koreans are a people of Mongolian stock, although some few scientists believe that there is a Caucasian element in their make-up as well. Despite the fact that the Koreans have been dominated by many other peoples — Chinese, Mongols, Manchus, Japanese, Russians, and Americans—they have managed to keep their own culture and identity intact. They have their own language and literature. In fact, when the Koreans were in control of their own destinies, they isolated themselves from the rest of Asia, and their country became known as "The Hermit Kingdom."

Nine out of ten Koreans depend for their livelihood on agriculture. Seventy-five per cent of the people live directly on the soil. Rice is the major crop, and it is produced by back-breaking labor with few tools. Most of the rural people live in small villages, but in the northern interior isolated farmhouses are not unusual. The Korean house is substantially built with mud walls, and the floors are radiant heated from the kitchen fires. Houses are poorly provided with windows. Most houses have thatched roofs, although the better off often use tiles.

The Koreans do not use beds as such, but build mud platforms along the wall which are also internally heated.

Korean life centers about the home. Women do not occupy too high a position and are made to work very hard, although they do have considerable freedom. Children are held in high esteem and receive much affection. Filial piety is regarded as the highest of virtues. On the death of the father, the eldest son becomes the inheritor and head of the family. White is the national color of Korean dress, both men and women wearing white garments. Young girls, however, go in for brilliant colors, with reds and yellows predominating.

The Korean people have suffered many tragedies in history but one of the greatest came in modern times when war tore their country apart. Many Koreans perished, many more lost all they possessed and became homeless refugees. Yet with patience born out of their hard life, the people of Korea set about rebuilding their homes and country when peace came.

Christianity was introduced into Korea by Koreans who returned from a diplomatic mission to China. The early missioners had to be smuggled into the country and many were put to death. There are also many Korean martyrs, put to death by a hostile government. Today in the South the Church is finding new strength with large groups being baptized each year.

Baseball is the most popular of the exports America has made to the Japanese people.

Many people on a little land is the story of Japan. Over a hundred million people, or half the population of the United States, live crowded on the four islands that make up modern Japan, and which together equal the area of California. Of all the problems that Japan faces, the growing population and lack of land is the greatest.

The origins of the Japanese people are difficult to trace because they are very fused. The Japanese are the result of a mixture of peoples who came from Indonesia, Malay-Polynesia, and Asia (Mongoloid). The culture of Japan is largely from China, although Korean and Indian traces are to be found, and in recent years the West has had a strong influence—particularly the United States since the end of World War II. In the big cities, Japanese youth dress in American styles, chew gum, dance to the latest American rock, talk baseball, and go to night clubs. Actually, these changes are mainly confined to the big cities and for the most part are only surface changes, for underneath Japanese life goes on in its old ways.

The Japanese have all the frugality of the New Englander. Their wooden houses have paper doors and walls, a bare minimum of furniture, and are heated by urns with a few embers. Their diet is almost monastic, consisting mainly of rice, raw fish, and vegetables. Their beverage is green tea. The family dines together, sitting on the floor. Each

Dressed in her New Year's kimono,
Kimko plays a game of shuttlecock.

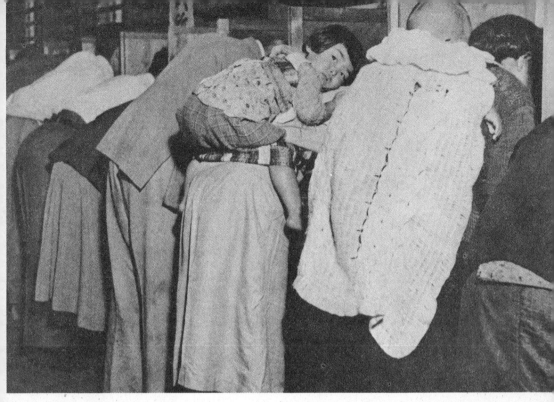

Although they don't vote, even children go into the polls in newly democratic Japan.

member has an individual small table-like tray. Meals are usually eaten in silence, punctuated only by the clicking of chopsticks and an occasional belch, the latter being a polite expression of satisfaction. The floors are always spotless because the Japanese never wear shoes in the house and thus the *tatamis,* or straw mats that cover the floor, remain clean. At night, thick quilts are spread on the floor as beds. Often, the pillow is a Spartan wooden block.

The Japanese are also a very ceremonial people. Politeness is regarded as the highest of virtues. They surround many acts with formalism and ritual. The tea ceremony requires long training before the precise graceful motions are

mastered. Flower arrangement is another art. Japanese gardens are arranged with great skill, so that they give an impression of being much larger than they really are. Even the Japanese theater is greatly formalized.

Despite the fact that Japan is industrialized more than any other nation of the Orient, it is still a country of farming people. The average Japanese lives in a small village and owns his own farm. His home is electrified, and his children have good educational opportunities. The Japanese farmer has a green thumb, and produces the highest yields per acre of anywhere in the Orient. The American farmer can have no idea of what intensive farming means until he visits Japan.

Farm madonna

Every bit of flat land is used and terraces are cut into mountainsides. The crops are planted right to the edges of the narrow roads. Villages are often crowded against hillsides to leave the flat land for intensive farming.

By nature the Japanese is a religious person. In fact, a Japanese may belong to several different religions at one and the same time. For example, there are 77 million Shintoists, 47 million Buddhists, and 3 million members of fractional sects other than Christianity. These totals come to more than the entire population of Japan. There are also well over a half million Christians, divided almost equally between Catholics and Protestants.

Christianity was brought to Japan by Saint Francis Xavier in 1549. It had considerable success until suppressed by violent persecutions. Catholics suffered a severe blow in World War II when the two atom bombs dropped fell on the most Catholic areas in the country. About half the Catholic Church in Japan was wiped out in these two atomic bombings.

While the work of conversion is slow, the Church has a much greater influence in Japan than its numbers would indicate. Another extraordinary fact is the large number of vocations from the small total population. Added to the foreign missioners at work there, no country in the world has as high a ratio of priests to faithful.

Ainu elder—member of a dying race

The original inhabitants of Japan are a people called the Ainus. The Ainus were in Japan at the time of the Stone Age. They are a Caucasoid people with light eyes and heavy beards. Their language is like no other. The best scientists can do is guess about their origin. (One guess: they came from Europe, probably around Russia.)

For many centuries the Ainus resisted the encroaching Japanese. They did manage to preserve their identity although they were slowly driven northward. Today the last remaining Ainus are on Hokkaido, the northernmost island. In recent years they have been marrying the Japanese, and it seems safe to predict that in another generation or two they will disappear entirely.

The Ainus are said to be the most hairy people in the world. They never had a system for writing, so their history was lost. Ainu words found their way into the Japanese vocabulary. For example, the Ainu word for "volcano" is *fuji*, also the name for Japan's most famous mountain. However, the Ainus have now adopted the Japanese tongue. In a recent survey, only two Ainus were found who spoke the pure Ainu language. Like many of our own Indian tribes, the Ainus seem to have lost the will to survive and to retain their identity as a people.

The Ainus had a religion that centered about the bear, and even today the bear plays an important role in their festivals. What culture the Ainus developed had its center around this big lumbering beast. The bear was the heart of their folklore. The main festival of the year was the Bear Festival, when a bear would be killed by many cruelties. The Japanese have banned this festival but it is still often carried out in secret, usually in winter.

Ainu dress was ornate and cumbersome. The women wore long heavy shell and bone necklaces. The heavily bearded men dressed in flowing garments and wore a crown, the front of which was fashioned to resemble a bear's head. They carried spears, swords, and bows and arrows — reminders of their hunting prowess.

Few Ainus ever became Christian. They were a people apart. No missions were established among them, although there were missions on Hokkaido. Today, the remaining Ainus make their living as tourist attractions, again a similarity with some of our own Indians. They put on their old dress and for a price pose for travel-loving Japanese tourists. They carve tiny figurines from wood which they sell as souvenirs.

It is sad to think that within a few years one of the earth's first human families will be no more. But that is the history of modern times. Simple and peace-loving people find it hard to exist in today's aggressive world. The Ainus managed to hold off the Japanese for many years but modern civilization was their undoing. In 1915, there were 200,000 Ainus, today but a few thousand.

This hard-working Filipino farmer lives in a Catholic land that has too few priests.

The people of the Philippine Islands are a tumultuous mixture of races and cultures. The Philippine Islands are a crossroads of Asia where many different peoples met and fused. The islands themselves occupy an area about as large as New York and New England combined, and are the home of more than 36 million people. Despite the fact that they are protected by large bodies of water, many invasions were made on them. Malays, Indonesians, Mongols, Spaniards, Japanese, and Americans have controlled the islands at various times.

Although anthropologists count about a hundred different tribes in the Philippines, the vast majority of the people are Filipinos, descended from Malayan and Indonesian ancestors. Of all the cultures that were brought to the islands, the Spanish seems to have had the greatest influence. While the Filipinos have taken over many aspects of American life, their basic culture and traditions are Spanish with their own adaptions.

In the cities, life is a curious blend of old and new. Filipino men dressed in tarong-bugalogs, shirts made of pineapple fiber and worn without being tucked into the trousers, stand at drugstore counters drinking Coca-Cola while outside, jeeps transformed into buses

Planting rice

Student at Santo Tomas University, a school begun 25 years before Harvard.

The Filipinos are ready to talk about their schools, hospitals, and skyscrapers, but reluctant to tell visitors about some of the primitive tribes that live in their country. There are well over a half million Moros, a Mohammedan people, formerly famous as pirates. They live in huts, raised on piles above the sea, and make their living as fishermen and pearl-divers. The Moros are of Indonesian origin and their sacred dances, which every girl must learn, were borrowed from Indonesia. The Moros are a very independent people whom the Spaniards and Americans found hard to control. Even today groups of them live in fierce isolation.

There are also a half million pagans—Igorots, Ifugaos, and Kalingas. Among these people, the women wear only skirts and the men loincloths. Tattooing is common. The Igorots formerly had the reputation for head-hunting, and they recorded their conquests in their tattooing. They are excellent farmers who dislike civilization.

The Ifugaos, who wear even less than the Igorots, are also excellent farmers, and their terraced rice fields where water is channeled into each plot, is a fantastic sight. Among the Kalingas, children are married almost as soon as they are born. The original inhabitants of the islands remain today in the Negritos who rarely grow over five feet tall, have beards, hunt with poisoned arrows, and consider snakes a delicacy. There are 30,000 Negritos remaining.

screech around corners. The men will go home to meet wives who will be dressed in a patadiong—nineteenth century Spanish style—and sit down to meals that are borrowed from the cooking skills of India, China, Spain, and America.

In the country, the Spanish way is even more evident in the slow tempo of Filipino life—food, wine, siestas, guitar playing. The country people are farmers who work their land with primitive methods, plus the aid of water buffaloes.

From the Spanish, the Filipinos also received their Catholic Faith. Unfortunately, for many years there has been a lack of priests. As a result, many churches have fallen into decay and the people have gotten out of the habit of many religious practices. But underneath, the old faith remains.

Mountain Igorot

THE
WORLD'S MAJOR LANGUAGES

AND THE NUMBER OF SPEAKERS

A. Individual Languages

Mandarin (China)	605,000,000	Italian	59,000,000
English	333,000,000	Telugu (India)	51,000,000
Russian	206,000,000	Punjabi (India)	50,000,000
Hindi (India)	192,000,000	Tamil (India)	48,000,000
Spanish	192,000,000	Korean	47,000,000
German	120,000,000	Cantonese (China)	46,000,000
Arabic	109,000,000	Marathi (India)	45,000,000
Bengali (India)	108,000,000	Javanese	43,000,000
Portuguese	108,000,000	Min (China)	38,000,000
Japanese	105,000,000	Turkish	37,000,000
Malay-Indonesian	86,000,000	Annamese	34,000,000
French	80,000,000	Polish	34,000,000

B. Language Families

Indo-European (Teutonic, Latin-Romance, Balto-Slovak, Indo-Iranian, Greek, Celtic, Albanian, Armenian)	1,500,000,000
Sino-Tibetan (Chinese, Thai, Burmese, Tibetan)	800,000,000
Afro-Asiatic (Arabic, Hebrew, Berber, Amharic)	150,000,000
Uralic-Altaic (Finnish, Hungarian, Turkish, Mongol, Manchu)	100,000,000
Japanese-Korean	152,000,000
Dravidian (Tamil, Telugu, other Indian languages)	130,000,000
Malayo-Polynesian (Indonesian, Visayan, Maori, Malagasese)	150,000,000
Mon-Khmer (Southeast Asia)	30,000,000
African (Nilo-Saharan, Niger-Kordofanian, Khosian)	150,000,000
American Indian (Mayan, Aymara, Quechua and 100 others)	18,000,000

Chapter 9

Indonesia

STRADDLING the Equator, between Asia and Australia, are a group of 3,000 incredibly beautiful islands whose land area is larger than the states of Texas and Alaska combined and whose population is in excess of 125 million. These are the fabulous Spice Islands or East Indies to which Columbus was sailing when he discovered America and misapplied the term Indies to the Caribbean area. Stretching one-eighth of the way around the earth, the islands and their people are gathered under a single government, called the country of Indonesia, formerly known as the Dutch East Indies.

Most of the people of these islands are easy-going Malays who speak 250 languages of the Indonesian, Polynesian, and Melanesian families. The prevailing religion is Islam, brought by Arab traders in the twelfth century, but modified by local beliefs based on ancient Hinduism. For example, the Indonesian believes that the soul which resides in the head leaves the body when a person sleeps and that therefore one should be wakened gently in order to give the soul the chance to return.

There is considerable contrast in the islands of Indonesia. Java has the densest farming population of anywhere on earth while Borneo, now renamed Kalimantan, is practically empty in its interior. Head-hunters still roam some of the islands while Bali has become synonymous with a tourist's paradise. The people of Indonesia are the bridge between Asia and the Pacific world—bright, cheerful, happy-go-lucky, impetuous.

A NEW LAND OF OLD PEOPLES

The people of Sumatra live in a changing land. Although Sumatra is the nearest Indonesian island to the Asian mainland, being separated from Malaya by the narrow Strait of Malacca, until recently it was a wild jungle land, home of head-hunters and pirates, and even today parts of it are still unexplored.

The sixteen million people of Sumatra live on an island about the size of California. In the north dwell the Achinese, who take their name from their former kingdom, Achin. Expert seamen, the Achinese were once pirates. They are fanatical Moslems who refuse to recognize any government over them.

South of the Achinese are the Battas, former head-hunters. Many are still pagans, although large numbers have been converted to Islam and others to Christianity. In the central highlands live the Menandkabau, a progressive farming people who build fantastically gabled longhouses which they artistically decorate and paint a bright red, and raise on stilts. A related family group occupies each house, with each family having its own one-room apartment.

The people of Sumatra grow tobacco and tea. They also harvest rubber and palm oil from plantation trees. Recently large reservoirs of oil have been discovered. In South Sumatra there was a great empire in the eighth century and the Buddhist university there was the largest in Asia, drawing its scholars from India and China. Today little remains as reminders.

There is an incident from Sumatra's history that might have a lesson for the modern world. In the days of the great southern empire, the army of that empire challenged the mountain people to battle. But instead, the mountain people persuaded the challengers to decide the quarrel by a fight between two water buffaloes, declaring that it was foolish for people to die over a dispute.

The people of Borneo live on a thrice-divided island. Borneo, larger than the state of Texas, is the third largest island in the world. The greatest part of the island with four million people out of a total of six million is Indonesian. Then there are the British protectorate of Brunei, Sabah, and Sarawak, each with a half million people. There are over seventy-five tribes on the island.

Along the coasts of Borneo, or Kalimantan as the Indonesians have renamed it, live Malay farmers and fishermen. Rubber and rice are also produced here. There are many small, neat towns. The people in the coastal areas are mostly settlers from Java.

Once away from the coast, the traveler finds himself in the wild and primitive interior where the pagan hill tribes live. Although these people are usually referred to as Dyaks, they are broken into many sub-tribes. The Dyaks themselves are friendly and inquisitive. They wear short tight sarongs fastened with belts of silver coins. They live in communal houses, grow rice, and harvest forest products. Beyond them live remote hill tribes, some of whom are thought to be still head-hunters, of whom little is known.

A Laki tribesman from the island of Sumatra. His formal dress is only for the most solemn and elaborately festive occasions. He formerly lived under Dutch colonists.

The Javanese live in the most densely populated farming area in the world. If you can imagine sixty-two million people living in New York State and trying to make a living off the soil, you will have a picture of Java today. In order to exist, the Javanese have had to cultivate every bit of arable land, even terracing the mountainsides, and then depend on tropical lushness to produce extraordinary harvests on a year-around schedule.

Java is the home of ancient man. Until the recent discoveries in Kenya, the oldest human skulls were found there in 1891 and 1940. The people of Java today are descendants of Malays who emigrated there as early as 2,000 B.C. Since they came from different areas, there are differences among them today. For example, on Java alone three languages are spoken: Sundanese, Madurese, and Javanese. In the beginning, the Javanese were animists who developed a complex civilization. Shortly after the time of Christ, Hindu influences from India filtered into the island, resulting in an impressive artistic and religious civilization. In the thirteenth century Islam put an end to Hinduism. In the sixteenth century, Islam's advance was halted by the coming of the Spanish and Portuguese, but wherever the religion of Mohammed had taken root it was not displaced.

Despite their closeness to poverty, the Javanese are a happy and contented people. Time means no more to them than the opportunity to enjoy life. Tradition is much more important than change. Work will be forsaken at any time if there is a festival or dance or theatrical in which to take part. Every Javanese has an innate sense of beauty and courtesy. Gambling is one of his greatest passions, and a cockfight will always collect a cheering, excited crowd.

Each Javanese family which dwells outside the few large cities has a small square house surrounded by banana trees. The house has plaited bamboo walls, a packed-earth floor. The roof is tiled because the former Dutch rulers decreed the end of thatch roofs as breeding grounds for rats. Standing in front of his house, the farmer sees rice fields reaching up to volcanoes. As he looks, he will pray to the Rice Goddess for a bountiful harvest.

Beauty and grace mark the Balinese.

310

Indonesian wedding couple in adat dress

This New Guinea mother speaks Pidgin — a combination of Malay, English and German.

This Filipino Morion pageant reenacts in Holy Week the passion and death of Christ.

The Man Who Stole His Wife

OFTEN JUST BEFORE dusk, Sameh and his friend Rapung take a walk along the beach below Sanur. Sometimes they stroll in silence, a luxury permitted old friends, and gaze out over the long strip of sand made gray by the receding tide. On other occasions they sit on one of the colorful outriggers, carved to resemble a *gadja-mina*—a mythical beast half-elephant and half-fish—and watch the mountains change under the setting sun from indigo to purple to black. Most of the time, however, the two old friends talk, often recalling the days of their youth.

"*Inge!*" Sameh often says with a sigh. "Bali is changing. It is not what it used to be. Aluminum for our roofs instead of thatch! Blouses for our womenfolk!"

The island of Bali lies south of the equator, about halfway between the Malay Peninsula and Australia. It is one of the volcanic islands that make up one of the world's newest countries—Indonesia. Only two miles of swift tidal currents separate Bali from Java and it is believed that at one time the two islands were joined. Bali itself is a green 2,000 square miles of extremely fertile land, studded with volcanoes, and densely populated.

Sameh was born on the day of the great earthquake of 1917. In fact, his mother's labor pains started with the first of the earth tremors. When the ground began to shake, his father and some women relatives helped his mother out of their bamboo house. A mat was placed in the shade of a large frangipani tree. While one woman supported Sameh's mother's back, a second helped to relieve the pains by massage, while a third soaked a shoot of coconut palm in water and then held the shoot over the expectant woman's head, allowing the water to drip into her mouth—this was an extremely effective charm against the *leyaks,* evil spirits that live on unborn children.

Within an hour after Sameh was born, the volcano Batur exploded in violent eruption. Despite the shaking of the earth, mother and child had to be carried under a pavilion to escape the hot white ash that rained down. While the population of Bali increased by one with the arrival of Sameh, it decreased that day by over 1,300—people who perished when Batur erupted. Also lost were 65,000 homes and 2,500 temples.

When Sameh was forty-two days old, he and his mother underwent the traditional ceremony of purification. For this occasion, he was given anklets and bracelets of brass to replace the black strings that he had worn since birth to ward off evil spirits. His ears were pierced and a thread run through each ear. A pouch containing amulets was hung about his neck. In this pouch were a piece of his own umbilical cord, glass beads, bits of coral and tiger bone.

At the age of three months, offerings were again made to the gods in Sameh's name, and the threads in his ears were replaced by earrings of gold. When he was one year old (actually 210 days because the Balinese calendar does not correspond with the Gregorian year), new offerings were made at the family shrine. He was blessed by a priest and had his hair cut. For this latter operation, his head was shaven clean except for a lock in the front which was to be allowed to grow to protect him against harm. He also received two names on this day: a secret name from the priest and his personal name of Sameh.

As soon as Sameh was able to walk, he was largely left on his own. He was allowed to toddle anywhere in the village and to spend his day with other children. He was seldom reprimanded and never spanked by his parents. At the same time, he was not pampered. As a result, he grew up self-reliant and unusually mature when compared to children of the West.

By the time Sameh was seven, he was already helping his father at work both at home and in the fields. With his father, he set out the rice shoots and cared for the fields, and with the rest of his family assisted at the annual harvest. He took care of the family buffaloes, began to learn to read and write in Balinese, and understood a smattering of Malay. At this time too, he covered his nakedness with a colorful batik skirt—a long piece of cloth that he merely wrapped around him and tucked in at his hips.

At the age of thirteen Sameh had his teeth filed. The act was a type of coming-of-age rite. His teeth were not filed to points as is the custom in parts of Africa but simply to an even line. Filed teeth are necessary if the Balinese is to enter the spirit world after death, and the operation must be performed according to set ritual and by a man specially trained for the task.

Sameh grew up in a rigid system of etiquette and taboos. He belongs to the Sudra caste, the class of the common people. The social system of Bali is based on Hinduism, transplanted from Java, and with Balinese adaptions. The result is somewhat like that in certain areas of Latin America where people practice a strange combination of Catholicism and pagan worship. The Balinese cult of ancestors and Balinese animistic beliefs have so colored orthodox Hinduism so that it would hardly be recognized by a Hindu from India. In Bali many civilizations and cultures met and melded — Malay, Polynesian, Hindu, and Chinese.

RELIGION AND nationality are identified in the Balinese mind. If a man becomes a Christian or Mohammedan, he is no longer a Balinese. He departs from the social life of his people, and in some villages is officially declared to be "dead." For this reason, conversions to Christianity are hard to come by. Religion holds the community together, providing the reason for daily acts, art, drama and festivals. It takes considerable courage for a family to cut itself off from relatives and friends and embrace a new way of life.

Sameh lived with his family on a small plot of ground that contained a number of buildings. The home was built and occupied according to the laws of magical harmony. Inside a mud wall, the various pavilions of the home were located and blessed by a priest. In one corner was the family temple and opposite it the sleeping quarters of Sameh's parents. Near the gate was an open pavilion where the family received and entertained guests. Across the hard, earthen yard was another smaller house where Sameh's grandmother and an aunt lived. A fourth house was used by Sameh and his brothers. Behind this pavilion was the kitchen, granary, and rice threshing area.

EARLY EVERY MORNING before dawn the crowing of the fighting cocks awakened all the members in Sameh's family. The women made their way to the village spring to get the morning's water. When they returned, they swept the hard earthen yard. The menfolk meanwhile had bathed and started off to the rice fields. They did not breakfast but each carried a palm leaf of cold boiled rice that had been prepared the night before. The rice would be eaten towards mid-morning.

When the women had filled the large water pot near the kitchen, they set out unhusked rice from the granary to dry in the sun. Then a fire was started and the day's cooking begun. While Sameh's mother prepared the rice, his grandmother and aunt scraped coconuts and fried the shreds in coconut oil to use in the hot, peppery rice sauce.

The Balinese have very catholic tastes in food. Except for taboo foods they will eat almost anything that walks, crawls, swims or flies. Crickets, bees, flying ants, porcupines, birds and eels are among preferred delicacies. Meat is used mostly on festive occasions but vegetables and fruit are used regularly. Papaya, coconut, eggplant, sweet potato, pineapples, oranges, acacia leaves, ferns, and bananas are among the most common. The vegetables are always cooked, often in the rice sauce, while the fruits are eaten raw.

While the women do the regular daily cooking, it is the men who prepare the food for feasts and banquets. Cooking for banquets and feasts often takes days and the most subtle sauces are prepared. Giant turtles, a general favorite, are cooked in a variety of ways. Roast stuffed pig is another favorite. Sameh learned to cook at an early age and he was often called on to act as chef at village feasts.

When the evening meal is finished, the family drifts off. The older men of the village gather at the village hall to chat and drink palm beer. The women meet to gossip. The young folk rehearse dances or practice in the village orchestra. Unless there is a dramatic show or a festival, all are in bed by ten o'clock.

WHEN SAMEH was sixteen years old, his mother died. A Brahmin priest was immediately summoned and messengers were sent with the news to distant relatives. The death lamp, made of bamboo and white tissue paper, was hung outside the compound gate. The corpse was placed in the guest pavilion. The priest who had arrived meanwhile consulted his oracles and declared that two days hence would be an auspicious day for burial.

The events that occurred during the next few days were more like a festival than a funeral. There were processions, singing and dancing and feasting. Cremation towers were built, decorated with colored paper ornaments and tinsel. Guests crowded the house and on the cremation day a great banquet was held. Then the village band appeared, fireworks were set off, and a procession formed. It was pure bedlam.

When the cremation spot was reached, the corpses were passed from hand to hand and placed in new coffins which were set in the towers. The priest sprinkled holy water, prayed and went into a trance. The mob tried to pull mirrors and decorations from the tower before they were burned. The orchestra played louder. A fire was started by friction and soon the towers were ablaze. There was a carnival atmosphere to the whole affair. When the fire burned down, the remaining ashes were collected in an urn and taken in a procession to the sea. By this time it was already dark. The ashes were spread over the water. Then all those in attendance bathed to cleanse themselves and returned home.

Sameh was eighteen years old when he decided to get married. He made up his mind quite casually one night. A Balinese opera troupe was presenting a show in his village. Sameh like the other young bucks was doing a bit of flirting while waiting for the drama to begin. He was talking and joking with Ktut Adi when suddenly he realized that she was everything that a Balinese girl should be. Her small, rounded face was set off by black, shining hair. Her nose was small, her lips full. Her skin was golden brown. She walked with the litheness and poise that would be the envy of any professional model. During the course of the play, Sameh proposed marriage and was surprised to hear her accept him. It was agreed that Sameh should steal his bride three days hence.

EXCEPT FOR KTUT ADI, his father, and the few friends he needed to help him, Sameh kept his plans secret. On the appointed day, Ktut Adi was on her way to the village spring when Sameh, Rapung, and several friends jumped from behind some bushes and seized her. Ktut Adi put up a struggle as is the custom, but her biting and kicking availed her nothing. She was taken to a hide-out—Rapung's home in a neighboring village. The kidnaping had been observed and reported to Ktut Adi's father who dashed around trying to discover who had stolen his daughter and to organize a search party.

Special offerings for the gods had been sent to the hide-out by Sameh before the kidnaping. As soon as the bridal couple arrived at the place, Ktut Adi ceased her struggles. She checked the god offerings. The marriage was then consummated. The offerings were important because they made the affair legal. Meanwhile Sameh's father and friends approached Ktut Adi's parents who pretended great outrage even though they approved of Sameh. At last they gave consent to the wedding and a bridal price was agreed on.

When the money was paid to the girl's father, Sameh and his bride left their hiding place and returned to Sameh's home. A priest was consulted about a lucky day for the solemn wedding ceremony—a public confirmation of what had already taken place. The day was decided upon within the prescribed forty-two day limit. When it arrived, the priest blessed the couple, sprinkled them with holy water, and offered prayers for a fruitful and happy life together. Thus Ktut Adi officially gave up her ancestral gods and adopted those of her husband.

Not long after, Sameh built a home of his own. There with Ktut Adi he lives in peace and happiness. Unlike many other Oriental lands, in Bali there is an equality between husband and wife, and a mutual respect. Sameh provides for his wife and she in turn manages his home and finances. In the years that have passed, five children have come to bless their home—three of them boys who will carry on the ancestral name and traditions.

These are the things that Sameh recalls when he walks with his friend Rapung on the beach below Sanur at sunset. They are memories of a full and happy life.

In the Spice Islands, time has stood still for three hundred years. In 1546, Saint Francis Xavier arrived in the Moluccas, known as the Spice Islands because of the abundance of nutmeg, cloves, and mace they produced. He established Christianity there and later was to hear that hundreds of his Christians were put to death by Mohammedans. If he was to return to these islands today, he would find them little changed. The volcano on Halmahera which he used to illustrate a sermon on Hell is no longer active but the life of the simple island people follows a traditional pattern.

The people of the Spice Islands live in simple bamboo and thatch huts, grow sugar cane, coconuts, cassava, and bananas. When the bananas are ripe, they are content to let their farm plots run down.

The people of the Spice Islands are poorer than those on Java or Sumatra. They live in a backwater that receives little attention. A mixture of Melanesian, Polynesian, and Malay races, they received little of their culture from Asia. Some of the islands are still Mohammedan, others Christian.

The people of the Lesser Sundra Islands were little touched by the culture of Indonesia. The Sundranese cultivate maize and roots rather than rice as on the main islands. Settlers from crowded Java have been spreading into these southern islands in recent years.

One item worthy of note is that in recent years large numbers of converts to the Catholic Church have been made on Flores and Indonesian Timor. On Flores, whole areas have become Catholic. On Timor, the Church doubled in a decade and is today a quarter of the population. The whole of Indonesia is heavily Moslem, two out of three Indonesians following that faith. There are two and a half million Catholics. The constitution guarantees freedom of religion, but fanatical Moslems militate against Christians, and in some areas there has been outright persecution, usually due more to intense nationalism than religion. Today Indonesia maintains diplomatic relations with the Holy See.

The people of Celebes are color-conscious. Celebes is the most fantastically shaped of all Indonesian Islands. The people of this island are noted for their love of color. The coastal Buginese wear sarongs of fuchsia and turquoise, or silks striped pink, purple, and orange. The inland Toraja tribes wear bright colored loincloths and paint their wooden houses red, green, and white. Celebes (now known as Sulawesi) is an island of neat villages. The people raise maize and rice and gather copra for sale. Like all the island people of Indonesia, the Celebese are a happy, contented people, living in a true tropical paradise.

Temple life and religious superstitions overshadow the lives of the Balinese girls.

SO YOU WERE BORN

Let's pretend that, as the sun came over the horizon this morning you were born into this world of three

1. COLOR

As one of 350,000 babies born today, you have

1 chance in 2 of being born in China, or India;

1 chance in 4 of being born in one of the remaining lands of color;

3 chances in 9 of being born in a white man's land.

You have only 1 chance in 20 of being born in the U.S.A.

2. LIFE SPAN

If you are born in India, you have 3 chances in 4 of dying within twelve months.

If you live to be a year old in India, you then have a 50-50 chance of growing to maturity.

If you are born in the U.S.A., you have 19 chances out of 20 of living to be a year old.

If you are born in the U.S.A., you have an average chance of living to be 71 years old.

3. HEALTH

If you are born black, brown, or yellow, you have 1 chance in 3 of being chronically ill all your life with malaria, intestinal diseases, or tuberculosis.

If you are born white, better living conditions make the chance very small that you will be chronically ill; if it comes you'll have care unknown to others.

THIS MORNING!

and a half billion. What are your possibilities as you take up your life on this planet? Small chance you'll be a Catholic American.

4. FOOD

Regardless of your color, you have:

1 chance in 3 of suffering from malnutrition through insufficiency of the right kinds of food.

1 chance in 5 of being hungry all your life, and at times starving from famine.

5. WAY OF LIFE

If you are black, brown, or yellow, you have:

3 chances out of 4 that you will never know how to read or write;

2 chances out of 3 that you will live all your life in a mud hut with dirt floor, thatched roof, no chimney.

6. RELIGION

You have:

1 chance in 7 of being a Catholic;

1 chance in 7 of being a non-Catholic Christian;

2 chances in 7 of being a Hindu or a Confucianist;

3 chances in 7 of belonging to other non-Christian beliefs.

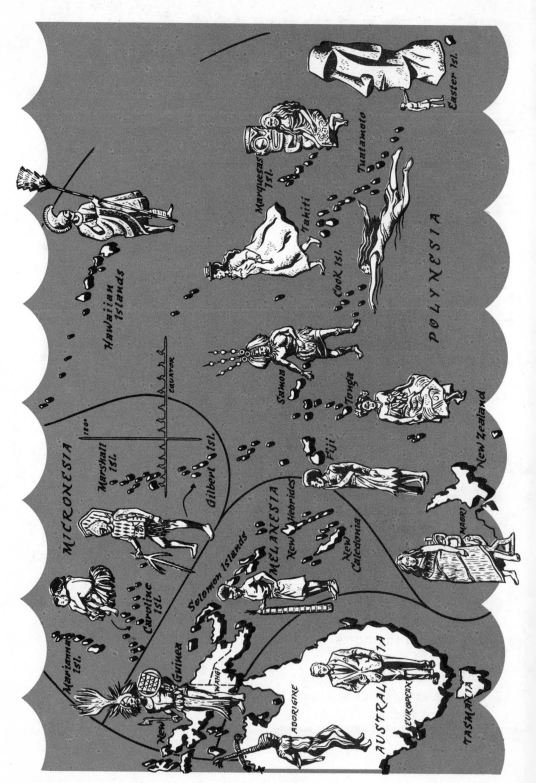

Chapter 10

The Island World

THE PACIFIC OCEAN is the largest thing in the world. It contains half of the earth's water and covers a third of the earth's surface. For centuries, men have explored this tremendous vastness, yet even today there is much that is unknown about it.

Rising out of this expansive sea, like the myriad stars in the heavens, are countless thousands of islands. Some of these islands are large, like the Australian continent. Most of them are small dots in this great sea. There are high islands which are in reality the top of mountain peaks rising up from the ocean floor. There are low islands, just a few feet above the waves, which are coralloid, or formed from the skeletons of billions and billions of small sea animals that have gathered together over the centuries.

People live on most of these islands, and their origins are as mysterious as their island world. In the eastern part of the ocean live the brown-skinned, handsome Polynesians (People of Many Islands). In the north and central Pacific are the Micronesians (People of Small Islands) who are darker and shorter than the Polynesians. In the southwest corner, around Australia, live the Melanesians (Black Islanders) who are of Negroid origin. Finally, there are the Austral-Asians, the original people of Australia, New Zealand, and Tasmania.

From the best scientific evidence, the Pacific peoples came from Asia, Africa, and South America. True cosmopolites!

These Australians on a beach near Melbourne represent Europe's racial contribution.

Australians live in a land of wide open spaces. Australia is a country as large as the United States but with fewer people than New York. Ninety-five per cent of the people of Australia either came from the British Isles or are descended from English, Scotch, or Irish forebears. In their far-off "down-under" land, the Australians have recreated British life and customs. Australian cities are modern counterparts of English cities, and Australian homes might be anywhere in the English countryside; yet, they have their own overtones.

Australians claim that they speak English but their language is even further removed from English than the language of the United States. They speak of England as "home"

but few Australians have ever been there. They have a fierce independent spirit, making their own laws, yet recognizing the English Queen as their Queen. They claim to be democratic but their laws allow few Oriental or colored persons to immigrate.

Two out of three Australians live in cities. One city, Sydney, contains a fifth of the population, and another fifth is in Melbourne. The cities are industrialized but most of the products manufactured are used locally. Australia is too far removed to compete in the world market. As a result, goods are expensive in Australia.

Two-thirds of the country is called the Outback. It is desertlike. Rich mineral deposits have been found.

There is a racial mystery about the aborigines who originally settled in Australia.

Between the Outback and the cities is the "country." Here live the farmers and cattle and sheep raisers. Most of these people live isolated lives, coming to the city once a year to attend a national "county" fair. Wool is the largest single export of Australia.

The original settlers of Australia were the aborigines who arrived there ten thousand years ago. The aboriginals are a Negroid people and some of them today are among the most primitive inhabitants of the earth. They wear no clothes, do not build houses, live on grubs and roots. Others have accepted a little civilization and live on reservations. There are a large number of aboriginal half-breeds.

Some of the aborigines, particularly those of mixed blood, work on the ranches. They are reputed to be expert trackers and possess keen senses of sight, hearing and smell. There are about thirty thousand aboriginals and fifty thousand halfcastes scattered throughout Australia today.

Tasmania, an island about as large as Scotland, is part of Australia. The original inhabitants, similar to the Australian aborigines, are now extinct. The last Tasmanian died in 1876. Today the island is inhabited by almost 400 thousand people of British descent. They engage in agriculture, dairying, livestock raising, sheep breeding, and mining.

The Papuans are close to the Stone Age.

Melanesia is a black man's world. The Melanesian Islands lie northeast of Australia, including all the islands extending from New Guinea to the Fijis. Melanesians are very dark skinned. They are short, frizzly-haired, and have broad, flat noses. They are primarily farmers, using the sea only when necessary. Outside of these similarities, Melanesians differ widely among themselves. There are a hundred or more languages in Melanesia, originating from three separate roots; as the result, a *lingua franca,* called Pidgin, has been developed. For example, the first sentence of the Lord's Prayer, as translated by Marist missioners, says: "Papa belong me, he live him long topside heaven."

The people of New Guinea are called Papuans. New Guinea, an island as large as Texas but with two and a half million people, is one of the last remaining wildernesses in the world. Few white men have ever penetrated this savage and wild island, inhabited by warlike tribes, some of the pre-Stone Age.

New Guinea is a man's world, for only males hold social status. Women are used to take care of children, tend the garden, and raise livestock. A man may marry as many wives as he can afford. Social accomplishments and prestige are gained in hunting, boldness in warfare, singing, dancing, and wood carving. Papuans believe in evil spirits and are very superstitious. They are wonderful naturalists, able to identify all plants, birds, and animals.

There are Pygmies on New Guinea who are very poor because they live in a pre-Stone Age culture. Their favorite food is beetles and their larvae which they find in tree trunks. The Pygmies are a peaceful people, live in grass huts, and wear only loincloths.

Solomon Islands. Many an American G.I. became familiar with the inhabitants of the Solomon Islands during World War II. Once these people were so unfriendly and treacherous that Europeans avoided them. Cannibalism was widely practiced. Missioners were martyred and Christianity had a hard time getting a foothold. Today most Solomon Islanders are Christians

These Medlpe boys of New Guinea study their ABC's during an island-wide literacy drive.

who live simple lives despite the fact that they were thrust into modern civilization overnight by World War II, adding C rations and chewing gum to their regular diet of yams and pork. The Solomon Islanders have a fine artistic sense that is shown in their decorations, wickerwork, and pottery.

New Caledonia. The people of New Caledonia are Papuan, but show traces of having mixed with Polynesians. Whites and Orientals have invaded the island because of valuable deposits of nickel and chromium. A century ago the Kanakas, as the French named the New Caledonians, were cannibals. They were fond of drinking and they practiced abortion. Today, they are declining in numbers and in a generation or two may become extinct.

The Fiji Islands mark the end of Melanesia. Three tribes inhabit the Fiji Islands—Fijians, Bure, and Yalantini. A little more than a century ago they were the most savage cannibals of the Pacific. Sailors avoided the islands fearing shipwreck and certain death, and the tribes made war on one another to get victims for their roasting ovens. Today, Fijians are a peaceful and friendly people.

The Fijians and other related tribes occupy two hundred islands in the Fiji group. They are dark, frizzly-haired, tall and muscular. Their features are more regular than those of the Papuans, thus showing Polynesian influence. Unlike the Papuans, the Fijians do not load themselves down with ornaments. A simple teeth necklace suffices for decoration.

327

A newly ordained Papuan priest (left) poses with his cousin who wears festive dress.

The Fijians do not like to work. When the British set up sugar plantations on the islands, the Fijians were happy to lease their lands but refused to give their labor. As a result large numbers of Indians were imported into Fijiland. Today the descendants of these Indians still work on plantations while others control the commercial life of the islands. The Fijians are content to play rugby or become policemen. During World War II many Fijians were scouts.

To see the Fijians at their best, one must visit them in their villages, away from the Indian cities. Here they live life as it was generations ago. They hold songfests, drink kava (native beer), and remind visitors that there is nothing that cannot be put off until the morrow. For special occasions, they have a fire walking ceremony that is spectacular, to say the least.

Most of the Fiji Islanders are Christians, divided between Catholics and Protestants. Most Fiji children attend school. The islands have a developed credit union system, established by a Catholic priest. About one out of every five people in Melanesia is Catholic. There are Melanesian priests, Brothers and Sisters. It was the work of the missioners that transformed these once savage islands and did away with many of the crude aspects of their culture. Marist priests and Sisters, Jesuits, and Columbans deserve the credit for the changes that have been made.

This young Samoan typesetter works for a Catholic publication of the Marist missioners.

Micronesians are the inhabitants of small islands. Several thousand years ago, after the Melanesians had occupied their islands, another group of Malay people began to move out into the Pacific. They had enough contact with the dark Melanesians to become a people of mixed blood. Since the islands they settled were all small, they were given the name of Micronesians from the Greek word meaning small.

The world of Micronesia includes the Marianas, Marshalls, Gilberts and Carolines. On a few of these low atolls live more than several hundred people, all leading simple lives, growing what food they can, wresting more from the sea. They do as little work as possible.

Micronesia is directly north of Melanesia. Although Micronesians are today a friendly people, they have a history of opposition to the white man and at one time were cannibals. The islands of Micronesia, while lying astride the equator, are cooled by the ocean breezes. Water is a precious commodity to Micronesians because there is little rainfall and on some islands the only drinking water to be obtained is that which is filtered through the sand.

Ethnologists believe that the Micronesians originated in the southeast part of Asia, around Cambodia. Physically and in language they differ from the Melanesians and Polynesians, even though there has been intermarriage.

329

Fiji Island policeman

The people of Micronesia have been unable to escape being caught up in the turmoil of the modern world. Because their islands occupy strategic positions, they were bitterly contested during World War II. Also this area has been used for testing atomic weapons. The Micronesians who lived on Bikini were all moved from their homes to islands far distant so that Bikini could be destroyed in a single blinding flash.

Other islands of Micronesia have become strategic air and naval bases. Guam is a typical example. For many years this island was held by Spain. The inhabitants absorbed Spanish blood and Spanish culture. They became known as Chamorros. After the United States occupied the island, the Chamorros were introduced to American ways. Their old village life was destroyed. Coca-Cola replaced coconut milk and cowboy films provided entertainment in place of the traditional dances and ceremonies. The people of Guam, mostly Catholics, thus became entoiled in the twentieth century. Their islands, however, remain beauty spots. Thatched roof houses are set in groves of stately palm trees that sway and whisper before the steady trade winds.

There is bright sunlight and a deep blue sky. Over this pleasant scene one hears the steady roar of the sea as giant breakers fall over coral atolls and the white spume races into sandy beaches. There is beauty in Micronesia, and it is God's beauty.

Easter Island is a great riddle.
Before we pass into the Polynesian world, Easter Island should be considered because of the riddle it presents scientists. The island was discovered on Easter Sunday, 1722, by a Dutch sea captain, who made a brief visit and passed on. It was fifty years before it was visited again. The people of the island were Polynesians—poor, dispirited, diseased. Most unusual was that the island was covered with gigantic stone carvings, heroic sized busts of individuals. No one on the island knew anything about the statues or their history.

Who carved these tremendous rocks, what they represent, and what happened to the carvers are mysteries that have never been solved. Some believe that the Easter Islanders were the ancestors of the South American Indians, as similarities between Andean carvings of Peru and those on Easter Island have been noted. One theory has all the Easter Islanders sailing on to Peru to begin a civilization there. Another theory is just the reverse. This explains the carvings by having South American Indians journeying to Easter Island on balsa rafts. A group of Scandinavian scientists attempted such a journey some years ago and recorded their findings in a book, *Kon Tiki,* that was a best seller.

Whatever the explanation, it has been lost to us. Easter Island remains one of the mysteries of our world but it is only one of many, many mysteries.

A typical fuzzy-haired woman of Fiji

The Polynesians are among the world's greatest navigators. While the Melanesians and Micronesians settled down, the Polynesians sailed on and on, exploring and colonizing the far islands of the eastern Pacific. They built great outrigger canoes, held together with coconut fiber. In these they went to all parts of Oceania. Without the aid of charts or compasses, they found their way back and forth across the vast sea. On many islands they left groups of colonizers. They settled on islands as far apart as New Zealand and Hawaii, across the great expanse of the Pacific Ocean.

The Polynesians were and are a people with a sense of tradition. They had minstrels and bards who sang Polynesian legends, handing them down from generation to generation. One such legend tells of how Polynesian explorers sailed into a region of snow and ice, where white mountains pierced the sky. This description fits Antarctica, and it is quite possible that these hardy seamen journeyed there long before the white men discovered the region.

Polynesians lead a happy, carefree life. Fish from the sea, taro root, and coconuts can be had for the taking. Tidal currents carry away garbage and refuse so that their villages can be kept clean. Polynesians themselves are very clean. They bathe daily, keep their clothes spotless, and dress attractively. They learn to swim almost as soon as they learn to walk. They love children and lavish affection on them. Although they live daily with beauty, they never grow tired of it.

The coming of the white man into Polynesia was a mixed blessing. The white man brought Christianity, a religion now professed by nearly all Polynesians. He also brought many comforts and luxuries from the white world. But some of his other gifts were not to be prized. He brought diseases unknown to the Polynesians and against which they had no immunity. Thousands upon thousands died in epidemics. Leprosy was unknown in Polynesia before the white man came; so too was smallpox. Often in return for friendship, the white man carried off islanders as slaves. It is difficult to add up a balance sheet.

Maori say "Hello" by rubbing noses.

This Maori mother wears a garment woven from flax plant and decorated with feathers.

New Zealand is the homeland of the Maori people. When the first British colonists arrived in New Zealand, they found the islands inhabited by a handsome, tall, brown-skinned people called the Maori, who resisted the white intruders as bitterly as did the American Indians. The Maori are a Polynesian people. They were not the first settlers of New Zealand. There was probably a Melanesian people there before them. The Maori killed off the men and absorbed the women with the result that some Papuan features show up from time to time among Maoris.

Although the Maori have no written language, like other Polynesians they preserve their traditions through songs and stories, handed down from one generation to the next. The Maori developed a higher civilization than other Polynesian groups because life for them was not as easy as on other Pacific islands where nature supplied food and shelter. The Maori were given to cannibalism, believing that by eating a person they absorbed his strength and virtue. They were also head hunters.

They were ruled by kings and sub-chiefs. There were three grades of society among the Maori—nobility, freemen, and slaves. Maori life was governed by an elaborate system of taboos. The men were warriors and the women workers. Maoris love decoration. In the past, tattooing was common. Maori homes were substantially built and artistically decorated with elaborate wood carvings.

334

Today, the Maori live in peace with the white men. They number about 227,000 against a white population of three million. They are good citizens who have equal rights and representation in the government. They are mainly farmers and sheep herders. They work hard on their land, educate their children, and preserve their ancient traditions. Many of them are Catholics, while others are Protestants.

The white population of New Zealand is mainly of English, Irish, and Scotch ancestry. Half of the population lives in cities and towns; the rest is engaged in agricultural and pastoral pursuits. New Zealanders are proud of their beautiful country and they beam with satisfaction as they tell visitors that they have permanent pastures all year around with no need for stables for their cattle and sheep. Wool and dairy products have brought wealth to this country.

New Zealanders are unusually healthy. They have the lowest infant mortality rate in the world and one of the lowest death rates. The country has an excellent educational system with good technical schools and a university. For recreation, the people of New Zealand go in for horse racing. Every small town has its race track and substantial sums are wagered.

New Zealand is an example of how people of different races can get along. The brown and white men of the country have learned to respect each other. New Zealand is an example for other lands.

He is a Polynesian elder of the Pacific.

The Samoan has a natural permanent wave.

A Polynesian mat weaver of Oceania.

Tonga is one of the best places to study Polynesian culture. Because Tonga is off the main line of ocean travel, the two hundred islands that make up this tiny kingdom have been able to preserve Polynesian culture to a remarkable degree. The ruling family of Tonga (also known as the Friendly Islands) goes back a thousand years. The Tonga people are said to be the handsomest of any Polynesians. The young men are skilled at boxing and wrestling. The Tongans are Christians, practically all of the Protestant faith. One Protestant missioner became Prime Minister, but the British Government removed him from office in favor of a native.

Tahitians have been called the most carefree people in the Pacific. Next to Bali, no Pacific island has received as much attention as has Tahiti in the heart of the Society Islands. There are sixty thousand people on this island, people of all possible mixtures— Europeans, Polynesians, Chinese, Eurasians, Chinese - Polynesians, European Polynesians, and so on, who make their living from copra, vanilla beans and tourists. Tahiti has night clubs that play jazz and an ersatz culture like no other island in Polynesia. The Tahitians are extremely handsome with well formed bronze bodies, flashing white teeth, and black curly hair. They are hospitable and friendly. Despite the fact that most of them have been converted to Christianity, they carry out many of the superstitions of their ancient worship.

The Tahitians are an easy going people who do as little work as possible. Their thatched huts are poor but they spend little time indoors. Their one aim in life is to seek enjoyment. Drinking to excess is common.

There are many other islands in this section of Polynesia, each rivaling the others in beauty. One is Huahine, where the people still build their villages on stilts over water in the ancient Polynesian manner. The people of this island wear European clothing but aside from that the old ways of life are preserved.

As far as the races go, Hawaii is the Pacific crossroads as these children demonstrate.

Parental love is the great common denominator between all the peoples of the world.

Hawaiians are Americans who live in a land of sunshine and flowers. Hawaiians make their homes on nine habitable islands whose total land area is larger than Connecticut but smaller than Massachusetts, and which contain over three quarters of a million people.

The original settlers of the Hawaiian Islands were Polynesians who originated somewhere in Southeast Asia. They were skilled seafarers who had a tremendous drive to see over the next horizon. They migrated across the wide Pacific, colonizing various islands, making their last stop in Hawaii. They carried seeds, such as sugar cane, but depended for most of their food on the sea and the natural plant life of the islands.

Several groups, each with its own chief, settled in Hawaii. Just before the arrival of the white men, one chief, Kamehamema, was able to make himself king of all the islands.

There is a question of when the first white men arrived in the Hawaiian Islands. Some historians believe a group of Spaniards were wrecked there in 1555. In 1778, Captain James Cook discovered the islands and named them the Sandwich Islands, after an English nobleman. The Hawaiians killed Cook the following year. His discovery, however, attracted other ships and soon the islands became a regular port of call for the New England whaling vessels and various trading ships. Chinese were the first settlers; and then as the sugar industry was developed, Japanese, Portuguese, Koreans, Fili-

Old Visayan woman from Cebu

Hawaiians live close to the sea. This is a hukilau, or traditional fishing party.

pinos, and Puerto Ricans followed. Today, because of intermarriage between the various peoples, there are very few Hawaiians entirely of Polynesian blood. The Japanese are the largest single group, representing a fourth of the population. People of Caucasian stock make up one-third of the population of our Fiftieth State.

Over half the people of Hawaii live on the island of Oahu where the city of Honolulu is located. Hawaii, the big island that gives the group its name, has less than a hundred thousand people; Maui and Kauai even less. Most Hawaiians make their living from agriculture and tourists. Sugar and pineapple are the main crops. Many of the plantation workers are very

poor and live in sub-standard housing. Other Hawaiians are engaged in the raising of beef cattle. The middle and upper classes have American standards of living. The Hawaiian labor unions are doing much to promote living and working conditions similar to those found in the United States proper, which is called the mainland.

Protestant missioners arrived in the islands in 1820, and shortly thereafter Catholic missioners came from France. One of those missioners was Father Damien, the Apostle to the lepers on Molokai. Today one out of every four Hawaiians is a Catholic. The Church has an extensive system of schools and parishes on all the islands, with a university in Honolulu.

A Sundanese
of West Java

What Is a Christian?

IT IS SURPRISING how many things in life we take for granted without questioning or investigation. We seldom stop to think about the air we breathe, or our rights as American citizens, or even what our religion really means. All of these things are of great importance, and on the last our eternal destiny depends.

What is a Christian? Simply, a Christian is a person who follows Christ and His teachings fully and completely. We say fully and completely because to do any less would make the person at best only a partial Christian.

Some people can accept the incomprehensible mystery of the Blessed Trinity but cannot give assent to Christ's teaching on divorce. Others find no difficulty in admitting the magnificent doctrine on the Blessed Eucharist but stumble over the question of birth control. Still others find no trouble in professing the Incarnation, but are unwilling to admit in practice the equality and brotherhood of man.

It takes more than the pouring of water to make a Christian. It takes a lifetime of living. A Christian proves his or her philosophy not by words alone but mainly by deeds. In short, Christianity means vital action and not mere lip service.

Christian living does not exist solely for or within the family. Neither does it exist solely for or within the parish. It exists for the entire world. Christ did not die for a few chosen individuals but for every individual who ever lived or will live. Therefore, as Christians we must also live for every individual in the world — not only for people we know and love but also for the most remote person of whose very existence we are not even aware.

Christ established a missionary Church. He was a missioner Himself. Everyone who calls himself or herself a follower of Christ must be as mission minded as He was. Missions are as essential to Christianity as the Ten Commandments.

Missions are not a work of supererogation—something in which we engage after other needs are taken care of. Missions must be an integral part of our living—a regular part of our Christian life.

Christ does not expect each of His followers to leave home for the ends of the earth. It is only to a proportion that He gives this type of vocation, although it seems evident that He gives the calling to many more than the few who answer it.

But Christ does expect each of His followers to engage as fully as circumstances allow in the work of the missions. He expects those who adopt His name and teachings to burn with His zeal for souls. And as has been said above, this zeal is not localized but is universal in its scope.

The evangelization of the world has been slowed down and hampered by the failure of Christians to grasp this essential idea. There have been periods in history when Catholics fully understood their obligations in this matter. As a result, those periods were times of great Christian penetration and conquest. Then, for one reason or another, the scope of Christianity became limited in the minds of many, with the result that religion was personalized and lost its universal outlook.

Anyone who calls himself or herself a Christian is in effect calling himself or herself a follower of Christ. To be worthy of the name and to be sincere in the calling, the Christian must be prepared to follow Christ completely. And this means accepting the entirety of Christ's doctrine.

Therefore, every Christian is a missioner concerned with the salvation of all souls everywhere.

INDEX

People and Places Mentioned in this Book

345

Russians, 8, 27, 176, 187ff,
  295, 306
Rwanda, 230

Sabah, 309
Sabines, 168
Saint Kitts, 103
Sakais, 271
Salvadoreans, 97
Samnites, 168
Samoans, 235, 335
Samoyeds, 188, 192
San Blas, 79, 98
San Marino, 164
Santhal, 261
Santiago, 79
Saracens, 212
Sarawak, 309
Saudi Arabia, 208
Savora, 261
Saxons, 150, 154, 171
Scandinavia, 33, 57, 154ff
Scandinavians, 150, 154ff, 161, 171
Scotch, 9, 57, 138, 149, 150, 154, 324, 335
Scotland, 154
Seminole, 37, 65
Semites, 23, 190, 212-214, 217, 233, 249, 250
Senegal, 219
Sentinels, 266
Serbia-Croatians, 177
Serbo-Croatians, 176
Serbs, 176ff
Seri, 80
Shangallas, 250
Shangana, 236
Shans, 269, 270
Shawnee, 65
Shelter, 35
Sherpa, 261
Shintoism, 216, 300
Shipibo, 119, 120
Shoshone, 65
Siam, *see Thailand*
Siamese, 272
Siberia, 26, 33, 58, 107, 192
Siberians, 192
Sicilians, 149
Sierra Leone, 219
Sikhs, 8, 258, 261
Sindhi, 261, 268
Singapore, 271
Singhalese, 261, 266
Sino-Tibetan, 306
Siouan, 65
Sioux, 9
Slavs, 140, 155, 168, 171, 172, 174,
  176, 177, 184, 185, 189
Sleeping, 38
Slovaks, 172, 174
Slovenes, 172, 174, 176ff
Snake, 65
Society Islands, 336
Solomon Islands, 326ff
Somalia, 210

Somalis, 210, 214, 236
Songhay, 219
Sotho, 226ff, 233, *see Bausto*
South Africa, Union of, 226ff, 230, 231ff,
  306,
South America, 106ff, 167
South Americans, 107ff
South-West Africa, 230ff
Soviet Union, 51, 155, 156ff, 168,
  174, 185, 187ff
Spain, 34, 70, 80, 166ff, 171, 304
Spaniards, 131, 151, 166, 302-304, 338
Spanish, 34, 60, 66, 68, 70, 79, 99,
  103, 138, 151, 164, 166ff, 168, 214,
  289, 306, 310, 331
Spanish Americans, 70ff
Spice Islands, 318, *see Indonesia*
Suahili, *see Swahili*
Sudan, 210, 242
Sudanese, 210
Sudras, 260, 265
Suk, 247
Suku, 248
Sulawesi, *see Celebes*
Sumatra, 308, 318
Sundanese, 310
Sundra Islands, 318
Sunni Moslems, 204
Swabians, 171
Swaetians, 191
Swahili, 236ff, 248, 249
Swati, 261
Swazi, 233
Swaziland, 233
Sweden, 128ff, 154, 155, 156ff
Swedes, 66, 149, 155, 176
Swiss, 34, 36, 172
Switzerland, 34, 172
Syria, 204
Syrians, 204

Tahiti, 336
Tahitians, 336
Taita, 236
Taiwan, *see Formosa*, 27, 288ff
Taiwanese, 288
Tajki, 204
Tamils, 261, 266, 267, 306
Tanzania, 218, 222, 227, 235ff, 245ff, 247
Taoism, 216
Taos, 65
Tartars, 35, 189, 192, 285
Tasmania, 323, 325
Tasmanians, 325
Tchoud, 176
Tehuana, 79
Telugu, 261, 306
Temne, 219
Teutonic, 28, 306
Teutons, 150, 151, 154, 155-161, 162,
  166, 167, 171, 172
Thai, 306
Thailand, 35, 272